My Business Is Now North

Of grief and love

Anthony Sobb

My Business Is Now North

Of grief and love

PEPPER PRESS

First published in 2024 by Pepper Press, an imprint of Fair Play Publishing.
PO Box 4101, Balgowlah Heights, NSW 2093, Australia

www.fairplaypublishing.com.au

ISBN: 978-1-923236-09-7
ISBN: 978-1-923236-10-3 (ePub)

© Anthony Sobb 2024

The moral rights of the author have been asserted.

All rights reserved. Except as permitted under the *Australian Copyright Act 1968* (for example, a fair dealing for the purposes of study, research, criticism or review), no part of this book may be reproduced, stored in a retrieval system, communicated or transmitted in any form or by any means without prior written permission from the Publisher.

Cover design and typesetting by Ana Sečivanović
Front cover photograph by Luna Marina

All inquiries should be made to the Publisher via hello@fairplaypublishing.com.au

A catalogue record for this book is available from the National Library of Australia.

Dedication

This book is dedicated to my family: Kim, Jackson, Louis and Oscar.

It is also dedicated to anyone dealing with grief. May your business be north.

'A compass, I learned when I was surveying, it'll ... it'll point you true north from where you're standing, but it's got no advice about the swamps, deserts and chasms that you'll encounter along the way.'

Abraham Lincoln, from the movie *Lincoln*

*'But there was no need to be ashamed of tears,
for tears bore witness that a man had the greatest
of courage, the courage to suffer.'*

Viktor E. Frankl, *Man's Search for Meaning*

CONTENTS

Dedication vii

Foreword 1

Preface—Here, Now and North.. 3

Introduction... 5

Part One: Those Moments.. 7
    Monday 21 May 2018 8
    The Long Way Home.. 9
    Kimberly Irene Frances Sobb 11

Part Two: The Emails 15
    October 2014—Moving Towards a Terrible Storm 16
    November 2014—This Deep, Dark Hole.. 20
    December 2014—Dependable Men.. 29
    January 2015—The Noosa Debacle 36
    February 2015—Hot Noodles and Mindless TV 40
    March 2015—Not Even in America... 45
    April 2015—A Quantum Leap... 48
    May 2015—Marcia Brady or Cindy?... 51
    June 2015—The Champ 54
    October 2015—Twelve Months On From the Diagnosis 59
    November 2015—A Points Victory... 63
    January 2016—The PET Scan is Clear 66

March 2016—A New Personal Best 70
April 2016—A Brief Taste of Relative Normality 73
May 2016—Degrees of Separation 79
June 2016—The Shadow of Radiation 83
July 2016—Cementing Treatment 87
August 2016—The Dreaded Mask 90
October 2016—Pseudo-progression 96
November 2016—The Yellow Submarine 104
December 2016—Absolute Denial 109
January 2017—No Retreat, No Surrender 114
February 2017—Bruce and the Hope Estate 120
March 2017—High-maintenance Patient Spouses 124
April 2017—Like Sisyphus, She Picked Up the Boulder 133
May 2017—Two Hearts are Better than One 135
June 2017—The Kim Sobb Resistance 142
July 2017—Hunting Invisible Game 148
August 2017—Returning Home 154
September 2017—Only Give Up Tomorrow 162
October 2017—It Always Seems Impossible 171
November 2017—Only Half of Anything 177
December 2017—This Must Be the Place 186
January 2018—Her Courage to Get Busy Living 196
February 2018—Oven Mitts 198
March 2018—The Delicate Art of Lymphatic Massage 203
May 2018—We Had Our Rituals 208
Monday 21 May 2018 213
May 2018—The Journey Has Ended 214

Part Three: Unravelling 217
    That Moment 218
    Travelling South 224
    The Grief 227

Part Four: The Strength 241
    The Fight 242
    The Dog House 245
    The Support 247
    The Medical Profession 249

Part Five: Travelling North 255
    El Camino (The Way) 256
    Travelling North 265

Part Six: And So It Goes 267
    And So It Goes 268

The Complete Playlist 270

Further Reading and Viewing 272

Acknowledgements 273

About the Author 274

Foreword

On October 15, 2014, I opened an email.

I opened it like we open a million others, inside the comfortable confines of my office, only to recoil immediately upon reading its first paragraph.

I remember pushing my chair back.

That first email laid out the unimaginable and the beautiful, both of which you'll soon have the honour to experience. And thus began an intimate, collective journey of words, tears, and laughs, for all of us, via a series of love letters addressed to those of us who loved the Sobbs but written very much for Kim and her boys.

'As most things in life do, it morphed,' Anthony writes, and morph these letters did …

… Into a true masterpiece of human resilience, viewed through the lenses of a thinker and the heart of a lion.

Those of us who know 'Sobbie' well are familiar with his self-deprecating refrains:

'Yet again, I'm humbled and a little embarrassed at how dumb I can be, and how wise Kim is.'

He is right about one thing: from the first time you met Kim Sobb, you felt like you had met a movie star in real life—one of the heroines of the plot, always.

But Anthony Sobb, as you'll soon sense, is a leader. He is a leader beyond any I have ever met—and I ostensibly train leaders for a living! And like all leaders—every single one, surely—he did not always feel up to the task, but he kept moving forward.

For none of us have all the things we need in this life.

As Anthony puts it early on, the things we need have the capacity to grow within us:

'In time, Kim and I developed these skills together when challenged, but neither of us were those people yet.'

This book shows us the possibility of who we can become—and also perhaps who we always have unwittingly been. It unveils the veiled—and that which is veiled in humanity is often that which is strongest within us. It takes us on journeys to some of the world's most beautiful places, buoyed by a philosophy that is told here in so many brilliant quotes from famous souls, but that more importantly is shown here by Anthony and Kim.

Show, don't tell, a great storyteller once told me—and here we are shown. Or in Sobbie's inimitable voice:

'I find it ironic, possibly poetic, that the day after the procedure, Kim and I will celebrate our thirtieth wedding anniversary. When initially diagnosed, they said we would never make it. I guess she showed them.'

As an academic myself, I am struck by Anthony's typical humour when he mocks his lack of academic acumen, and yet, I would hope this is a book that every first-year medical student reads.

To be shown, not told, what it means to heal a human life, as these future physicians embark upon a career to perform that very superhuman task.

As I look down, it turns out that I am writing these words exactly nine years after I opened that first email. Now, fortunately for all of you, dear reader-friends, you are about to share in a journey that was once a gift to a few, but that now can be read by the many. It is a tale that will reframe your path in ways that you too shall never forget, and that will forever imprint your own thinking.

Lucky you. You get to be shown where 'north' truly is.

Bo Bernhard, Ph.D.
Vice President of Economic Development University of Las Vegas, Nevada (UNLV)
Philip G. Satre Chair, University of Nevada, Reno (UNR) & UNLV
Professor, UNLV Harrah College of Hospitality
Professor, UNLV Department of Sociology
October 15, 2023

Preface—Here, Now and North

Cancer is an intrusive disease. It is insidious and disruptive. It is unfair, inexplicable and at times all-consuming—physically, mentally and emotionally.

Cancer touches all of us. It exists within some of us, sometimes leaving without even a whisper, other times grabbing hold and strangling our lives into unrecognisable shapes. Like love and life, every cancer experience is different. It can sharpen the remaining days of our lives into aching vividity or soften them through the blur of medication.

My greatest wish for you is that you don't have a cancer story. Yet I'm certain it will touch your life—most likely it already has. An estimated one in two Australians will be diagnosed with cancer by the age of 85. More than 400 people a day in Australia receive a cancer diagnosis. But these statistics are meaningless when it happens to you or your partner, a relative or a friend, someone in your community … Cancer doesn't always happen elsewhere and when it arrives in your life, it is shocking.

But there is hope.

Some people survive cancer. Some die with cancer. And yes, some die because of cancer. The future is neither hopeless, nor set in stone, as you will discover when reading this book. The medical profession's understanding has never been greater and keeps getting better, maybe even a little because of people like my beautiful wife, Kim.

I'm not even sure that mine is a cancer story though I know it is a love story. It is also a war story and an adventure story. We experienced romance and horrors, fought hard and went to places few, if any, have been before. You, too, might have a cancer story. Know that you can set the narrative. You can make yours into a different story, one of love, of mystery and discovery and of heroes.

For me, the initial purpose of writing this story was to have something tangible that represented Kim, or at least some part of Kim's life. I thought the tragedy and circumstances in which her life was cut short and the beauty of her as a human being at the very least deserved that.

But, as most things in life do, it morphed.

Writing a book was certainly not intentional, but like the natural meandering of a river, it took its path and developed.

At the time of concluding this book, it is over five years since Kim passed and nearly ten years since the day she was diagnosed. The last five years have been filled with deep, deep grief, so dark it's almost impossible to articulate. I am not sure if this makes any sense, but in the darkest moment, it was not a matter of wanting to die. I did not want to live, not like this, anyway.

But I began my journey towards a distant light. And that is where I am today.

With no particular destination, I head north and out of the darkness. And that's the thing. North is not a destination or a place. It is a way, a direction, and I believe that is all we can hope for in life, to have a way, a direction.

Introduction

At approximately 11.00 am on Monday 13 October 2014, I received a phone call from my wife, Kim, that changed our lives forever. From this, emerged the '*Kim Updates*'.

My initial purpose for these updates was one of trickery, the sleight of hand of a magician. If I gave enough minutia and detail while writing in the narrative form, Kim and I could elude everyone.

The Sobb family, being Anthony, Kim, Jackson, Louis and Oscar, have always been a tight subset, purposely keeping a safe distance from others. I am sure many family members and friends possibly found it odd. Some even misconstrued it for superiority or arrogance. The fact is, we simply enjoyed our own space. Perhaps it grew from both Kim's and my early feelings when we eloped from our respective families to start a new tribe.

So, on hearing the unexpected news of Kim's diagnosis with late-stage terminal cancer, the last thing we wanted was to have our solitude invaded, even when the intentions were good and meaningful because Kim was 'my friend', 'my sister' or 'my relative'.

I had to devise a distraction. Hence, I hatched my great plan to write these detailed narratives, giving just enough description and information to keep the invaders at bay.

Well, that's how they began.

The more I wrote, the more I found solace in making sense of a situation that made no sense at all. The notes progressed to reflections and sometimes love letters to my wife.

And that's the irony. I had gone from hiding Kim and myself away to eventually revealing our intimate story and love for one another to everyone.

I never intended to turn these writings into a book, and while I am no writer, I have a story to tell. Apart from sharing Kim's incredible story of courage, this is a story of profound grief. My aim is to show that in the depths of deep grief, we can eventually find our way out.

As you follow our journey, you soon realise that the title of this book, *My Business is Now North,* was my sign-off. It is a morphed version of the final line of an incredibly moving speech given by the famous British Commander, Lieutenant Colonel Tim Collins before the troops entered Iraq. I love its sense of purpose, commitment and direction. It became my whole mindset fighting alongside Kim during our battle with cancer. I still use it to this day.

This book is certainly not the sum of our life, or anyone else's life mentioned in this book, but rather a chapter so intense and so life-changing, it could have easily been another whole complete life. Thank God it wasn't.

It is important to remember this is not our whole story. A sense of privacy prevents me from sharing everything. In short, it is a detailed account of one chapter in our lives. The rest? Well, that's between Kim and I.

My business is now north.

Part One:

Those Moments

Monday 21 May 2018

While in Mexico City Airport, heading to the departure gates and en route to meet up with the boys, Kim collapsed into unconsciousness. I worked on her as best I could on the floor of the terminal, but she died in my arms. I'm sorry. I couldn't save her.

Ant

The Long Way Home

'Darling, you're going to have to try to remain lucid or they won't let you on the plane,' I said as Kim drifted in and out of consciousness.

'If you wanna get out of here, you've gotta talk to Ant,' she wryly replied, paraphrasing from the movie *Mad Max 2*.

And, for the last time in her life, she made me smile.

At Mexico City Airport, I swung into commando mode, somehow pushing her wheelchair, loading up her oxygen and carrying our luggage, shooing off well-meaning people wishing to give assistance.

After checking in, Kim asked to go to the bathroom before we boarded our flight. From the moment I met Kim, any and every trip was prefaced by a trip to the damn bathroom. But by now, I was well accustomed to the whole modus operandi of taking Kim to the toilet. I still remember one of the earlier times when she sat there and burst into tears, explaining she had lost her dignity and that I had not signed up for this.

'It's an honour for me to do this, and I did sign up for it,' was my reply.

However, this time was very different.

She slumped over every couple of minutes, her speech becoming more and more slurred.

I attempted to wake her up. All I got in reply was a groan and glazed eyes.

Redressing her was difficult. She was like a rag doll.

In my scrambled panic, I just wanted to get her to the boarding gate as our flight had been called. My heart pounded. Subconsciously, I knew everything wasn't right, but my mind would not accept that.

We made our way out of the bathrooms and into the heavy human traffic of the public walkway in Mexico City Airport. As we did so, Kim's limp body slid out of the wheelchair and onto the cold, hard linoleum floor. I knelt by her, and her eyes temporarily opened.

It finally dawned on me like a tremendous punch to the gut.

The penny finally dropped.

Kim was dying.

I looked into her eyes.

'Don't you fucking die on me, don't you fucking die on me!' I screamed.

In her eyes, I saw fear. Not acceptance. Not peace. But fear. Fear of death. No romantic embrace of peaceful finality.

'Ant, get me out of here,' she was saying to me.

Belatedly, I started CPR. First the breaths, then the pumps.

I looked across at her.

Nothing.

I felt people stepping around us or staring as they walked by.

As I started my second set of CPR, an arm pushed me aside and a voice screamed in English, 'We are doctors.'

Like a numb zombie, and on my knees, I moved aside.

After an eternity, the older man and younger woman, both doctors returning to the United States, turned to me and explained they were sorry, Kim was dead.

I curled up next to her body, taking her hand and placing it on my cheek. I simply lay there. I don't know how long for. Seconds. Minutes. I was unaware of the crowd that had gathered.

In my mind, it was just Kim and I.

I returned to some form of awareness when a Mexican official, along with the two doctors, grabbed me by the arm and pulled me off her. The airport official could barely speak English. Luckily, the American doctors spoke Spanish, and they explained that Kim's body needed to be taken away. They also explained their plane was about to leave and the official would not let them go. With the little wit I had left, I produced the medical certificate I had obtained from the doctor in the hotel lobby the night before, which stated that Kim was terminally ill with stage 4 lung cancer. The official begrudgingly allowed the doctors to leave.

With the American doctors gone, I was alone with the Mexican Airport officials. In their broken English, they explained I needed to remove all Kim's jewellery before they transported her body.

I gently removed her rings from hands withered by disease and the toxicity of chemo and radiation, then lay back down next to her body. I watched crowds of people walk past us. Some stepped over us, others turned their heads, and some made the sign of the cross.

I had this incredible sense of being alone, of lying next to something or someone I deeply loved who no longer existed.

It was like falling into an abyss.

Kimberly Irene Frances Sobb

The year is 2014.

Kim is extremely attractive, with an elegant, slender physique, blonde hair, a beaming complexion and an eye for fashion. Practising as an instructing solicitor in Sydney's Director of Public Prosecutions in the Court of Criminal Appeal, life is good. With a successful professional career, three healthy sons, a loving but flawed husband and blissful domesticity, she's as sharp as a tack with a wicked sense of humour—just what you expect from a criminal prosecutor. A law graduate from the famous University of Sydney, she is articulate and well-read.

She spends summer weekends at the beach and winter weekends supporting her husband, Anthony, and middle son, Louis, as they compete in Surf Life Saving Inflatable Rescue Boat (IRB) carnivals. She is the glue that keeps the Sobb family together. None of the men in her family can match her intellect. But never once does she appear lofty before them. They're her boys and she is their girl. She gently navigates and guides them in the fine art of how to communicate with one another—beyond physical confrontation.

She is selfless. Every boy's birthday is an event to be celebrated. She supports every football game from the sidelines. And yes, every parent-teacher interview is spent defending her boys when I know she is secretly disappointed that they inherited her husband's brains.

Jackson Cage Jeffrey Sobb is Kim's firstborn. Named after the Bruce Springsteen song, *The Jackson Cage*, he has Kim's blonde complexion. A deep thinker, he has always been concerned about the well-being of others. These are wonderful traits in life, but terrible inside the ring. For this very reason, both his mother and I had great trepidation during his bouts in boxing. Jackson immerses himself in his work, often working ridiculously long hours at the restaurant and bar he manages.

Louis Sobb's first word was 'no'. A man of few words, he is straight to the point. Sitting between elder brother Jackson and younger brother Oscar, he is named after the famous heavyweight boxer Joe Louis. Louis and I often train together at my gym, the Dog House, for hours on end, many of them with little or no words spoken. He is the man you want by your side when your back is to the wall. He is a prolific trainer, a tough and talented boxer and a mixed martial artist with an incredible sense of loyalty and duty. Right now, he's considering a career in the Police Force.

Oscar Atticus Sobb is Kim's youngest son, named after boxer Oscar De La Hoya and Atticus Finch from *To Kill a Mockingbird*. Sensitive and never afraid to speak his mind, he is battle-hardened from having two older brothers. Kim, knowing he would be her last child, spoils Oscar and he is happy to oblige. Ever the opportunist, he often pays the price for this by being tormented by Jackson and Louis. This being said, growing up, Oscar's playgrounds often echoed with, 'That's Louis Sobb's brother. You better leave him alone.' In 2014, Oscar is attending his first year of boarding school at St Joseph's College, the same place I graduated from.

Kim grew up in an era where it was common to pursue further tertiary education based on one's Higher School Certificate mark. With Kim's superior intellect, she chose law. However, due to her gentle nature and love of animals,

I can't help thinking that in another life she would have taken up veterinary science. Kim and our German Shepherd, Reuben the Wonder Dog, spend their spring and summer afternoons together on long walks through our local bushland. They return with stories of adventures encountering snakes or of Reuben defending her from other dogs. The famous Sobb family Easter Show days are never complete without a visit to the Dog Show and a viewing of the performing police German Shepherds, where without fail, Kim repeats, 'They're not as good as my Reuben.'

I'm Anthony, Kim's husband. I've built a career around my passion for food, wine and bringing people together. Travelling the world with Kim by my side allows me to pursue my appetite for bringing new tastes and experiences back to Western Sydney where I am the CEO of Fairfield RSL, a club I am gradually transforming into a world-class leisure facility.

Kim's strength and loyalty, especially to her family, are matched only by her beauty and fragility. She has a wonderful passion for travel, characterised by a yearning to see and experience new cultures. Yet she can still stand beside me, holding my hand as we devotedly sway to the beat of our fifteenth Bruce Springsteen concert.

It is before October 2014. Life is good.

Part Two:

The Emails

October 2014—Moving Towards a Terrible Storm

Wednesday 15 October

I trust you will forgive me for sending a blanket email such as this.

However, owing to the circumstances, I would like our friends to be aware of the current situation. Kim and I believe you deserve to know, and it allows me to immerse my energies into looking after her and the family. I also trust you will forgive my self-indulgence in sharing my thoughts.

For approximately eight weeks, Kim has been experiencing increasing pain in the back of her head. We looked at various treatments such as acupuncture and physiotherapy, though Kim has an amazing pain threshold. Eventually, Kim got referred for an MRI scan.

Soon after, I received a phone call that has changed my family's life forever. 'Ant, I'm with the doctor and it's not good,' were Kim's words.

The doctor explained that Kim has advanced stage lung cancer, and it has spread to her bones.

Kim has never smoked in her life.

The results of the CT scan we had on Monday will be shared with us on Thursday, and our oncologist will map out a timeline and plan. Right now, Kim is in a lot of pain.

The older boys are angry, and I have the unthinkable task of attempting to explain this to our youngest boy, Oscar, when he returns home from St Joseph's College boarding school this weekend.

I have chosen to share this news with as many friends as possible, as I believe you have the right to know. But also, from a selfish perspective, I don't have the strength to tell this story over and over to each of you. I prefer to keep my reserves for Kim and the boys.

The other reason I'm sharing this is because in the future, Kim and I may simply wish to retreat into one another. I know you will respect this. Those who know us recognise we do nothing without each other, be it ringside at boxing, in the stands of St Joseph's College, freezing at IRB surf carnivals or just sitting at the dinner table. We do everything together.

Right now, I feel like our family has been cast adrift and we are moving towards a terrible storm that will only end in pain and tragedy.

Friday 17 October 2014
Thank you for all your texts, emails and messages. Kim has read every one of them. Some I have read numerous times whilst sitting in waiting rooms. You can't possibly realise their value.

I apologise for not getting back to you individually, but my number one priority is looking after Kim and the boys. Being able to send group emails such as this helps. Repeating the updates over and over feels like reopening a wound.

A lot has happened in the last week relating to Kim's condition. She had a further CT scan, four separate visits to St. George Hospital on Wednesday and an incredibly painful biopsy today. They inserted a needle into Kim's back with no general anaesthetic to obtain the sample from her lung. Her arms are swollen, purple and extremely sensitive from all the cannulas and needles she has received during numerous tests.

You'll be happy to know that I dutifully carry around not only the numerous medical results such as CT scans, MRI scans, x-rays, bone density reports and lung biopsies, but also her makeup kit. Cancer may be strong, but Kim's wish to always look her best is even stronger. During today's painful lung biopsy, I swear some of the expletives she yelled out would have made our friend Johnny Lewis and all the boys at Newtown Boxing Club blush. Louis Sobb was equally impressed when I told him.

Our meeting with the oncologist at the cancer ward filled in a lot of blanks. We are now sure that Kim's primary lung cancer has spread to the bone in her C3 vertebra—hence the excruciating pain in the back of her head—and, unfortunately, also to a lymph gland. This is not good news.

Kim will have a PET scan early next week which will tell us with 98% accuracy if, or where, any further cancer is located that the MRI and CT scan did not detect. We meet with the neurosurgeon next week to investigate the possibility of removing the C3 vertebra altogether. We'll also look at attacking the lung and affected lymph gland with chemo and radiation therapy.

I've been blessed not just with incredible friends, but also an unbelievable Board and executive management team at work. This has enabled me to get things done quickly.

I won't lie. There are moments of sheer despair. However, my aim is to keep these to a minimum and the Sobb family focused and positive. We refuse to capitulate.

With this all said, a significant factor is how Kim's body will react to the treatment. The doctors are amazed at her physical health, so that's a great start. My job is to ensure her emotional and mental frame of mind is as good as it can be. A lot of this comes down to her mindset during pain management and our mantras of 'we're not pulling up stumps' and 'let's celebrate small victories'. This is where our journey is thus far, and while I wish this curse upon no other person, this situation has even further bonded our love for one another.

Tuesday 28 October 2014
So much has happened, and articulating all this to you assists me greatly, both therapeutically and cognitively.

Jackson, unwittingly, has been wonderful for Kim by virtue of his naturally happy and cheerful demeanour. It's also fortunate that his new role as the restaurant manager at the Riley Street Garage is all-consuming and keeping him occupied.

Louis, by nature, is always quiet and I'm keeping a close eye on him. However, he has been an unbelievable help by taking Kim to appointments when I've been unable—a responsibility you would wish upon no son.

We have had great support from the Joey's community of St Joseph's College. Oscar's boarding co-ordinator has played an incredible role in supporting him and acting as a conduit between Joey's and our family.

Kim has good days and bad days, both physically and emotionally. One cruel continuum she speaks of is the Groundhog Day of waking every morning with a thumping pain in the back of her head and the knowledge she has been diagnosed with cancer.

For those of you who know me, this is all very much a matter of 'go hard or go home' and I took on the role of trainer and drill sergeant immediately. I placed an alcohol ban on the house and I'm overseeing all Kim's dietary requirements which now consist of nothing but green protein shakes.

Dutiful to me, mindful of my ways and ever-wise, Kim eventually pulled me aside and quietly said, 'Remember, I'm not just a patient to you, I'm your wife, and if I decide to have one glass of champagne now and again, it's a reminder that I'm living my life rather than sitting out a sentence.' Our usual 'date nights' do consist of Kim having a glass of champagne, so I'm humbled and a little embarrassed at how dumb I can be and how wise Kim is.

OCTOBER 2014—MOVING TOWARDS A TERRIBLE STORM

In relation to treatment, the neurosurgeon believes it is far too dangerous to operate due to the tumour's position in C3 and around the spinal cord. As a result, Kim commences extensive and intense radiation therapy each day for the next four weeks, starting Monday.

Our chemo oncologist is waiting for the results of the lung biopsy. As a non-smoker, she may have a mutation version of lung cancer which apparently responds extremely well to chemo tablets. We will know the answer to this on Friday. However, he did say not to be too hopeful. If this is the case, we will move to regular chemo via blood transfusion, which has some distasteful side effects.

Whilst the news about treatment hasn't been great, I simply see it as a couple of early rounds being given to our opponent. Our aim is to have Kim there at the sound of the bell of the twelfth.

Watching her being prodded, poked and put through some incredibly uncomfortable and intrusive examinations and tests is nothing short of humbling. The irony is that she is giving me strength.

Thank you again for all your well wishes. They mean so much to both of us, and I know you respect our need to focus on the battle at hand.

My business is now north.

November 2014—This Deep, Dark Hole

Monday 3 November 2014

The situation Kim and I find ourselves in doesn't come with a manual, so it's very much a day-to-day and 'deal with it as it arises' situation.

Kim has started her intensive radiation treatment, with chemo also starting this week. Despite the numerous horror stories you hear about the treatment, we welcome it as an ally rather than reject it as a foe due to its side effects. The radiation treatment lasts four weeks, with four weeks on the lung but only two weeks on the vertebrae because the doctors are fearful of damaging the spinal cord and arteries. It's an intrusive and confronting treatment that takes place in a clinical and cold environment, magnified because Kim suffers from claustrophobia. Yet, she stoically turns up time after time, humbling my preconceptions of bravery and strength.

Our most recent news hasn't been what we hoped for. Our chemo oncologist says Kim's form of cancer does not have the mutation commonly found with non-smokers that responds well to chemo tablets.

The other not so good news is our neurosurgeon confirmed they won't operate to remove the tumour on Kim's C3 vertebra due to its proximity to her spinal cord and arteries.

Enter our incredible friend, the famous boxing trainer Johnny Lewis, who, over the last twenty years, seems to pop up at the right time whenever I've needed help. Johnny did what Johnny does best, quietly making things happen in the background. Through Dr John O'Neill, a well-known Australian doctor associated with boxing, Johnny organised for us to see the world-famous South African neurosurgeon Dr Marc Coughlan, who has worked alongside other legends such as Dr Charlie Teo. It's usually a six-month wait to see Dr Coughlan, and that's if he decides to take the case. Johnny got us in to see him within a week. The appointment is on Wednesday, and we are holding onto hope that he may find a way to remove this tumour.

The role reversal is unmistakable as I dutifully follow Kim around from treatment to treatment and doctor to doctor like a bumbling personal assistant. On my trusty iPad, I frantically take notes as doctors regurgitate mountains of information we can barely digest at the time. Kim's pain appears to be getting worse, which creates a lot of anxiety. She's on a lot of pain medication and we're attempting to manage it the best way we know how. Our oncologist tells us the radiation treatment should begin to ease the pain.

Kim and I are taking refuge in my gym where I lock the doors and we train together to the sounds of Bruce Springsteen and Dragon. Here, we have a temporary escape from the world. We stretch, then she pounds the treadmill while I do my session. Kim is as fit as a mallee bull and as beautiful as a spring deer. She continues to do what she does best, which is managing me.

At our recent daily weigh-ins, I developed growing concerns about her weight loss. In my infinite wisdom, I decided to take her out for dinner every night. After a week, she pulled me aside.

'Ant, you know I really love it when you cook for me.'

Yet again, I continue to climb this steep learning curve and, yet again, she treats me with love and dignity.

That's not to say we don't have our moments. For instance, we constantly battle over her not carrying her medication around.

'If you think I'm going to stop nagging you about this, you've got another thing coming. You're going to back down before I ever do,' I told her, exasperated after the umpteenth incident of finding her without it.

'That's why I want you in my corner,' she said and burst into tears.

It's ironic how times of sorrow and pain can be transcended by simple gestures from people. The team from North Cronulla Lifesavers have been great, and it's comforting to know they're there in the background. Kim loves the tranquillity of walking along the beach or being rejuvenated by floating in the sea. Even so, last week while coming home from the beach, she explained that she felt like we had both been diagnosed with cancer, to which I replied, 'The day you got it, I got it.'

'Worry does not empty tomorrow of its sorrow; it empties today of its strength.'

Corrie ten Boom

Tuesday 4 November 2014

Were we still numb from the news of the recent diagnosis? I don't know. But we were totally unprepared for our first experience and introduction to chemotherapy. To this day, the word 'chemotherapy' brings on feelings of anxiety. In hindsight, our initial oncologist had possibly become numb to the needs of his patients in not preparing us. Regardless, that awareness came later, after much pain, tears and effort.

The drive to the hospital that first morning was surreal. Kim sat in the passenger seat like a zombie, staring out the window. Me being me, I just couldn't stop thinking, 'This can't be happening to us? This happens to other people.'

As we pulled into the car park of the hospital, Kim stared ahead, almost in a trance, giving the impression she wasn't going to move. I gently touched her on the arm.

'Come on, darling. We can do this. I won't leave your side.'

Begrudgingly, she became more present, unbuckled her seatbelt, and together we walked hand in hand into the hospital, like dead men walking to an execution. I don't think either of us had ever been so frightened in our lives. All I knew is I couldn't let Kim have a sense of anything other than I was in total control and her guardian.

Once we got to the entrance of the chemo ward, it was as if somebody had shocked Kim out of her trance-like state. She squeezed my hand.

'We are not doing this, Ant. Take me home now,' she said in total defiance.

With that, she attempted to turn me 180 degrees back towards the exit.

Despite trying to physically overwhelm me, we did not turn 180 degrees. There was a momentary pause as we looked at one another.

'I mean it, Ant. Let's go home now,' Kim said in a louder and more authoritarian voice.

I had to think quickly, as we both knew we weren't going home. We had to drink from this cup despite its pain and bitterness. We just needed to figure out a way we were going to do this. In time, we developed these skills together when challenged, but neither of us were those people yet. In a millisecond, I decided a calm, confident, pragmatic approach would be the avenue that best serves us.

'Listen, Kim. Going home is not an option. Going through with this chemo is going to help us, and I'm not going to leave your side.'

She broke down and wept.

'OK, Ant. Just don't leave,' she murmured, clinging to me.

So, there we were. Two lost, frightened souls clinging to one another outside the entrance to the chemo ward, one weeping, and the other frightened and pretending that everything was going to be ok.

And, with that, hand in hand, we opened the door and crossed the threshold to the world of chemotherapy.

I didn't know what to expect. Neither of us did. It was the journey of cancer, all wrapped up in one room, a spectrum of nationalities, ages and genders. It contained all the stages of cancer, from those who looked quite well and healthy, through to those who looked close to the final days of life. If you were perceptive enough, it was like looking into your future.

And that was tremendously frightening.

They led us to our designated bed where the nurse inserted the cannula into Kim's virgin veins and the process of intravenous chemotherapy commenced. Lasting around three hours, it felt like an eternity. I stared around the room, attempting to piece the puzzles of the patients and their carers together.

Who were these people before they were diagnosed and found themselves here? What kind of lives did they live? What would they say? What would they never say? Collectively, all our futures were too frightening to contemplate.

It was a sad place. What little hope anyone had would be drained whenever they saw those in the later stages receiving their treatment. It was then I worked out I had to devise a distraction to get Kim through future treatments. I bought the latest iPad and some double earpieces, and requested Kim tell me twenty films she would like to watch.

This would become our 'north' through chemo.

Friday 7 November 2014

Kim has finished her first of four weeks of intense daily radiotherapy. Her pain medication has caused her face to swell slightly which makes the claustrophobic radiotherapy mask she has to battle with each day even harder.

Kim's first week of chemo treatment was also extremely confronting and again proved cancer's lack of discrimination. Getting through that first day was nothing short of heroic.

We also met with Dr Marc Coughlan—the South African spinal neurosurgeon Johnny Lewis organised for us. Of all the numerous doctors we have seen recently, he was the first to move away from his desk, sit directly in front of Kim, look her in the eye and genuinely ask, 'How are you feeling, Kimberly? I'm terribly sorry, this must have come as a great shock to you. Are you OK?'

That gesture alone was unique and pivotal. He went on to explain he had reviewed all the information supplied by Kim's bumbling, but ever loyal, personal assistant, yours truly.

Dr Coughlan believes he can successfully remove the C3 vertebra with little or no damage to Kim's arteries or spinal cord. He had also taken the liberty of speaking to a lung cancer surgeon specialist, Dr G, whom he believed could successfully remove Kim's lung cancer tumour.

In this deep, dark hole, asphyxiated by nothing but bad news, we finally got some hope.

I have a close group of friends who talk about the power of hope, and nothing captured this better than that moment. Dr Coughlan is off to the States next week to attend a spinal neurosurgeons' convention where he will discuss Kim's case amongst other things.

He is prepared to operate on his return, which will be in approximately two to three weeks. After the operation, Kim will spend four days in hospital. After a few weeks of regaining her strength, our plan is to operate again. This is when Dr G will remove the lung tumour.

From Kim's perspective, the simple, or from a surgeon's perspective, extremely difficult, removal of these tumours—especially the one giving her such pain in C3—is an act of cleansing and one she is looking forward to.

In the meantime, Kim will continue her treatment and endure all the pain and anxiety that comes with it. This bumbling PA's job is to keep the make-up kit close at hand until that moment she awakens from both these operations, and keep her positive, fit and loved.

By virtue of the wonderful support I receive at the workplace, I'm by her side for every treatment session, doctor's appointment and any other flotsam or jetsam that this new 'cancer world' has brought us.

I made her smile the other day when madly walking from one treatment appointment to another, complete with her large handbag and umpteen test results. I strode ten yards in front of her, surely looking like Dustin Hoffman from Rain Man!

'Anthony Sobb, you are a man possessed,' she screamed out, which in turn woke me from my Asperger's moment to stop and turn around.

'Well, my darling, I have a lot to be possessed about,' I replied in a comic, yet close, moment.

'Life's blows cannot break a person whose spirit is warmed at the fire of enthusiasm.'

Norman Vincent Peale

Monday 17 November 2014

Kim amazes me. Small things once taken for granted now take a monumental effort, but still, she never complains and stoically confronts her treatment every day.

She is still suffering from relentless pain, day in and day out. We've been managing it with some strong morphine-based painkillers. However, these give her anxiety and affect her mindset. So, we've reassessed and reduced some of this medication. The trade-off is Kim is now less anxious and in a better frame of mind. She no longer believes I started the Middle East War, shot Archduke Franz Ferdinand and single-handedly created global warming. I jest!

We also decided not to continue with one of our doctors. Through this whole ordeal, if Kim and I have learnt anything, it's the importance of empowerment, knowledge and self-belief. I knew our decision was inevitable within the first fifteen minutes of meeting him. He told us to make her will and that regardless of any treatment, the cancer was going to eventually kill Kim. His mindset seemed to be one of creating painless submission to the fight and elongating existence for as long as possible.

The great boxing trainer and motivator, Teddy Atlas, often spoke of fighters who make silent agreements with their opponent to survive the fight, rather than sparring to win. I believe this doctor's approach echoed that sentiment, which is the opposite to what Kim, and I believe. He also advised us against surgery with Dr Marc Coughlan—who tabled Kim's case to a panel of world-leading neurosurgeons at a conference in San Francisco last week. By the way, all of them agreed on the need to surgically remove C3.

Our tactic is simple. We will die on our feet rather than live on our knees. We don't want to simply exist. We welcome a fight to live. On Wednesday, we have a pivotal meeting with Dr Coughlan where we believe he will outline the schedule for surgery on C3 and the tumour on Kim's lung. After that, we anticipate Kim will need six weeks of intense chemotherapy. We must accept that the cancer must still be in her blood somewhere given that it metastasised from her lung to the C3 vertebra.

We will wear the side effects of the chemo as a badge of honour—or title belt—as we believe it's a necessary path on our journey to defeat the cancer.

Kim continues to be an incredible source of strength for me. Our isolated sessions together in my gym are incredibly welcome breaks from the world. Louis often joins us and our constant ribbing of each other about who has the fastest hands on the speedball amuses Kim greatly. I stole a glimpse of her yesterday at the gym and was struck by the irony of how fit and beautiful she looks, and yet here she is diagnosed with cancer.

'Where are you going? I'm going to pick a fight.'
Sir William Wallace—Braveheart

Friday 21 November 2014

For some reason, the intensity and negative side effects of radiation treatment for cancer are often overshadowed by that of chemo. Is it the loss of hair? The nausea or the bloating of the body that chemo brings on? I am not so sure.

I learnt during my immersion into understanding treatment that radiation is equally toxic and damaging. Amounts of treatment and the incredibly specific accuracy of its location are key. With radiation, fractions of millimetres inaccurately targeted to the body can be devastating, even fatal, for the patient. So, in Kim's case, when we are talking about treatment for the C3 vertebra, we are talking about the spinal cord. For this reason, a mask on the face and head needs to be used. The mask is tightly fitted so it pins your head firmly and still to the treatment table. When you then take into consideration side effects of coinciding treatments, such as chemotherapy, the face can swell. Hence,

affixing the mask to the face and then pinning it to the treatment table can become a laborious and painful challenge. Now when you further add Kim's claustrophobia onto this, one can't help but be humbled at Kim's courage.

This image is of Kim with her wonderful radiologist on the final day of radiation. Kim is holding a framed quote, which we read every morning as we walked out the door during her five weeks of radiation treatment.

> '... *Do you want me to fight? Huh? Do you want me to trade places with you? Do you? Listen. This guy (Holyfield) is finished. There comes a time in a man's life when he makes a decision—to just live. Survive. Or he wants to win. You're doing just enough to keep him off you. And hope he leaves you alone. You're lying to yourself. You're gonna cry tomorrow because of this. Do you want to cry tomorrow? Huh? Don't lie to yourself. Back this guy up and fight a full round ...*'
>
> Teddy Atlas, April 1994,
> during the fight, between rounds, the night Michael Moorer won
> the IBF/WBA heavyweight titles from Evander Holyfield by decision.

Tuesday 25 November 2014

We now have some firm dates and direction for Kim's treatment.

This Friday, 28 November, Kim will have a surgical procedure at the Prince of Wales Hospital. They will take a CT scan to check whether the cancer has spread any further, then insert balloons into the arteries surrounding C3 so our neurosurgeon will know whether the blood flow has been restricted by the tumour. Finally, they will inject her with a blood-thickening agent that will hinder any excess blood flow when they remove the vertebrae.

Then, next Tuesday, 2 December, Dr Marc Coughlan will operate on Kim to surgically remove the C3 vertebra as well as whatever tumour remains. He'll replace the C3 vertebra with a prosthetic.

The surgery will be approximately five hours and they will enter via Kim's throat. We anticipate approximately four days' respite in hospital with a couple of weeks at home to recover, then back in to operate and remove the tumour in her lung.

Today, we met with our radiation oncologist. While it is far too early to measure the results of the current intensive radiation treatment, he was amazed Kim had been weaned off any of the morphine-based pain management medication. He explained this is a good sign that the treatment has been shrinking the tumours.

A week can be an eternity when dealing with situations like this and whilst Kim and I believe we have no other option but to operate, Kim is becoming quite anxious. Knowing Kim, she has probably worked me out, but my tactic will be to keep her as occupied as possible.

The treatment has taken a toll on her, and her body has really taken a beating. Ironically, we still go down to the gym together and she'll pump out four kilometres on the treadmill and look beautiful the whole time.

My role of dietician and cook is because Kim couldn't boil water and thinks 'cooking' is a city in China! She is eating great organic food with Louis in charge of the vegetable and fruit shakes. Her body and mind will be fit for this fight.

I won't lie. Sometimes she frets that she has come to the end of her tether. During these times, we attempt to discuss things logically, rather than letting 'the monkeys' loose in her mind. She has been in or around the fight game for some time now and knows the importance of a focused mind.

Whilst obviously anxious and concerned about their mother, the boys are keeping blessedly distracted. Jackson is busy at the restaurant but continues to delight Kim with his lovely, innocent and sometimes moronic nature! He's always the first to hug Kim.

Louis is focused on his personal training and final Police Force exams while remaining quiet, dutiful and dependable. The other day, he followed me out into a strong rip current to help rescue a young boy and his father.

'Thanks for following me out, Son,' I said to him when the whole episode was over.

'I'd follow you anywhere, Dad,' he replied. I couldn't have been prouder of him at that moment.

Oscar has his busy life at Joey's. His boarding co-ordinator is keeping an eye on him and seems to have a knack for knowing when to reach out to him or let him be.

Louis is inquisitive about Kim's whereabouts, treatment, diet and so on while for Jackson and Oscar, their coping mechanism is to avoid the subject. At this time, that's possibly not a bad thing. Either way, I must keep my eye on all of them.

My business is now north.

December 2014 – Dependable Men

Monday 1 December 2014

Our procedure last Friday became a little more complicated than we expected. The surgeon cut and clamped the artery around C3, and Kim now operates with one artery. The area is clear for our neurosurgeon to remove the vertebrae and tumour. However, until now, we've found that when having procedures, everything that can go wrong usually does. For instance, when Kim had her second lung biopsy, they warned us there was a tiny chance her lung would collapse … and, of course, it did.

Friday was no different. Without boring you with the details, Kim spent the entire weekend in the intensive care unit. Everything that could go wrong so far has, but I welcome that. We are battle-hardened because of it. We're both still standing, and Kim is still fighting. Tomorrow is a big fight, and we welcome the battle.

'It always seems impossible until it's done.'

Nelson Mandela

Tuesday 2 December 2014

It's 4.00 pm on Tuesday afternoon. Kim has just come out of surgery. Surgeons Dr Marc Coughlan and Dr John O'Neill have both spoken to me and are extremely happy with the outcome.

Kim's C3 vertebra was removed and replaced with a prosthetic. All that was humanly visible of the tumour was taken out as well.

'We can never say hundred per cent, as there may be a cell here or there, but in my view ninety-nine per cent has been removed,' said Dr Coughlan. 'We will now use chemo to mop up any cancerous cells left in the area. Once this step has been completed, we look towards further surgery to remove the tumour on the lung.'

In short, Kim is in a lot of pain right now and quite beat up, but in my eyes, she's never looked so beautiful and strong.

'The credit belongs to the man who is actually in the arena, whose face is marred by dust and sweat and blood, who strives valiantly; who errs and comes short again and again, who knows the great enthusiasms, the great devotions, and spends himself in a worthy cause; who at the best, knows the triumph of high achievement; and who fails while daring greatly, so that his place shall never be with those cold and timid souls who know neither victory nor defeat.'
Theodore Roosevelt

Friday 5 December 2014

Kim spent two days in the high dependency unit after the operation.

It took a lot out of her and was an extremely anxious time for both of us. She was incredibly brave leading into this complicated and dangerous surgery, and the high dependency unit was a much better experience than the previous weekend's nightmare in intensive care. The unit seemed more seamless in delivering their care, and Kim and I were far more prepared after being very specific about her postoperative pain management medication.

Owing to the tumour being so close to her throat, and the entry point being through the throat, there was a massive amount of swelling. Breathing was difficult, which magnified her anxiety. Even swallowing water was impossible. After the third day of not being able to consume any food, the doctors brought in a speech pathologist who coached Kim through techniques of how to swallow. This eventually led to her being able to eat tiny amounts of pureed food. She has lost an enormous amount of weight.

Kim will be discharged from hospital tomorrow.

Her neuro team, Dr Marc Coughlan, Dr John O'Neill and now thoracic surgeon Dr G, will have a planning meeting next Tuesday, along with our new chemo oncologist Dr C, to schedule Kim's upcoming lung surgery followed by her chemo treatment.

So much has happened to Kim in a short amount of time, yet she dutifully places one foot in front of the other and marches forward with little complaint. I continually remind her to visualise the tumour and cancerous C3 vertebra literally leaving her body.

The surgeons assure us that the removal of the lung tumour is far less complicated and less invasive. We look forward to Kim being tumour-free before Christmas—unless the PET scans say otherwise.

The chemotherapy is certainly not something to look forward to, but Kim realises that like many things in life, some things just need to be done. I have absolute faith that this beautiful, heroic individual will accept what needs to happen.

Oscar visited Kim in hospital, and I think it really shook him up. We had a long talk last night and I continue to reassure him. Jackson, despite his busy schedule, was also able to pop out and see Kim and, as confronting as it was, I think it comforted him to see that his mother was in such expert hands. Louis sits his final exam today for the Police Force at 3.00 pm but he's made a Herculean effort to juggle his study with extensive visits to the hospital.

Upon waking from her operation, I was holding one hand and Louis the other.

'My two dependable men,' she mumbled.

Friday 12 December 2014
The following photo was taken last Wednesday, exactly eight days after Kim had major surgery to remove her C3 vertebra and a tumour wrapped around her artery the size of half a fist. Kim could still pump out a treadmill session while Louis and I trained at our gym.

The downside is Kim has dropped to a worrying forty-nine kilograms and there appears to be some nerve damage in her mouth, tongue and throat. Dr Coughlan assures us this will heal in time and reminded us how major the surgery was. Kim still finds swallowing extremely hard and is continually reverting to the speech pathologist's techniques.

The excruciating pain caused by the tumour is now gone, replaced by the much-welcomed lesser pain of the post-op surgery around the neck. However, our dream of being tumour-free by Christmas seemed out of reach because regular operating theatres close next Friday.

Our thoracic surgeon had been hard to pin down, but enter our co-ordinating surgeon, Dr John O'Neill. By working with Kim's bumbling assistant (who can be as annoying and persistent as a mosquito on a summer's night), we now believe Kim will have the tumour removed from her lung next Thursday or Friday. Our dream of being tumour-free before Christmas will come true ... just!

Our thoracic surgeon will work closely with our new oncologist once Kim has recuperated from this surgery—it will be her third in four weeks. The oncologist will prescribe her chemo and possibly a further radiation regime. This is as far ahead as we want to look right now.

I continually mention to Kim the importance and value of sometimes just being the plodder, head down, putting one foot in front of the other.

'Continue to do this, Kim,' I say, 'and before you know it, you'll look back and be a mile from where you started.'

I reminded Kim that eight weeks ago we had just been diagnosed and literally told before we had even finished introductions and pleasantries from our other oncologist to 'draw up her will'.

Now here we are preparing to be tumour-free.

Physically, Kim's body is in incredible shape and her history of looking after herself is absolutely paying dividends. Emotionally, it has been tough. I cannot even imagine how someone could mentally prepare for a situation such as this, but still, she amazes me.

Yes, there have been moments, and it has broken my heart to give her the tough love speeches where I refuse to lie down, to capitulate or to cry with her. I reinforce that I wouldn't be doing my job if I did—as much as I'm drawn to it at times. To Kim's absolute credit, she simply bounces back.

Monday 22 December 2014

Kim is currently convalescing in Prince of Wales Hospital after her lung surgery with the cardiothoracic surgeon, Dr G. He was suggested to us by Dr Marc Coughlan and Dr John O'Neill, the surgeons who were brave enough to perform the procedure of removing Kim's C3 vertebra and tumour.

Dr G's agenda was to remove the primary tumour on Kim's left lung. Whilst possibly not as complex as the first and second surgery, it was equally invasive, with a lot more trauma in relation to pain and recovery. He completed the two-hour surgery last Friday. Two agonising days in intensive care followed.

Dr G informed me the tumour had shrunk as a result of the radiation treatment and that he had successfully removed it. He did have some concerns about the lymph nodes. The bumbling assistant (who has now taken on the role of 'Dr Sobb') reminded the good Dr G that the PET scan showed no cancer in the lymph nodes. The qualified thoracic surgeon respectfully enlightened the 'hack Dr Sobb' that PET scans are only ninety-eight per cent accurate—the scans were taken approximately eight weeks ago and that this was standard protocol. He also placated me by saying this could be a result of scarring from the radiation treatment. Hopefully, we will know either way before Christmas.

Kim is still on a drip with self-administered pain relief and has a drain attached to her lung. All the respective doctors have passed comments on how well she is recovering. While positive from a medical perspective, both physically and mentally, I think she has had enough.

The next chemo will not be until February next year—in eight to ten weeks—to enable all her wounds to heal as chemo treatment makes patients highly susceptible to infections. The treatment will be an extremely intense dosage as both an inpatient for one day and an outpatient for another twelve weeks. For me, this break between treatments will be all about Kim's emotional and physical recovery. It's about time this bubbling assistant earned his keep!

Unfortunately, it looks like Kim will be in hospital for Christmas Day, so we'll deal with that. I'll make some dishes and bundle the boys and some presents up to the hospital. Not the Christmas we expected, but there are a lot of people around the world in a worse situation than us.

Kim's emotional state mirrors that of her physical state. Yes, she is beaten up and will need time to recover. How could one not need time to emotionally recover from three months ago being a healthy, fit, successful lawyer with a loving family and a bright future, to this?

After waking from her most recent surgery in intensive care, the first words she mumbled were, 'I'm doing this all for you.' Hearing those words and seeing all she has gone through gives me the energy and motivation to keep going and do it all again if I had to, though that's easy for me to say.

At home, Oscar has settled in since returning from boarding school and has a newfound love of coming to my gym. Perhaps it's the new equipment I've just purchased as his Christmas present, but either way it's keeping his mind occupied and off the situation Kim and I are in. Even so, the reality of what is happening to his mother is sinking in. We had a frank discussion last night where he became very inquisitive and specific in relation to Kim's situation. I had been quite vague in the past to protect him. This time I answered all his questions and, unfortunately, he has lost much of his blissful ignorance and innocence. He refuses to see Kim at the hospital, and I recognise this as a coping mechanism for him.

I felt cheated that we couldn't properly celebrate the recent results of Louis passing his police entry exam. Not Louis, though. He has stoically continued to train and dutifully assists me around the house and with Kim. He says very little but does so much. His attitude is strong and positive, but his silence speaks volumes. I'm keeping a close eye on him as his staunch loyalty and dependability are creating signs of fatigue. He continually rings me to check in or find out where I am.

Even though Jackson has kept busy at work with long and late hours, his workplace has closed for two weeks which presents him with a lot of downtime. Jackson is not used to this, and my aim is to keep him as occupied as possible. He's upbeat and happy, though, and his attitude brings a lot of comfort to Kim.

I'd like to share with you an irony that recently occurred. As an eighteen-year-old young man, I came across this wonderful poem that I kept in my wallet. I had forgotten all about it. Last week, thirty-four years later, while sitting outside intensive care, I rediscovered it. Frayed and almost illegible, I reacquainted myself with its words. Little was I to know as an eighteen-year-old young man how poignant it was going to become. I draw great courage and strength from its words.

My business is now north.

DECEMBER 2014—DEPENDABLE MEN

Tired and lonely,
So tired
The heart aches.
Meltwater trickles
Down the rocks,
The fingers are numb,
The knees tremble.
It is now,
Now that you must not give in.

On the path of the others
Are resting places,
Places in the sun
Where they can meet.
But this is your path,
And it is now,
Now that you must not fail.

Weep
If you can,
Weep,
But do not complain.
The way chose you—
And you must be thankful.

Dag Hammarskjold

January 2015—The Noosa Debacle

Monday 12 January 2015

Kim's health is an all-consuming situation, with a pattern of highs and lows. The euphoria of leaving hospital on Christmas Eve was premature and short-lived because in our ignorance and haste to return home, we had no pain regime program in place. Within a week, we were back in the Prince of Wales emergency department for a horrendous six-hour stint sitting in the hallways seeking help for Kim's extreme pain.

Fortunately, we came across a doctor who took the time to fully enquire about Kim's situation. This eventually resulted in a full evaluation from the Pain Management Care Unit along with further CT scans and x-rays.

The scan showed inflammation of the lymph node that we were already aware of. We are due a biopsy report on it from our oncologist next Thursday, along with our upcoming chemo roster. The other outcome from the scans was discovering that Kim had a fractured rib. Our best guess is this resulted from her most recent lung operation where they entered through her back.

Anyone who has ever experienced fractured, broken or bruised ribs knows the extra pain Kim endured would have been excruciating. Again, her pain tolerance overwhelms me. So, the outcomes from our lengthy stay in the corridors of emergency at Prince of Wales were identifying the fractured rib and a pain management regime of approximately thirty tablets a day!

Kim and I have always loved Noosa, so, in preparation for Kim's upcoming chemo in February, I planned a week-long trip to Noosa Heads. In this picturesque holiday location in North Queensland, I hoped she could recover and ideally put on approximately three kilos. Due to the timing of the lung surgery, we couldn't fly up, so I booked an overnight rail sleeper which takes approximately fourteen hours.

Even the best thought-out plans can go wrong, though. It ended up being a complete disaster for poor Kim owing to her inability to move with any ease.

JANUARY 2015—THE NOOSA DEBACLE

On arrival in Noosa, my PA, Julie, and I swung into action, searching for ways to get her back home. In the end, we discovered that with a blood-thinning injection, we could create a twenty-four-hour window of opportunity for a domestic flight home. With this planned, Kim, my mother Nola, Oscar and I attempted to enjoy Noosa, but it was bittersweet.

As with Kim's physical wellbeing, her emotional state is extremely fatigued. At the not-so-low points, we discuss logic. I speak to Kim about treating the cancer with utter contempt.

'We can't let it stop you from doing what you really want to do.'

However, it's a constant battle. During the lowest points, we cling to each other, or maybe I simply cling to her. How could Kim not feel emotionally cheated after having her life kidnapped from her? I continue to reassure her not to despair about feeling fatigued, as I have enough strength for both of us. Again, easy for me to say. In reality, our life may never be the same. Nonetheless, that doesn't stop me from attempting to get back as much as I can for Kim.

It's the little things that make all the difference: the fellow member from North Cronulla Life Saving who wore their father's prized bronze medallion after his battle with cancer to show support for Kim, the brief texts, the phone calls, the messages, the way Kim held my hand in the plane and said, 'I don't want to give your hand back.'

The little things have never been so big.

Selfishly, I am happiest when I'm with Kim, and that is where I am.

Thursday looms as the day for the lymph node biopsy report and chemo itinerary. It seems ominous, but my intention is for us to come out fighting.

Friday 23 January 2015

We needed a little time to digest the results of the biopsy on Kim's lymph node and let the dust settle. The result, as you've possibly guessed, was not the one we were looking for. The biopsy proved positive for cancer in the lymph node. That being said, it doesn't change matters in relation to Kim's treatment.

Kim begins her intensive chemotherapy in the first week of February, consisting of four cycles of treatment every three weeks. The treatment requires Kim to stay overnight where they will administer the chemo and closely monitor her. This differs from what had been reported to us earlier and is certainly different from the initial chemo administered prior to her surgeries.

In relation to pain management, Kim has weaned herself off all prescription pain-relief medication. When considering the massive doses and strength of the drugs she was on, this is an incredible feat—I will never boast about my boxing ten-rounders ever again! Kim is still in pain but has chosen clarity rather than the clouded mind brought on by the medication.

Weight gain is hard, and she still weighs approximately forty-nine kilos. Swallowing is still difficult, though the speech therapist has assured her that her vocal cords are not damaged.

However, owing to the complexity and massive intrusion on her throat because of the surgery, it may take some time for them to come back to normal. The therapist has also given Kim exercises for her tongue and mouth. Coughing and clearing her throat are an absolute no-no regardless of the strong, continuous urges to do so. Much to Kim's anguish, Louis diligently follows her around the house and pounces on her should she even appear like she's going to clear her throat or cough—he'll make a great cop!

I've got Kim back to the gym and on the treadmill doing two kilometres a session at a slow pace. These are some of our most memorable moments; Kim on the treadmill, Oscar on the weights and Louis and I skipping and whaling away on the bags to Dragon and Bruce Springsteen. I really can't describe how close we all feel to one another during these times. Nothing gets said, but we all know it.

Emotionally, it's still a rollercoaster for Kim; a glance in the mirror, putting on certain clothes or even an innocent look from a stranger can trigger off emotions. However, true to form, we've logically discussed the situation and being the champion that she is, she gets back up and marches forward.

My work colleagues and the Board of Directors have been nothing short of incredible. It's given me the flexibility I've needed to juggle 'the dailies'. Mornings are the hardest for Kim, both physically and emotionally, so it's my job to start each morning with motivation. God, she must be sick of my voice and turns of phrase!

Once up, I prepare her antioxidant fruit drink with some variety of protein such as scrambled eggs, and of course, her usual double shot of espresso with milk. Despite losing her appetite and the absolute chore of swallowing, she'll dutifully follow my instructions and finish everything. Hopefully, we will tackle the weight situation when we meet our nutritionist.

In the meantime, I'm hoping to squeeze in a short break away between chemo treatments to make up for the Noosa debacle.

Jackson has returned to the whirlwind operation of Riley Street Garage Bar and Restaurant, and Louis is now pursuing an application to work as a camp counsellor in California during the summer while he awaits the further progression of his Police Force application. He continues to train hard and we're looking to schedule a fight soon. Oscar has been an absolute champion while home from boarding school. Up at Noosa, he dutifully hung out with his parents and grandmother, never complaining once—a tough call for a sixteen-year-old boy. He returns to boarding school next week. He is now the tallest of all our boys and is really filling out. He possesses a wonderful sense of humour and continues to be his own man.

Despite all the horrific events that have unfolded since the diagnosis in October, I've discovered that somehow Kim and I love each other even more than I imagined and that she possesses this incredible well of energy that she selflessly passes on to me and the boys. As crazy as it sounds, I feel blessed.

I recommend a four-minute YouTube clip called *'The Mind'* by a philosopher called Alan Watts. During some of the recent tough times, I have sought refuge by viewing it.

As Kim and I prepare for her upcoming chemo, I say to her, 'We will refuse to be victims.'

My business is now north.

Playlist:
Alan Watts, *The Mind*, courtesy of alanwatts.org

February 2015—Hot Noodles and Mindless TV

Monday 9 February 2015

Kim's physical health update is mixed. Her throat is healing excruciatingly slowly, with eating and swallowing still laboriously slow. The twenty-or-so-inch wound on her back has become reinfected for the third time. We are currently on a massive dose of antibiotics in a race to have the infection cleared so we can start chemo on Wednesday.

Chemo will be a half-hour transfusion at the Prince of Wales Cancer Centre, followed by transfer to a ward where another dose will be transfused over a five-hour period. The second dose is extremely toxic, and Kim will need to stay in overnight for observation.

In the lead-up, and to help her body cope, she has received a vitamin B injection and folic acid. On the day, and the day before, she will take doses of steroids. She will combat the side effects of nausea with drugs and as we move further into the cycles, fatigue will progressively get worse.

Hair loss will only take the form of thinning, so Samson, aka Kim, is relieved. She will receive four cycles in total with each occurring every three weeks. After the second cycle, we will conduct further CT and PET scans where we can measure the success of the treatment. There are contingencies, but I don't think it serves any purpose to discuss them at this point.

Physically and mentally, Kim is nothing short of phenomenal, though she has her moments. To not have moments in this situation would border on being inhuman. I don't think it serves a purpose to further articulate this. However, when these moments do transpire, they are dark. We have each other and my aim is to ensure we move forward quickly away from them.

A large part of Kim coping so well mentally is her disciplined approach to her physical regime—and maybe a little duress from the boys and me! She has ramped up her speed on the treadmill and increased her distance to three kilometres. On top of that, she now includes a hand weight curl regime for her upper body.

Last Sunday, she donned the bikini and came out to North Cronulla with me. Those moments wading out the back of North Cronulla are truly wonderful. I take her hand and gently negotiate through the breakers until we're out treading water together and discussing how beautiful and clean the ocean feels. While chemo looms like a nemesis, we will always have my gym and North Cronulla beach as our spiritual oasis and haven.

As close as we are as a family, each of the boys is so different in their own ways. The opening of the National Rugby League (NRL) season has been a good distraction for Oscar. He continues to produce these incredible film clips about his beloved South Sydney Rabbitohs. I think he welcomed returning to Joey's, but as per usual, we are reminded of the harsh reality by the little things. Oscar couldn't kiss his mother goodbye on his return to boarding school because he had a cold. We couldn't risk infection for Kim coming into chemo. Nonetheless, he stoically negotiates through our situation and it's apparent his personality is developing while moving into early manhood. As we spend more time training together at the gym, we're talking more and sharing our thoughts, aspirations and experiences.

Louis just celebrated his twenty-first birthday and I think he will be happy if he never sees a drop of alcohol again. He is so disciplined in his approach to diet and training that any movement to the 'dark side' has major repercussions with his body rebelling. I kind of like that! He is currently finishing this incredibly long and detailed application to be a counsellor in a Californian summer camp. He is particularly looking at camps for troubled youth, specialising in boxing and fitness. Our hope is that this great life experience will dovetail into his call-up to the NSW Police Force.

Jackson is still working tremendous hours at the restaurant. He loves being mothered by Kim and this co-dependent relationship is good for both.

I continue to be Kim's shadow and possibly—let me change that—most definitely can be overprotective at times. I wander the hospital halls and waiting rooms with my portable travel bag, complete with handle and wheels. It holds a complete portable filing cabinet of documents containing all of Kim's results, along with further relevant information regarding anything to do with Kim's health. I think I must look like some sort of 'carpetbagger' or a comedic Charlie Chaplin as the 'Little Hobo'. Nonetheless, more than once, it's held us in good stead as overworked physicians bumble through notes in search of Kim's information. I'm usually the first to place the results on their tables.

Monday 16 February 2015

The Cancer Centre has appointed a nurse/cancer welfare person to act as our liaison officer. She informed us that the unique nature and intensity of Kim's treatment means the process is not as seamless as other treatments. As I explained previously, Kim receives two forms of chemo. One is at the Cancer Centre and the second is in a ward where she must stay overnight.

The night before, of course, was a sleepless one as we pondered what the following day held for us. As usual, I got up early, cooked Kim a huge breakfast, pushed, prodded and bullied her into getting ready and then waited … and waited.

By 9.30 in the morning, I rang the Cancer Centre who again told me we just had to wait for the phone call. My paranoia of Kim missing out on her treatment drove poor Kim demented. The day progressed into the afternoon and at approximately 3.00 pm, we received the call.

We arrived at the Centre and they took us into the chemo room. Initially, it was extremely confronting watching old, young, men and women, all at different cancer stages, receiving their treatment intravenously. I pondered how incredible these people were. I felt quite humbled by the way they were simply getting on with things. A young teenager with her mother, a more mature lady speaking to the nurse about her family, a Gen X-er, a young man obsessed with his iPhone; all different walks of life connected in this room.

We were the last to leave. They purposely co-ordinated our departure so we're not at the hospital for any longer than we need to be—transporting us, still on a drip, up to the special cancer ward. This is an old part of the hospital, and we shared a room with a French lady who spoke no English and another middle-aged 'lady' with the vocabulary of a soldier on R and R in Phuket.

Kim's evening meal was already on the bed. It was cold and looked about as appetising as something Kim would have cooked herself. As you know, Kim can't boil water! I quickly drew the curtains around our bed and set about making this space our own.

After setting Kim up, I politely placed her food tray at the nurses' station and went on a reconnaissance mission to find real food. My aim was to put something in her mouth that had strong flavours to counter the metallic taste chemo brings on. I also wanted the food to bring her comfort.

I wandered the streets of Randwick and came across a cook-to-order noodle bar where I went about ordering the hottest dish they had, bought chopsticks and napkins, and quickly made my way back to Kim and our bunker.

I set up a table on the bed where we civilly dined on our noodles together—just the two of us, hidden from the world with the only reminder being a cannula in her arm and the chemo bag it was attached to. The noodles were hot and never tasted so good as they did that night with Kim. With dinner finished, I set about for us to watch the most mindless TV programs we could.

Visiting hours finished at 8.00 pm. I stayed until 9.00 pm, ensuring I had her iPad set up with movies to watch. Kim knew she was going to be in for a long night. We accepted that, and I promised to be there first thing in the morning. I made my way through the hospital halls back to the car, realising that as much as I love her, I had no idea how brave and strong my wife could be. We talked again at length on the phone while I was in the car on the way home.

I arrived at the cancer ward the next morning to find that 'Frenchie' still refused to speak any English, so, of course, I greeted her in my pathetic version of French and that warmed the room up a little. To my amazement, I discovered that the 'lady' had befriended Kim! Kim had her bags already packed and whispered, 'Get me out of here now, Ant. This lady is mad.' I hastily obliged.

The first forty-eight hours weren't too bad as the steroids masked the nausea. On Saturday, Valentine's Day, the nausea hit. Kim refused to cancel our Valentine's Day dinner and politely pretended to sip her champagne through dinner, looking beautiful. Still feeling unwell on Sunday, I took her down to North Cronulla where she received some slight respite by wading in the ocean. Then I literally dragged her kicking and screaming to the gym. She sulked for the first twenty minutes whilst on the treadmill but proceeded to pump out a three-and-a-half-kilometre personal best! At the end of training, she capitulated and admitted she felt better after her session, both physically and emotionally.

So, this is where we are now after our first cycle. After the second cycle, our oncologist will conduct further PET and CT scans, which will enable him to measure the effectiveness of the treatment. I predict that each cycle of chemo will pretty much run the same as the one I have just described, only we'll be a little wiser and I possibly won't be so paranoid about her missing the treatments.

Currently, I'm working on getting Kim to Bali in between chemo treatments, as they occur every third week. The aim is to get her into a villa in Seminyak or Ubud where she can rest while I do some work, studying some of the restaurants and their fit-outs. With her birthday coming up in April, she has requested a family trip to Uluru, the famous Aboriginal site in outback

Central Australia, followed by travel on the Ghan to Darwin. My aim is to ensure this eventuates.

Kim and the boys remain tight, and, in true Sobb fashion, we continue to make fun of one another at every opportunity. Kim has received no special favours to this point!

We move forward and refuse to capitulate and become victims. While many matters relating to this disease are out of our control, we retaliate by surrendering them and dealing with what we can control on our terms.

My business is now north.

March 2015—Not Even in America

Monday 30 March 2015
Kim's time in Bali was a great respite for her both physically and emotionally. She rested much of the time and even gained some weight. When I think back to recent darker times after those three major surgeries where she dropped to forty-seven kilos, it's just outstanding to contemplate Kim's resilience, determination and strength. The Sobb family jibes have returned to where she is regularly called a 'fat mess' and it is this taste of our family's pre-cancer normality that keeps us all pushing forward.

Our trip finished with two days in Singapore where I had some work to do at the Marina Bay Sands Casino. Kim used her time wisely—well, in her opinion anyway—to purchase four pairs of shoes and a handbag. It appears our gym sessions have not only given her physical strength but also retail strength!

We arrived home on the Tuesday night with doctors' appointments and scans starting on the Wednesday.

As great as the trip was for Kim, we were straight back into the fight within twenty-four hours of touching down in Sydney. We started with a CT scan to check on the progress of the chemo treatment, and a blood test to check our cell counts were safe enough to commence the third cycle of chemo the following day.

Unfortunately, the CT scans were not exactly what we wanted. The results showed that while the cancer appears not to have spread anywhere else, the tumour in the lymph node has seen moderate growth.

As a result, our oncologist decided to proceed with our third cycle of chemo, however, we will make the decision to accept the fourth cycle based on the results of a more accurate PET scan. Otherwise, we will look at possible further radiation treatment.

I spoke to the doctor about options for surgical removal to which he replied, 'Not even in America would you find anyone to take on such a surgical procedure.' With that as my guide, I immediately began to research our options for surgical removal. As a result, we have an appointment this Wednesday with a surgical oncologist from St. Vincent's called Dr H. I will present Kim's latest reports and scans to him.

Should this appointment prove unsuccessful, I will utilise a contingency of our now good friend, the South African Dr Marc Coughlan, who has connections worldwide, to possibly source a surgeon prepared to take on this procedure. In short, the battle continues.

I assure Kim we will still be in the fight as long as she keeps herself physically in shape, both nutritionally through diet and physically by our regular workouts at the gym. So, we wait with bated breath for our appointment with Dr H from St. Vincent's Hospital and the result of our PET scan.

Emotionally, Kim is nothing short of a champion. She stoically gets up each morning feeling less than a hundred per cent but fights the good fight. I cannot begin to imagine how one wakes up each morning to face this—yet she does.

As we move further into our battle, the dark times seem a little darker. It is here that I turn our conversations to logic rather than emotional anecdotes. I also choose between empathy or tough love. Sometimes I get it wrong, and to this day Kim has always forgiven me. She never uses it as ammunition for emotional blackmail. Any self-doubt I may have, Kim simply washes it away.

On Good Friday, we leave for Kim's highly anticipated trip to Uluru where we will stay for three nights with the boys. From there, the boys will return home while Kim and I continue up to Darwin on the Ghan train. After two nights in Darwin, we will return home to face the results of the PET scan.

In the meantime, Kim and I greatly anticipate Oscar's return home each weekend from boarding school. With the football season just commencing, we look forward to afternoons on the sidelines and sitting in the stands of Joey's with our usual flask of hot soup. Huddled together, we cheer for the cerise and blue, the colours of Joey's. It sounds so simple, but it gives us great joy.

Louis' trip to America as a lifeguard for the Marist camp in June is proceeding well. He has an appointment coming up with the U.S. Consulate to approve his visa. In relation to the Police Force, while Kim and I were away, our family home had an impromptu visit on a Sunday afternoon from two burly policemen wishing to interview Louis. The purpose of the impromptu interview was to get an 'unrehearsed' version of the police applicant and their family life.

Here's what they got: Louis shooting hoops with his mates in the front drive while his grandmother and two brothers screamed wildly at the TV while watching the South Sydney Rabbitohs. Add to this the blood-curdling barks from Kim's German Shepherd, Reuben, and what you have is a normal situation for a Sunday afternoon at the Sobb household. The following week, both our neighbours received similar impromptu visits in relation to Louis' application.

Things must have seemed OK as they brought his physical examination forward to last Sunday, which he passed with great success. They informed him the next step will be a psychological examination—God help us!—followed by a full medical. They explained that should there be no issues, he could be down at the Police Academy as early as September. Louis has been incredibly patient and focused through this whole process. With everything else going on in our household, it's great to see him progressing.

Jackson continues to work incredible hours and, on top of this, much to his mother's great pleasure, he has re-enrolled in the final unit of accounting to complete his Advanced Diploma in Hospitality. Reuben continues to shadow Kim wherever she goes. She often tells me of waking from her afternoon sleep to see him staring at her loyally like a centurion. She finds great comfort in her partner and protector.

My business is now north.

April 2015—A Quantum Leap

Monday 20 April 2015

Kim's physical update today is significant in many ways. The tumour in the lymph node has grown and a small new cancer was found in the pubic bone.

The doctor decided to review our supposed fourth and final cycle of chemo alongside a far more accurate PET scan. There's no point in receiving any more chemo if the tumour continues to grow. After returning home from Uluru, Kim and I nervously attended the PET scan appointment. With great trepidation, we came to our oncologist appointment for the results of the scan, fully prepared to expect the worst.

However, as per usual, and working in his own time (not ours), God blessed us with a result showing a significant decrease in the tumour's size in the lymph node, while the growth in the pubic bone remained minimal. So, they ordered us straight up to the cancer unit for the bittersweet fourth cycle of chemo.

On entering the ward, it appeared all the staff were aware of Kim's result, and that it was her birthday, and their enthusiasm was overwhelming. Kim was quite emotional, but it was just the news she needed to hear.

Once Kim was settled in and I had gone through my usual ADHD preparation of her immediate area, I went to a quiet place I knew in the hospital. There's possibly not a square metre I don't know about at the Prince of Wales Hospital after spending so much time there.

I just needed some time to digest what was happening.

I said a short prayer of thanks and, for some reason, pondered what Jesus must have gone through in the garden of Gethsemane. Up until now, I have realised that what could go wrong, has gone wrong for Kim and I. However, He blessed us now at this eleventh hour with this news. Please don't misunderstand this result. We are far from where either Kim or I would like to be in relation to her health, but it's a round. Kim deserves it and we'll take it.

Our appointed cancer nurse later explained to Kim and I that in her time, she had never seen anybody as physically strong as Kim on their fourth cycle of cisplatin chemotherapy, and due to the results of the recent scan, we could go to an unprecedented fifth and sixth cycles. With this being said, the side effects are cumulative, and Kim was very ill in the days after treatment. It's now a matter of finishing the chemo cycles, reviewing scans and then looking at further contingencies.

So, in summary, Kim's physical health, while sick from the chemotherapy, is positive with its response to the treatment. The cancer has not spread, and the tumour has significantly shrunk in the lymph node.

Emotionally, Kim continues to be a champion. The trip was a welcome distraction, and despite the beauty and spirituality of Uluru, I think her highlight was simply being with her boys. Travelling on the Ghan afterwards was a quantum leap from our last train trip debacle. In all, I think Kim really enjoyed the step back in time with the experience. It really was like something out of an Agatha Christie novel.

Kim's physical and mental health is buoyed by her training, diet and rest routine which I meticulously keep her accountable to. Sometimes she has tears as I drive her to the gym, but dutiful as she is, she jumps onto the treadmill and continues to pump out five kilometres at level-five speed. Without fail, we walk out of the gym with Kim commenting on the euphoria she feels after training.

Kim has discovered the importance of not capitulating to the side effects of the treatment. She came down to the beach last weekend and sat for four hours to watch and support her bumbling old husband and athletic son Louis train for the upcoming IRB (inflatable rescue boat) Surf Carnival. She was so sick but never complained once. It truly is humbling when I consider the things I complain about.

Kim's looking forward to our upcoming winter carnivals with the IRB racing team. They often take place at regional beaches where we can simply get away for the weekend, while Kim also offers her support to the North Cronulla team.

Support from the Board and management at work has been nothing short of faultless. It's a constant reminder of the importance of gratitude and that no man or woman is an island.

With the aid of circulation stockings and regular exercises, she looks forward to joining me on my next trip to Vegas, where Kim will get some much-needed downtime after her sixth cycle of chemo. I will go off to my meetings while Kim rests and reads.

The boys are the boys, the absolute apples of their mother's eye—along with Reuben.

Louis recently sat for his police psychometric test, and we await news of the result and the final interview process. Understandably, he is hoping to hear the outcome prior to leaving for the Marist camp in the USA. His focus and patience have been outstanding. At training for the IRB, he's always the first to volunteer to crew for the less-experienced bumbling old guy (me). There is something bonding about us being in the boat together out in the surf. I'm certainly going to miss his company when he leaves in June.

Oscar continues to surprise me with his maturity at being able to read a situation. He is also beginning to display a wonderful sense of self- and social-consciousness.

Jackson continues to attempt to be all things to all people at all times and I'm constantly amazed at what he can fit into twenty-four hours. For Jackson, it's always about somebody else and that makes me extremely proud.

Reuben, Kim's little-known fourth and favourite son, continues to follow her from room to room each day as she goes about her housework. The therapy of his presence and company for Kim are unquestionable, hence I tolerate him!

We fought and won a significant round, but the fight is not over. It may never be over, so we will continue to keep throwing just one more punch.

My business is now north.

May 2015—Marcia Brady or Cindy?

Friday 22 May 2015

Kim's fifth cycle of cisplatin chemotherapy really knocked her around. True to form though, she came down to North Cronulla beach and rallied herself for an hour-long beachside walk while Louis and I trained with the IRB team. She could have easily chosen the effortless option of staying at home in bed, but she wanted to be with her boys and live her life rather than capitulate. Even so, the cumulative effects of the fifth cycle certainly lived up to expectations with its negative effect on her health, in both intensity and duration.

Kim continues to be extremely self-conscious of her speech and enunciation. Enter the bumbling, but tenacious 'Dr Sobb' who bullied his way into seeing one of Sydney's top neurologists to address the matter. The neurologist explained that Kim's surgeries, particularly the removal of the C3 vertebra, were extremely intrusive and would have caused massive trauma to her nervous system.

Our approach is to have another MRI scan. At worst, we will discover that the injuries are irreversible. At best, further surgery could release the pressure on the nerve endings where, in time, they will heal, and her speech could return to normal. In true Sobb fashion, no household member is immune to being a focal point of humour. Kim posed a wry grin at one point when we were discussing her speech and I commented that while she may look like Marcia Brady, she now sounds like Cindy! The journey has been a long and traumatic one. However, my aim is to leave no stone unturned and to seek clarification and knowledge on all options for treatment.

Kim will receive her sixth and final cycle of cisplatin, then move on to what is called maintenance treatment utilising the much less toxic and less traumatising chemo drug called Alimta. Whilst cisplatin's role was to destroy or kill the cancer, which at this point it has only partially done, the role of Alimta is to simply arrest the cancer. They administer this intravenously every three weeks and as an outpatient program. After a period of time, we will measure the success of the treatment and make appropriate decisions.

In relation to her physical wellbeing, Kim is the one who should have the fight name 'the Energiser', not me. I have now progressed her to the cross trainer where she pumps out approximately eight kilometres per session. She follows this with sets of hand-weight curls and a stretch down.

She receives physio each week as well as acupuncture. The acupuncture doctor has also supplied her with some Chinese herbs to burn and inhale—which stinks the bloody house out—and I soak her feet in near boiling water each night to assist her with circulation. Each morning, I ensure she has a hot breakfast, high in vitamins and protein, along with an antioxidant drink. Each afternoon, she rests. She then meets me at the gym for an afternoon training session. Any time in between, Kim is welcome to fill in at her own leisure!

As stoic as Kim is both mentally and physically, there are dark times. My role is to create distractions and events to keep not only Kim, but the rest of the family occupied. This is where moments like 'hey, let's go out for dinner tonight', or driving to a regional beach to compete in a surf carnival, take on monumental importance.

Jackson continues to take on further responsibility at the hip Riley Street Garage Bar and Restaurant, and he continues to be the first to hug his mother when he rises from his slumber on a Sunday morning.

Oscar announced he would like to travel with his mother on my annual trip to Las Vegas this year. This gave Kim great joy as we thought we had seen the last of our boys wanting to travel with their parents. My job will be to ensure it is something special for both of them.

Louis completed the final section of stage nine for his physical test, and we now wait with bated breath to see whether we progress to the final stage ten, which is a panel interview at Police Headquarters at Surrey Hills. Hopefully, this happens before he flies out to America for three months.

So, at this point, we are certainly at the crossroads in relation to Kim's treatment. I will work closely with the doctors to review the results of her scans. Whatever these results, Kim and I have never been closer, family values never more important, small things never so big and once apparent big things never so insignificant.

I recommend a two-minute YouTube clip called '*Live Fully Now*' by a philosopher called Alan Watts. I hope you get as much out of it as I do whenever I watch it.

My business is now north.

Playlist:

Alan Watts, *Live Fully Now*, courtesy of alanwatts.org

June 2015—The Champ

Monday 1 June 2015

1. Here is the Champ on the cross trainer during one of her sessions, now pumping out close to ten kilometres—before she moves on to core stomach and arm curls.

JUNE 2015—THE CHAMP

2. The Champ with a wannabe (aka Louis)!

3. The Champ with her bumbling doctor and trainer.

4. The Champ supporting her husband and the North Cronulla IRB Race Team at Windang Beach Tourist Park. It was freezing cold that night, so we turned up the heater, sat on the couch with a rug and ate pizza in front of the TV. It's one of my favourite nights with Kim.

5. The Champ pumping out some kilometres on the treadmill (with Kim's and my trusty gym partner, Louis).

It's now the eve of our sixth and final cycle of cisplatin chemotherapy. We should have received it last week, but we postponed it so Kim would be well enough to attend Louis' twenty-first/farewell party. Kim is being incredibly heroic, as we know that the cumulative effect of this treatment will make her quite sick.

We had an incredible moment down at the gym where, in a possibly weak and selfish moment, I became a little angry with the boys for not being as helpful as I would have liked in the setup of Louis' party. I also mentioned my concern about the side effects of Kim's final cycle of chemo. She simply walked up to me, put her hand on my cheek, and said, 'Don't worry about me, I'll be fine.' Talk about role reversal—it was now her getting me through this!

Louis' twenty-first was eighties themed with the beautiful Kim, of course, going as 'Roxette', complete with tight, leather, thigh-high boots and a blonde wig (that made her look like a cockatoo). She looked fantastic. As fatigued as she was from all her treatment, she was there at the end of the night after everyone left, helping me clean up.

After this final cycle, as I have said before, we will move to maintenance chemo. I am also investigating a possible move to a new oncologist at the Prince of Wales Private Hospital for several reasons. One is that, at this stage of our treatment, I think it may be a good opportunity for a change to one who is more gender appropriate. Another is being open-minded towards alternative treatment, as I have begun some initial investigation with the University of Western Sydney who offer an outpatient program and service for their Chinese medicine degree students. Whilst the doctor I spoke to said that the Chinese medicine at this point offers no cure, it certainly has statistical proof of success rates in containing cancer.

The boys and Reuben are all doing well. I'll give a further update later about the results of our recent MRI scan where the neurologist will see if we can repair any nerve damage affecting Kim's speech.

Whilst I'm a little tired, this compares to nothing Kim is feeling, and it is this resilience and strength in Kim that propels us forward with hope in our hearts.

My business is now north.

October 2015—Twelve Months On From the Diagnosis

Friday 16 October 2015

At the time of writing this email, Kim is not physically where we would like her to be. She is recovering from a major viral chest infection which we believe results from the massive damage caused to her immune system by chemotherapy. Yes, it's not ideal, but we're navigating our way through it.

These infections seem to arise approximately forty-eight hours after chemo treatment. So, in anticipation, I've asked our Chinese herbal doctor to up the ingredients of the herbal potion she takes three times a day to aid in strengthening her immune system. Most important is complete rest and an ultra-clean environment in the forty-eight hours post-chemo.

A positive outcome of these infections (that came complete with emergency runs to the hospital and tests till the early hours of the morning) was we got an unscheduled CT scan of her chest. This showed the pleasing results of the lymph node cancer area dropping from seventeen millimetres to eleven-and-a-half millimetres—a great result showing that radiation treatment continues to work months after the final treatment.

That being said, radiation has taken a hard toll on Kim's body. It's finished now and we await the results of the more accurate total body PET scan due on 2 November. This will be a significant test result as it will determine whether we continue with our three-week cycles of maintenance chemotherapy with Alimta. Should the results be good, we'll continue with the status quo, if not, we have contingencies in place.

While we were away in Southeast Asia, emotionally, Kim had never been better. However, on return, going straight into chemo—along with these infections—has been tough for her. Yet, like Sisyphus, she continues to pick up that boulder and carry it up the mountain.

I reminded Kim that almost twelve months ago we were diagnosed with stage 4 cancer, told surgery was not an option, prescribed such ridiculous amounts of so-called pain management that it virtually turned her into a zombie, and were informed by the doctors to 'get your affairs in order'.

Fast-forward twelve months and we found a surgeon who would operate and had three major operations within a six-week period, including the clamping of a major artery, a partial left lung lobectomy, the removal of her C3 vertebra which was replaced by a prosthetic, and the removal of a tumour the size of half a fist next to the C3 vertebra. In addition, Kim has endured two separate extended treatments of radiation, six major cycles of the highest form of chemotherapy with cisplatin and is now receiving maintenance chemo cycles of Alimta every three weeks. We take special Asian herb preparations three times a day and she has weaned herself off all prescription pain medication.

'The bottom line is, Kim, we are better off now than what we were twelve months ago,' I say to her.

Kim fulfilled her dream of visiting Angkor Wat in Cambodia and travelling through Vietnam on our last trip. She loved every minute. She also enjoyed having Oscar and Louis with her, and that on numerous occasions I had to dismiss myself to do some work!

While Kim is in some discomfort as she battles the chest infection, I put together a brief montage of photos to give you a visual of how she is travelling of late. She will be embarrassed about the one I put in of her in a bikini, but what the hell, she looks fantastic. It will be worth the trouble I am going to get into!

OCTOBER 2015—TWELVE MONTHS ON FROM THE DIAGNOSIS

MY BUSINESS IS NOW NORTH

The boys are all doing well. Jackson is settling into his new role. Louis is awaiting his final panel interview for the Police Force while training hard with me at the gym, and Oscar is tackling his final year at Joey's. The lesser known, but highly favoured younger son, Reuben the German Shepherd, continues to shadow Kim wherever she goes. I really don't know what we would do without him.

We attempt to continue with as relatively a normal life as we can until the results of our November PET scan.

My business is now north.

November 2015—A Points Victory

Wednesday 4 November 2015

Yesterday, Kim and I received the results of her most recent PET scan. These are considered the most accurate form of reporting on cancer activity. While CT scans may measure the size of tumours, they don't measure the activity of the cancer, which ultimately determines the progress of the disease.

During a PET scan, the patient is infused with glucose (in the form of fluorodeoxyglucose or 'FDG') and the scan highlights hot spots where the glucose is most aggressively being taken up. Cancer, by its nature, takes up glucose, so where there is FDG uptake, there is cancer. The measurement of this uptake determines the strength of its activity. Kim's June PET scan reported high FDG uptake in the lymph node and some activity in both the pubic and femur bones. We saw no FDG uptake in the lung or C3 vertebra owing to the lobectomy and surgical removal of her vertebra and tumour.

Yesterday, our oncologist reported that the results of the most recent PET scan showed Kim has no abnormal FDG uptake in any part of her body. On hearing this, both Kim and our oncologist became quite emotional. She claimed this was an unbelievable result. While reticent to say we are in remission, as the cancer is possibly just dormant within Kim's body, it is not active and has responded to the painstaking treatment Kim has placed her body under.

It's almost unfathomable when I cast my mind back to last October that the so-called surgical experts claimed her situation inoperable and her oncologist whispered me a timeline, told me to get Kim's 'affairs in order' and suggested the best approach was copious amounts of Endone to ease her pain and make her 'comfortably numb'.

Here we are, twelve months later, bruised and battered at the end of the twelfth round. It's not a knockout decision, but we will certainly celebrate a points victory from the latest PET scan results.

Our next step in Kim's treatment is a simple resting treatment. Kim welcomes this break from radiation and chemotherapy, and I can't emphasise or articulate the emotional and physical depletion it takes.

At this stage, our plan is a further PET scan in twelve weeks unless any further symptoms arise. Pending the results of this PET scan, we will decide whether to continue with appropriately targeted chemotherapy and/or radiation.

After what Kim has put her body through over the last twelve months, she welcomes being left alone to regain her identity as Kim Sobb—the mother, wife, solicitor, sister, daughter, daughter-in-law, friend and Reuben's mother—as opposed to Kim Sobb, the cancer patient.

We still have the unresolved issue of her respiratory system and have no hard evidence about its cause. I will continue to monitor these symptoms along with preparing her Chinese herbs three times a day and managing her diet and food intake. The shortness of breath, chest pains and coughing fits are becoming less as time goes on. Much to Kim's dismay, I have her back at the Dog House training already. Yesterday, we celebrated the PET scan results with an eight-and-a-half-kilometre cross trainer session!

The anticipated break in treatment has fed Kim's insatiable desire to travel and so the floodgates have opened! We're off to the UFC event in Melbourne where Kim will cheer for her 'Sister in Combat,' Ronda Rousey. Then we're up to Wategos Beach at Byron Bay for a three-day health spa and snorkelling at the Great Barrier Reef early in the new year. Dear God, she will send me broke!

Meanwhile, the pace of Jackson's new role in the RSL Club industry is a far cry from managing a hip CBD bar and restaurant. However, the management team are close family friends and are passing on a whole new set of values and skills Jackson will need in the future.

Louis was recently called up to his final panel interview at Police Headquarters. Louis and I prepared for hours, including preparing a file, conducting mock interviews and running through scenarios. To put it into the great words of Chuck Norris when questioned on how he felt pre-fight, 'We had a sense of calm and peacefulness as we knew we could not have prepared any better than we had.' Within fourteen days, we will have the answer on whether he will be called down to attend the Police Academy in Goulburn for the January intake.

'Little Buddy', or Oscar, continues to be a joy to his mother, and the two recently indulged in shopping together to purchase him a new outfit for his upcoming Year Eleven Formal. I'm the one struggling with him taking a girl other than his mother!

Kim has promised to ride in the IRB with Louis and I down at Cronulla this season. Louis, myself and many of the members of the North Cronulla Surf Life Saving fraternity are keen to uphold her promise.

Kim's courage throughout this whole ordeal is almost impossible to contemplate or articulate. The boys' commitment to family and their mother is nothing short of noble. Support from family and friends makes me feel quite humble ...

The small things have never been quite so big.

My aim is to ensure Kim and the boys enjoy this victory—as the fight is not over. It may never be over. This is a fact I am happy to accept as, if this is our destiny, so be it.

My business is now north.

January 2016—The PET Scan is Clear

Wednesday 27 January 2016

On Monday, Kim had her scheduled PET scan. Our last scan showed 'no FDG uptake' which we were over the moon about. Leading up to our recent scan, Kim was incredibly anxious, bearing in mind we were diagnosed as stage 4 and the type of Kim's cancer—non-small cell lung cancer—is regarded as one of the most aggressive forms.

We are fortunate enough to now have an incredible oncologist. I scared off, pissed off, or walked away from three others due to their negative or capitulating attitudes. This oncologist texted me the results as soon as she received the report as she understood the agony of waiting four days until our next appointment. The text, verbatim, was:

'Hi Anthony, Great news. The PET is clear. No change from last scan apart from improvement in the fluid around the left lung. No evidence of active tumour. Will give you a copy at the appointment. Cheers.'

Now we have two consecutive, clear PET scans. While it is important we don't get too carried away with ourselves, it's equally important, as I mentioned in one of my first 'Kim Updates', that we celebrate the small victories. This is certainly a significant victory when considering our early oncologist's diagnosis and timeline.

Kim is celebrating and here she is in her latest number which she purchased on our recent visit to Hamilton Island. Notice the youngest Sobb boy, Reuben, who is never far from Kim.

JANUARY 2016—THE PET SCAN IS CLEAR

This second photo is a Sobb selfie taken after a heavy training session at the Dog House. Notice the sweat on the mirror!

Oscar returns for his final year at Joey's this year. Equally, Kim and I look forward to our usual place at the Joey's football games, sitting in the stands, sipping hot soup and cheering for the cerise and blue. We really appreciated his effort during the Christmas break to actively participate in the family household. Numerous times, I witnessed situations where he refused the temptation of being with his mates or doing what he wanted so he could spend quality time with Kim and myself.

Louis' first three weeks at the Police Academy have certainly been challenging. He is one of the youngest of a large intake of 200 recruits. The drill sergeants have been tough taskmasters and dropping him off there was reminiscent of dropping him off on the first night at Joey's all those years ago. They lost two recruits in the first forty-eight hours, with another walking after the first week.

Louis finds the academic work a challenge, but I know he is equal to the task. He scored quite well in a recent physical test which has given him great confidence. He locks himself in his room each night to study and, straight after class, leaves the Academy to train at the Goulburn Police Citizens Youth Club (PCYC). The local boxing trainer, after watching him do his bag work, enquired if he would be interested in some sparring. He agreed, knowing that the local boys were going to try to 'touch him up'. He must have done reasonably well as they immediately asked him to join the boxing team. To his credit, he declined, saying he needed to focus on his work at the Academy. He returns home each Friday night for the weekend and he and I both miss each other's company immensely. However, he is where he needs to be.

Jackson's new role has brought many challenges and long hours, but he always ensures he finds quality time with his mother.

I'm not sure what the future holds in relation to treatment for Kim as we don't see our oncologist until Friday. The mapping out of treatment in such a situation and scenario such as Kim's is quite unique. Even the good 'Dr Sobb', with his hours and hours of research, has found very few, if any, cases remotely similar. However, that doesn't mean I won't stop trying.

Even our oncologist can't explain our results, but simply says, 'Whatever you are doing, just keep doing it.' So, I will continue to prepare the high-protein breakfasts complete with antioxidant shakes each morning, prepare Chinese herbs three times a day and push her through fitness sessions and core strength work each day at our Dog House gym. Most importantly, we will continue to keep our own counsel, stay positive and refuse to capitulate.

Thank you again for lending me your ear.

My business is now north.

March 2016—A New Personal Best

Monday 7 March 2016

Here's a quick pictorial update on Kim.

Kim parasailing on Sydney Harbour last Sunday morning with her wingman and minder, Louis:

MARCH 2016 — A NEW PERSONAL BEST

The Champ between rounds with assistant trainer 'Left Hook' Louis Sobb:

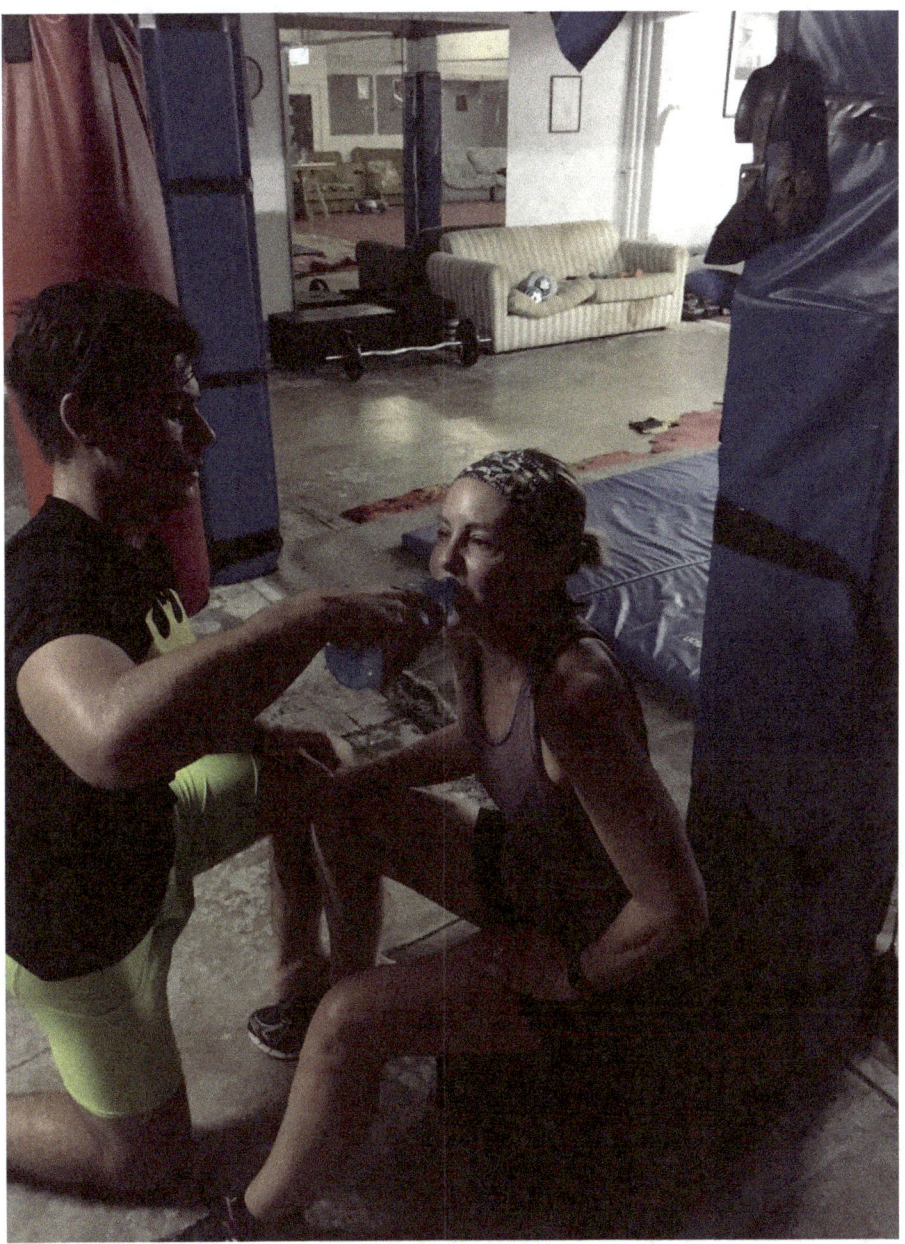

Just finished a new PB of 11.68 kilometres in thirty minutes on the cross trainer:

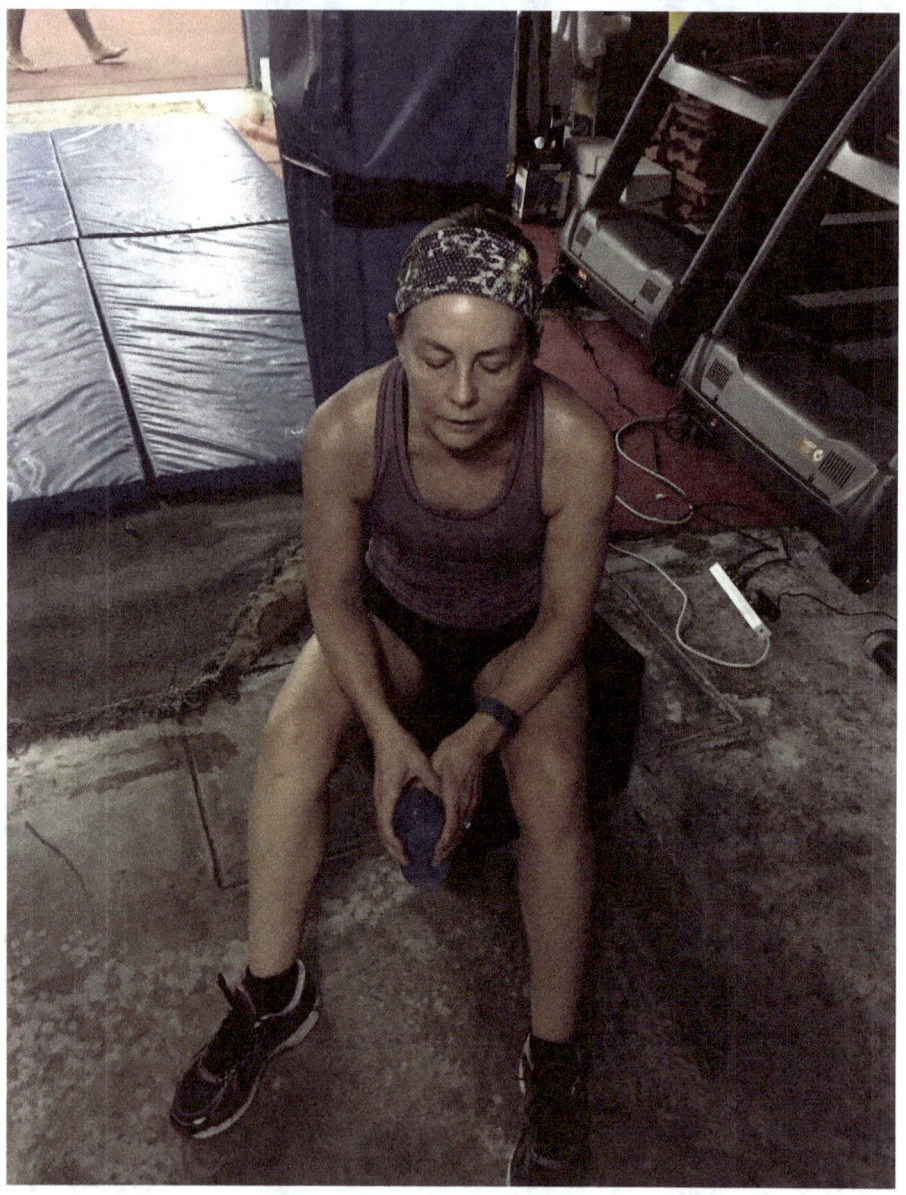

As you can see, the diagnosis has not and will not stop the Champ. Obviously, we have our dark days, but in all, Kim is an inspiration and a tower of strength. Our next scan is in April, which we look to with trepidation but hope in our hearts.

My business is now north.

April 2016—A Brief Taste of Relative Normality

Wednesday 13 April 2016

I share the following recent photos of Kim as they relate to a landmark promise she kept to Louis and me at the beginning of the surf life-saving season to suit up and come out in an IRB patrol session before the end of the season.

MY BUSINESS IS NOW NORTH

APRIL 2016 — A BRIEF TASTE OF RELATIVE NORMALITY

As you can see, Kim kept her promise. With Louis as the crewman and me as the skipper and driver, she screamed her way out through the North Cronulla breakers. On returning home, she couldn't stop talking about how frightening, yet exhilarating, it was. I know how much she was out of her comfort zone, yet she proceeded with the probable motive of keeping Louis and me happy. That's Kim, selfless to the core.

Kim achieves another milestone on Saturday, which is celebrating her birthday. Calendar dates such as these run in tangent to our newly embraced philosophy of mindfulness. This revolves around living neither in the past nor the future, but the ever-present now. Regardless, I say to hell with it and we will celebrate the day, celebrate Kim's life (and future) and drink a glass of champagne.

Kim is recently back from accompanying me on a food and restaurant trip to Bali. She patiently waited while I acquainted myself with managers and chefs, took photos and notes of fit-outs or was simply a pest, getting chased out of kitchens. While I obsessed with all things hospitality, Kim wisely immersed herself into the healthy and peaceful spa treatments.

On Monday, we attend our regular PET scan. It's almost a paradox of time. In one sense, it comes around so quickly, yet in another it's almost an eternity. The stakes, or the results, are just so incredibly high. I constantly remind Kim of how great she looks, how fit she is and that our regime of diet, Chinese herbs and exercise, along with faith, holds us in good stead.

I cannot imagine what it's like to mentally scan one's body at every waking moment with the slightest ailment potentially representing further activity and cancer. The way Kim conducts herself is nothing short of heroic and with a strength I can only aspire to have.

Again, we are fortunate enough to have the backing of an incredible oncologist who, rather than put us through the painstaking torture of waiting until our next appointment to get the results, texts them to me the moment she receives them. I find it almost inexplicable to understand this surreal waiting period for the results. I wish it upon no one. Yet, as I discussed with a very close friend, one can't fight the situation. To move forward, ironically, we must surrender, which is itself an incredibly brave and arduous task. The thought of surrendering to overcome is not new, but it is also not easy.

Should the outcome of the upcoming PET scan be positive and show no active FDG uptake (i.e., no active cancer), Kim has begrudgingly agreed to return to work two days a week. Should the alternative occur in relation to the results, the bumbling 'Dr Sobb' has contingencies as a result of much late-night research in my home office.

Wednesday 20 April 2016
The results of the PET scan weren't exactly what we wanted or expected. They showed Kim has developed a cancerous tumour on her L5, the lowest vertebrae in the lower back.

As usual, our oncologist was good enough to message me the results so I could prepare Kim before the appointment. The sheer act of having to deliver such news to your soul partner and the love of your life is indescribable. I wish this upon no-one. Upon delivering the news to Kim, she became ghost-like before my eyes. She was shattered. The recent months of no treatment and living as close to a normal life as possible may as well have been another life. The memories of the fatigue and sickness associated with treatment, the postoperative pain and rehabilitation and the fear of further activity just flooded Kim.

When I attempted to put this into perspective and find some positives, Kim initially batted these back to me, and I totally understand this. Fate gave us a brief taste of relative normality only to cruelly snatch it away from her. I wanted to lie down in exhaustion and cry with her, but we don't have that luxury.

Frustratingly for Kim, I went straight into fight mode once we reached the Prince of Wales Hospital for the appointment. Our oncologist explained the situation in more detail. At the risk of me being branded an imbecilic optimist, no FDG uptake was detected in areas that had previously displayed this, like the lymph nodes, pubic bone and femur. So, it is all clear bar the mild-to-moderate FDG uptake in L5.

Our oncologist suggested no systemic treatment, but rather an intense dose of radiation. As I may have explained previously, the adverse side effects of radiation treatment are extremely under-rated. If you speak to anyone who has had radiation, they will explain the horrors of this treatment. There was brief mention of surgery, but this revolved around it not really being an option—I immediately felt déjà vu.

Upon leaving the oncologist, we swung into action and I organised a CT scan for the next day. While a PET scan accurately measures location and activity of cancer, the CT scan gives size and measurement, similar to a photo image. The purpose was to get a starting point for measurement of treatment, but I also had an ulterior motive. CT scans are what surgeons review before considering an operation.

With the CT scans organised, we drove out of the Prince of Wales Hospital car park. When we got home, I texted the surgeon who eighteen months ago successfully completed the apparently impossible surgery on Kim's C3. Marc texted me straight back from Switzerland where he was delivering a lecture, saying he believed surgery would be an option. He flies back into Sydney on Monday, and I have scheduled an appointment to see him Tuesday morning.

So, Kim has a new cancerous tumour in L5 with no other active cancer at this point. Should Marc believe it is operable, we'll take this option immediately. If not, we revert to the intensive radiation treatment.

Thursday 28 April 2016
Dr Marc Coughlan returned from Switzerland on Monday and was good enough to see Kim on Tuesday morning. He reviewed the CT scans and believes we have several options.

The first is to completely remove the L5 disc, insert a screw and literally fill the cavity with cement. The second is a technique, 'I serendipitously discovered recently,' as he put it. It involves filling the cavity adjacent to the tumour with an epoxy-cement. This kills the blood supply to the tumour and thus the tumour.

The first is far more intrusive, while the second is a slight incision in Kim's back and an overnight stay in the hospital with virtually no rehab. Both are good outcomes. Both are enormously better options than intensive radiation.

Marc will decide which option based on the results of an MRI scan. If the tumour has emulsified itself into the bone, then we need to remove the whole disc. If it has grown separately and adjacent to the disc, we will take the less intrusive option of filling the cavity with the epoxy-cement and strangle the tumour to death.

Walking out of Marc's office, we organised MRI appointments. The results were couriered to his office and are currently at his desk, waiting to be reviewed. Marc assured me he would do the operation as soon as possible so Kim could be 'active cancer tumour-free' by this time next week.

Upon leaving Marc's office, my unbridled enthusiasm, though some may call it imbecilic optimism, simply couldn't lift Kim. As wrongly frustrated as I became, I needed to understand that while we are going through this together, it is her body and her emotions that are being battered, not mine. It is perhaps this situation that tortures me the most.

The three major surgeries of clamping her right major artery in the neck, the complete removal of her C3 vertebra and the partial removal of her left lung were intrusive, with painfully long recoveries not forgotten easily. Add on to that the dozens of intensive radiation treatments, the dozen or so highly toxic chemotherapies plus claustrophobic scans and hundreds of cannulas and you can understand her reticence.

My aim is to keep Kim positive and buoyant using logic. Yes, her disease is incurable and yes, it may come back and yes, we don't know where or when. But this is here and now and soon we will be actively cancer free. Up to now, we have smashed all the odds given to us by the doctors nearly two years ago. Marc Coughlan even spoke about possibly doing a paper on Kim, reporting her successful management and fight against this aggressive cancer.

Even so, Kim, emotionally, is broken and empty. She struggles to make any sense of the cruelty of fate. I keep reminding her I have enough strength for both of us. I can sense an anxiousness amongst the boys, and I feel the days of their blissful ignorance in relation to Kim's health have sadly passed.

On the family front, Oscar completed his HSC exam trials with Kim lamenting, 'If only one of my boys would have embraced academia ...' I humbly apologised for the strength of my gene contribution. Oscar trained with me during his break from school and I can attest that what he possibly lacks in academia, he makes up for in wit and humour. We dropped him back at Joey's on Tuesday night which I think will be a pleasant distraction for him away from home. He returns to his Joey's life of mates, rugby and some academia—probably in that order! For the first time in many years, we went up as a family and unpacked Oscar into his room. I think this act symbolised our family bunkering in together. Kim obviously felt it as she said, 'I'm so happy to be here with all my boys' (minus Reuben!).

We will not let cancer destroy our ever present here and now. That is ours to do with as we wish. Our choice is to live our lives and love each other. We prepare for the future with our positive nature and physical fitness, but ultimately, we surrender to God. It is not easy, but it is one day at a time. With that as our guide, we cautiously move forward with hope in our hearts.

The bell has sounded and now it's time to go to work.

My business is now north.

May 2016—Degrees of Separation

Tuesday 3 May 2016

The tumour on Kim's L5 appeared to be growing quickly because by Sunday Kim was experiencing sharp pains in her back. Dr Coughlan explained that at its current rate of growth, Kim would have experienced a loss of strength and trouble walking within three weeks. We made the trek up to the Gosford Private Hospital for Monday's procedure, as this was the only theatre Marc could book at such short notice.

He explained a summary of the procedure to me.

'I'm extremely happy with the procedure. Initially, I was going to fill the cavity with cement to starve and kill the tumour. However, when I got in there with the syringe, I could feel it and it was still quite soft, so I took the opportunity to pierce it and suck the whole tumour out. This also gave me the ability to get right in and fill the cement comfortably into the cavity, as well as pushing some of it up into the veins. Because the cement is so hot, it instantly kills any minute cancer cells that are not only in the cavity but also in the veins that they come into contact with.'

So, the procedure was a great success. Marc could not have been happier with the outcome.

There was a ten per cent chance of nerve damage owing to some of the cement spilling out of the cavity and onto the nerves. This appears not to have happened as Kim has no pins and needles in her toes and has full lateral movement of her legs and feet. Whilst reluctant to take any painkillers, owing to the previous terrible side effects of Endone and Targin, Kim has relented, which tells me she must be in quite a lot of pain.

Moving forward, I will give Kim a week off training to recover, but still maintain her Chinese herbs three times a day and the consumption of my high-antioxidant and high-protein meals and shakes.

While spending most of the day sitting in the waiting room at the hospital, I had a lot of time to contemplate many things. Strangely enough, my thoughts meandered to how fortunate we were to have degrees of separation through boxing. Johnny Lewis to Dr John O'Neill and then Dr Marc Coughlan brought us to this new procedure that few oncologists are aware of. As usual, it led me to the need to surrender. God will give me what I need rather than what I want.

The game has now changed and so will my strategy in managing Kim. Not so much in fitness and lifestyle (unfortunately, she will never escape her trainer!), but with treatment. Several new immunology drugs, with successful data and results in the treatment of non-small cell lung cancer, have now come off trial.

Thursday 19 May 2016
We've just finished a whole day of meetings with specialist oncologists to map out Kim's next steps. In the days leading up to these meetings, I did as much research as possible to bring myself up to date with the latest on treatment and products currently on trial.

Our first meeting was with our radiation oncologist who was reluctant to give the further radiation I requested to the L5 region. My rationale was that Kim's recent surgery may have left tiny cells of cancer which could travel to other parts of her body, multiplying and creating tumours. My thought process was to utilise the radiation to mop up anything missed during surgery.

The doctor initially declined my request, stating there was no data to prove this as a successful strategy. I promptly replied via email explaining that if anyone only relied on current available data for the use of treatment, how could one ever discover new possibilities or treatments? He finally relented and today Kim starts a three-week regime of radiation every day.

I don't know who I have pissed off the most ... our radiation oncologist or Kim. Honestly, I'm sure the doctors dread their appointments with us. I march in with my wheelie bag of data, madly taking notes on my iPad and questioning every strategy!

I have mentioned before the terrible side effects of radiation and it breaks my heart to know I have been the one who has initiated this, but we have to stay in fight mode. I remind Kim that had we listened to the initial advice of specialist oncologists we would not have found a surgeon to remove the C3 vertebra. We would not have been able to remove the tumours through a lobectomy on her left lung. We would not have received the extra two cycles of the highly toxic chemotherapy cisplatin, and we would not have had the recent tumour on her L5 lumbar removed.

Kim would have been comatose with Endone and just existing. One recent oncologist stated Kim would not see Oscar complete his HSC this year. Yet, here we are now, active-tumour-free, owing to Kim's incredible courage and undeniable trust.

On completing the radiation treatment, we will make an assessment about whether Kim takes up a brand-new form of treatment that has just come off trial based on a new immunology strategy. Simply put, our bodies' natural immune system has a set of brakes and for good reason. This new drug called Opdivo, also known as nivolumab, releases the handbrake on the immune system, allowing our natural system to identify and kill the cancer cells. It does have some negative side effects; however it is far less toxic on the body than chemotherapy.

I've been following the clinical trials of Opdivo for some time, and they have shown some incredibly positive results. Only in the last couple of months has it been taken off trial and made available. Our aim is to decide whether we take this drug immediately or wait for the results of our next PET scan in July, which gives time for Kim's body to fully recover from the radiation treatment.

I won't bore you with any further details on treatment, however from my perspective, I need to step up my game to ensure Kim's body is as strong as possible to recover from the radiation and prepare it for any future treatment. If she thought our sessions at the Dog House were brutal, they will be nothing compared to our new program. Diet will also become increasingly important along with our thrice daily intake of Chinese herbs.

In July, I head off on my annual business trip to the U.S. which I know Kim is looking forward to. I don't think I have met anybody who loves travelling more than Kim. During these trips, she patiently sits at restaurants while I dissect menus and fit-outs, or she immerses herself with a book by the pool as I wander gaming floors or meet with casino executives. I'm fortunate to have a Board of Directors who believe in the ethos and the benefits of allowing you to travel with your partner.

Meanwhile, sitting with one another sharing a flask of hot soup and cheering for the Joey's rugby teams each Saturday afternoon remains a high point. Kim will watch her lumbering old husband, along with her son, Louis, the fine young specimen, compete at the upcoming NSW and Australian Surf

Life Saving Titles at Mollymook. Dutifully, she will rug up and walk from lane to lane on the beach quietly cheering for her North Cronulla team, perhaps feeling a little embarrassed and sorry for her old man who is usually last to the boat—amongst his much younger peers may I add!

Louis is on a study break from the Academy at present. When not doing the study—that I usually have to oversee and prescribe for him—he is either taking personal fitness classes at the Dog House or quietly training with me as we listen to Bruce Springsteen, occasionally speaking a sentence or two over a two-hour session. He returns to the Police Academy in August.

Jackson, as with everything, has completely thrown himself into his new role as operations coordinator, but he is always the first to give his mother a hug. I often find him sitting on the lounge with her, his arm around her shoulder, watching TV.

Boarding school life at Joey's has been such a godsend to Oscar on numerous levels. He's able to escape there, away from the situation at home, with good mates, caring teachers and an ethos of great spirituality.

As we move on to our next phase of treatment through this extended radiation program, Kim is quite anxious—and rightly so. As wonderfully personal and caring as the treatment staff are, she is still grappling with the reality of 'How did I get to be here?', 'What am I doing here?' and 'I simply want my life back.' These questions have no answers but underline my love and admiration for Kim's courage and strength.

My business is now north.

Playlist:

Across the Border, Bruce Springsteen

June 2016—The Shadow of Radiation

Wednesday 8 June 2016

Here is Kim on the last day of three weeks straight of radiation treatment. As I have said before, the dedication of these staff and their relationship with the patients is really something special.

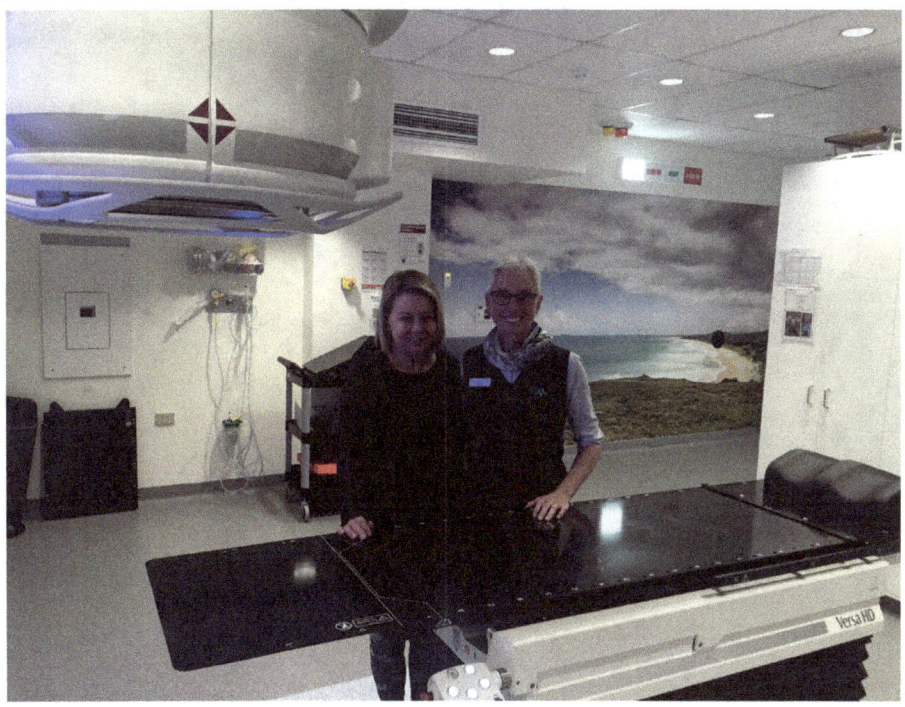

We attended Saturday rugby at Joey's. We sat in the pouring rain together from 10.30 am till 4.30 pm. Wouldn't have wanted to be anywhere else or with anyone else.

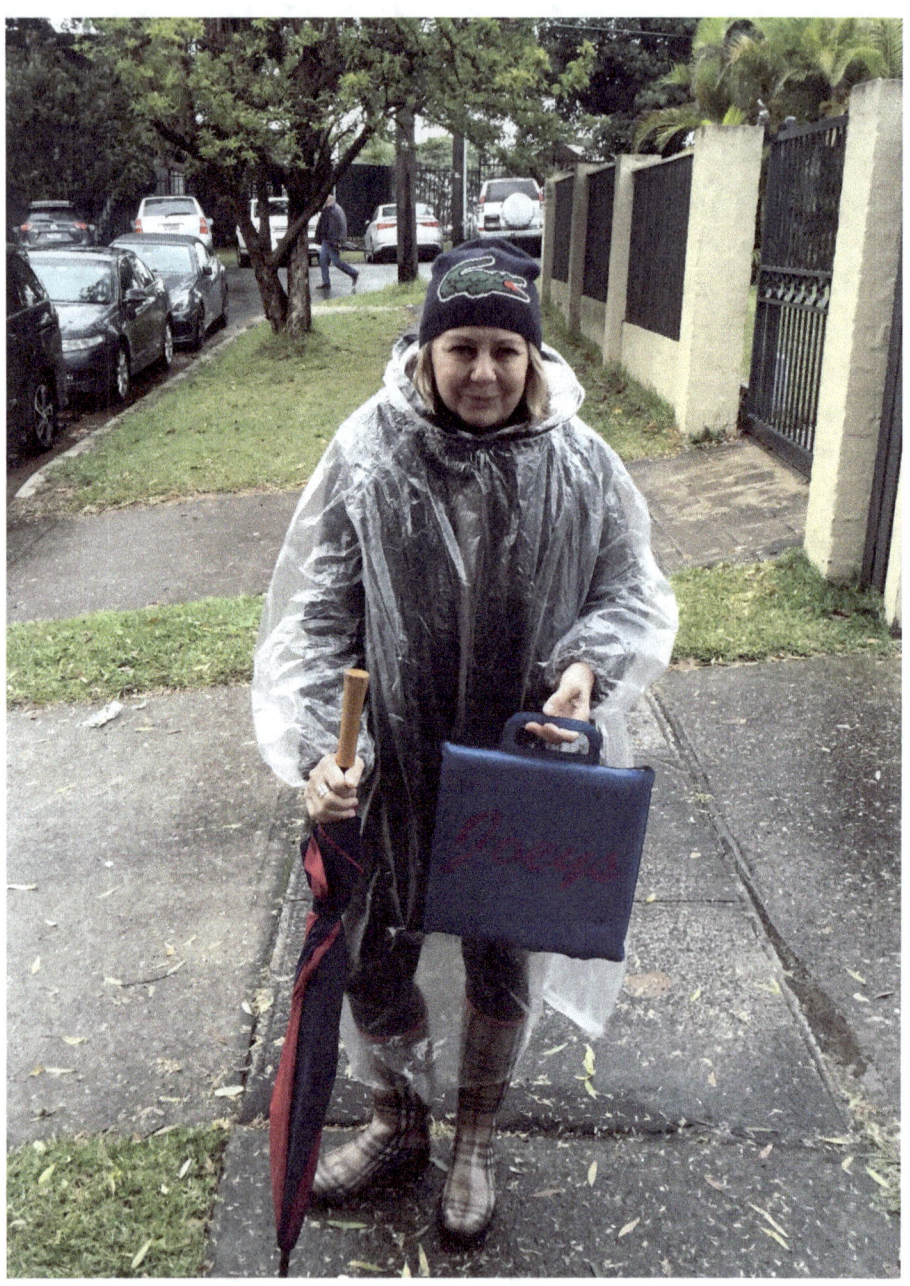

Our three weeks of radiation treatment are over. That Kim is still talking to me, given I argued for, then insisted on this treatment, is testimony to her incredible patience with the good 'Dr Sobb'. I possibly pushed the envelope a little too much when I suggested we bring the PET scan forward to measure the success of this radiation trial. I was quickly put into my place with a blunt 'no', and a matter-of-fact explanation that the radiation output on a human during one PET scan is the equivalent to approximately 1,000 x-rays.

I am learning to only fight the fights that really need to be fought, though Kim continues to trust me implicitly, which itself is quite humbling. So, now we wait until Wednesday 20 July when we receive our next PET scan. Based on the result, we will decide whether to begin the new intravenous immunology treatment of Opdivo for treating aggressive cancer.

The conclusion of the radiation treatment came as a huge and welcome relief. Apart from the physical side effects, the mental and emotional strain of waking up and greeting each morning to face radiation treatment was all-consuming. I purposely booked each treatment as early in the day as possible. That way, Kim could live without the shadow of the treatment ahead of her each day. It worked to a point, but one can only tweak and take so much.

Throughout the whole process, Kim was nothing short of stoic. I'm not saying we didn't have some moments. In fact, we had a few. I was tough when I thought the situation required it and attempted to be comforting during others. Even then, in many situations, I simply didn't get it right. We found ourselves in this situation with no warning and no instructions—just instinct and each other.

Between now and the next PET scan, I will keep the family as busy as possible. Louis has been doing extra study in between his own training sessions with me at the Dog House and taking private fitness sessions as a personal trainer. With whatever little down time he has had, he has either worked in the dock or literally scrubbed pots for me at Fairfield RSL, where I work.

In July, we will compete together at both the State and National Surf Life Saving IRB titles. And yes, I'm usually the last from the beach sprint to the boat, but that Louis wants to continue to crew alongside me is something very dear to us both.

For all the extra responsibilities Jackson now has in his new role and other day-to-day pressures, his generally positive demeanour and commitment to the family—particularly his mother—is heart-warming.

Oscar continues to develop into his own man. However, rather than yearning for independence, he seems to fuel the family members with the importance of us all continuing to do things together. I don't know if it is a symptom of the situation our family has found ourselves in, but it's his mindset at the moment and something I am quite happy to foster. While a common thread connects all the boys, they are three very different individuals with different needs at different times.

Until 20 July, Kim will loyally walk up and down beaches, rugged up against the winter cold to support her two men and the lifesavers in the IRB section of North Cronulla. I will also whisk her away to the U.S. with me where I will conduct my work while she gets some much-needed rest and rehabilitation before we step into the ring for our next bout.

We will not yield. We will continue to defy this situation.

My business is now north.

July 2016—Cementing Treatment

Monday 25 July 2016

Kim has had an extremely busy schedule. We returned home last Tuesday from my work trip in the U.S. for her to receive her PET scan on the Wednesday. Then we departed on the Thursday to the South Coast where Kim was the support crew for Louis and me to compete in the Australian IRB Surf Life Saving titles. I organised this on purpose to keep Kim's mind busy and distracted.

On the Thursday night, whilst down at the South Coast and sitting at the dinner table with Kim and Louis, I received a text from our oncologist outlining the results of the PET scan. She stated the scans showed the reoccurrence of lesions in the C3 vertebra and another new lesion in her pelvis. She also requested we begin treatment with the new drug Opdivo immediately. I pretended the text was from work, as looking at Kim across the table, she looked so vibrant and healthy. I simply couldn't do it.

In the ensuing twenty-four hours, in between races and making excuses to ring work along with some incredible support from my PA, I contacted our surgeon Marc, who has now become a friend, organised a CT scan at 8.30 am this morning and put a strategy in place, knowing it wouldn't be long until I had to tell Kim.

That time came on Saturday afternoon when she expressed concern about not hearing from our oncologist. After Saturday's races concluded, I sat Kim down and gave the news that every cancer patient dreads. Kim was devastated, and despite my attempts to explain that I had strategies and plans, she melted into a deep, dark hole. I can't put into words the darkness of that place. In her mind, whatever trickle of hope remained had been totally doused.

I took her out for dinner that night and she had her usual glass of French champagne. However, she was just empty. For those of you who understand, the beach and the ocean have a therapeutic and spiritual effect on some people and somehow, as if by God's good grace, the South Coast beach of Mollymook was beautiful.

The next day, Kim greeted Louis and I down at the beach as we prepared in the early morning for the upcoming races. Nobody would have known the pain she was carrying. She followed us up and down the beach, always giving us a special little wave before the starter's gun, a pat on the back when we finished, and a special hug for the old husband plodding back from the finish line.

After a lengthy conversation with Dr Marc, he believes he can remove the tumour from the prosthetic C3, which he initially implanted into Kim. He also believes he can utilise the same 'cement method' he used in Kim's most recent L5 operation on the current tumour in her pelvis. He marvelled at Kim's response to treatment and claimed a major reason for this is that she is so fit. While she remains fit, he believes he can continue to surgically assist us.

It usually takes six months to get an appointment to see Marc. However, our relationship is such that we have his personal mobile. He will be operating on Kim in the next seven days, such is his admiration for Kim and her fighting mindset. Once Kim has recuperated from what will be her sixth major surgery in eighteen months, 'Dr Sobb' will push for further radiation (Kim will kill me for this!) to the C3 region and pelvis as a preventative measure.

Kim will maintain her Chinese herbal preparation three times per day, as well as high-protein antioxidant supplements prepared by 'yours truly' and a training schedule equal to any competing athlete.

Thursday 28 July 2016

After a long consultation with our surgeon, Dr Marc, we have decided to leave the tumour on C3 to radiation treatment as it doesn't pose an immediate threat now. The tumour on the pelvis, however, is far more serious as it is large and growing aggressively. If left any longer, as it is weight-bearing, Kim will begin to have extreme pain and issues walking.

Marc is quite confident his revolutionary 'cementing treatment' will be successful in removing this tumour. He is currently teleconferencing with colleagues about mixing the cement with anaesthetic to reduce the intense pain Kim suffered after the last procedure.

This operation will take place next Monday morning at Gosford Private Hospital. Marc will perform this procedure via CT scan, and he believes the surgeon at this hospital is one of the best he has worked with. The following Friday, Kim will receive a CT scan for tattooing and preparation of the dreaded full facial mask, readying her for three straight weeks of radiation on the C3 vertebra and the pelvis.

I find it ironic, possibly poetic, that the day after Monday's procedure, Kim and I will celebrate our thirtieth wedding anniversary. When initially diagnosed, they said we would never make it. I guess she showed them.

I've attempted to keep this news away from the boys, as I believe they have enough on their plates. Jackson could be looking at a further promotion soon, so he is immersing himself—possibly a little too much—in his work. Oscar returns to Joey's for his final ten weeks of school. He has become a little anxious as he ponders what the future holds for him as a man. I write to him each week, as I did with the other boys, reminding him of the privilege he has in being at Joey's and the love and support that awaits him at home. Louis sits a major three-hour exam this Saturday, then God willing, will return down to the Police Academy in August. We continue to quietly train together. Reuben, the fat-mess giant Shepherd, remains glued to Kim's side, sparking fear into any poor person who rings our doorbell, delivery man or otherwise.

The news has not been what we wanted, but we have options, strategies, motivation and, most of all, hope in our hearts and the courage to fight. That doesn't mean we haven't had dark moments. I manage Kim's through a regime of exercise and mindfulness, and keep mine to a minimum, ensuring I am alone when they occur.

We have a tough week coming up, but we will fight the good fight.

My business is now north.

August 2016—The Dreaded Mask

Tuesday 2 August 2016

Kim is in good spirits and recovering from the surgery. Dr Marc is extremely happy with the procedure.

We made the trip up to Gosford on Sunday night to be close to the hospital, as we were scheduled in the morning. The positive was our hotel was approximately three minutes away from the hospital and, perhaps, the negative was you could rent rooms by the hour! Either way, it was an extremely anxious time. What mattered was that we were together.

Neither of us slept much that night. Bleary-eyed and fatigued, we made our way to the hospital early Monday morning. I kissed Kim goodbye as they wheeled her away and my final words to her were, 'Just keep punching hard.' She gave the traditional Sobb clenched fist.

The operation was three hours and took longer than expected owing to some technical complications, so it was with great trepidation that I read my text from Dr Marc asking me to meet him in the hospital coffee shop.

Marc, still fully gowned, came directly from the operating theatre and in his perfect Afrikaans accent said, 'That woman is amazing.'

He explained how they used CT scan imaging as a type of satellite navigator for the syringe to reach the bone adjacent to the tumour.

From there, he used his natural instincts to feel the bone, then tap the syringe with a hammer into the tumour where he sucked out a large amount of brown fluid. He said the tumour was approximately the size of a 50-cent piece. He filled the cavity with the cement formula containing anaesthetic. Marc explained this technique is still very much in its infancy, and to be honest, he was learning as he was going. He also said he was going to write a paper on it as this could potentially change the way we treat certain cancerous tumours.

He explained that while this new technique was showing success, much of it was also due to Kim's physical fitness.

AUGUST 2016—THE DREADED MASK

Such is our relationship with Marc, he gowned me up so I could be in the post-op area when Kim came to. When I arrived, she squeezed my hand, told me she loved me, then babbled on about how beautiful the trees were. Lord only knows what she was visualising!

By the time they moved her into a ward, I couldn't believe how well she was recuperating. The last time we had this procedure, she woke up with incredible pain and anxiety. This time, she woke with no pain and more like she was rising from a long sleep. This, of course, was the result of Marc learning from Kim and mixing a strong dose of anaesthetic into the cement.

Believe it or not, by 2.00 pm we were on the road and heading home. The anaesthetic will eventually wear off and we do have some pain killers. However, Kim is reluctant to take anything as she is determined to drink a glass of French champagne to celebrate our thirtieth wedding anniversary today.

Friday 12 August 2016

This morning was a milestone for Kim. She courageously completed five sessions of her radiation program with the dreaded mask. The following photo gives you an idea of what my incredibly brave partner went through every morning this week.

If you suffer from claustrophobia, as Kim does, you can imagine the anxiety she went through. To magnify this, they bolt the mask down to the bench for the treatment. Luckily, we had an incredible group of staff who allowed me into the room with Kim to hold her hand and go through our breathing and meditation techniques right up to seconds before the treatment commenced and the door closed.

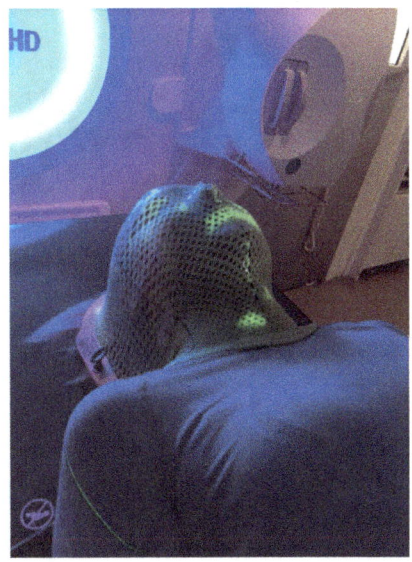

The first treatment on Monday was perhaps the worst, and the staff were even good enough to allow me to talk to Kim over the microphone during the treatment.

The doctor also cut her radiation program by one week. After doing further mathematical calculations on the massive amounts of radiation she's had to date, her body cannot accept the scheduled fifteen sessions, so it has been reduced to ten.

It's not even two weeks since her last operation to remove the tumour on her pelvis, but she continues to go to the gym. As she still suffers some pain from the operation, I have adjusted her program to favour the treadmill as opposed to the cross trainer. She really is phenomenal.

We begin her immunology intravenous drug program with Opdivo on 26 August. Whilst it has been hailed as a wonder treatment for cancer, it doesn't work for everyone. We hope we are one of the patients who responds to the treatment. Failing that, I'm looking at contingencies around further surgical options with Dr Marc, and the developments of a vaccination treatment program that is currently being trialled with some success.

Our next scan is in October, which also marks two years to the month we were diagnosed and given little hope with only drugs to numb our life.

Tuesday 30 August 2016

For the most part, Kim is in good spirits as you can see in the following photo. She's going to kill me when she sees this!

Actually, it was Kim's idea to pose for this photo as we 'dined' in Oporto, an Aussie chicken burger joint. We sent it to Oscar who claims to be starving at boarding school. Despite everything, she still has a sense of humour.

This being said, we still have down times as Kim believes our latest form of treatment is the end of the line. She certainly underestimates my resourcefulness and love for her.

AUGUST 2016—THE DREADED MASK

With radiation now thankfully behind her, Kim continues her fitness regime. This consists of me barking at her on the cross trainer for more effort, resulting in a new personal best of 11.89 kilometres in thirty minutes! Core strength work follows, overseen by her personal fitness trainer, none other than Louis Sobb. Some would observe it as one long constant argument on what is correct and incorrect form. However, I see it more like the mutual love between mother and son.

Considering everything Kim's body has been through, it's amazing what she does at the gym. I can't stress the benefits of exercise, both physically and mentally, to her recovery and the ongoing battle of this disease.

Treatment-wise, Kim took time to recover from the radiation. I think we worked out she's had approximately forty doses of radiation treatment in all. With the breakthroughs happening in new treatment, it is my opinion (good ol' 'Dr Sobb') that in the not-too-distant future we will remember chemotherapy and radiation as barbaric forms of treating cancer. That she is doing what she does in the gym is testimony to her bravery and resilience. She is my pillar of strength.

Last week, we commenced our first dose of the breakthrough immunology drug, Opdivo. We had to sign numerous waivers and stay back an hour after the treatment in the chemo ward for close observation for any negative reactions, such is the infancy of this drug and its treatment. Kim is only the second patient in the Prince of Wales Hospital to receive it, and the drug has to be ordered specifically for her. They make it up that morning for her as it only has a shelf life outside the fridge of approximately two hours.

Because the treatment takes approximately two hours from start to finish, and the treatment schedule is every two weeks, I have changed Kim's chemo oncologist to a private hospital much closer to home with a far more streamlined modus operandi. Little things like car parking, more natural light, larger chemo rooms, better staff ratios and general location take on monumental importance when simplifying the huge production of treatment into a fast, seamless event that the rest of one's normal life can flow around.

In the next few weeks, I head off to Singapore for work and, of course, my travel buddy Kim has already organised the sites she will see as I go about my business. Apart from quenching her appetite for travel, it also acts as a wonderful distraction from the results of our upcoming PET scan in October.

The boys are all doing well and the Sobb humour of paying each other out keeps us closely bound together, feet set tightly on the ground. It provides a healthy release from the situation we have found ourselves in.

Oscar is anxiously preparing for his upcoming High School Certificate (HSC) exams and concluding his school life. He understands that the Joey's chapter in his life is coming to a close. God, through Marcellin Champagnat's Marist Brothers, gave us one of the greatest gifts through this ordeal by supporting Oscar through Kim's illness with the staff and spirit of Joey's. I am sure Kim will also miss her wonderful Saturday afternoons watching Joey's boys playing rugby together!

Louis passed his exam for the Police Academy, but much to our surprise has decided he doesn't want to return for several reasons. After consultation with a close friend who worked directly with the NRL, he is attempting to establish a career as a high-performance strength and conditioning trainer. Despite my initial disappointment, my aim is to help Louis achieve whatever he wants to do. His personal training clients and the boxers he trains down at the Dog House keep him occupied, and he and I still enjoy the silence of each other's company whilst exercising together nearly every afternoon.

Jackson recently received a promotion and, on top of his busy work schedule, is attending Notre Dame University to complete a Business Degree. Kim 'the only academic Sobb' is so proud that finally one of her boys will attain a degree. Much to his mother's delight, he received a distinction for his first presentation at university.

Reuben, the fifty-three-kilogram baby Wonder Dog, still follows Kim around from room to room, listening to her idly chatting to him.

Kim begrudgingly attempts to return to work, albeit for two days a week, on the first Tuesday of October. I understand her trepidation, but as throughout this whole ordeal, she will simply get up, face her fears and place one foot in front of the other.

My business is now north.

October 2016—Pseudo-progression

Thursday 6 October 2016

During an airplane descent on our recent trip, and without warning, Kim experienced some excruciating pain in her left eye. I initially put it down to a change in cabin pressure. However, as the days progressed, she experienced further pain, blurred vision and swelling of her eye.

Immediately upon our return, I pressed our new oncologist to conduct a CT scan. Yes, I'm 'breaking in' yet another oncologist. With trepidation, she did so and within forty-eight hours, she requested a PET scan and then an MRI scan.

Apart from the return of cancer to her C3 prosthetic vertebra, Kim now has an aggressive tumour growing in the bone of her left eye socket. The tumour is growing into her sinus cavity and towards her brain. This is putting pressure on her eyeball, causing it to swell and impair her vision.

Our chemo oncologist referred us to a radiation oncologist who specialises in cancer issues relating to the head. Chemo is not an option for us anymore and we can't receive any further radiation to the C3 area.

However, while we were away, I made some 'Dr Sobb' assumptions and contacted our surgeon Marc Coughlan to give him a heads-up on the situation. He informed me he would be away when we returned, however, would be back at work on Monday 10 October, ready to operate as soon as possible.

Up to now, much of the medical advice we've received from oncologists has been typical, such as the use of traditional chemotherapy or radiation, avoiding what they called 'radical surgery' options. However, yesterday afternoon the latest oncologist suggested surgery, considering the position and aggressive nature of the tumour in the eye socket and Dr Marc's reputation.

By lunchtime today, I had all Kim's scans and reports, including the CT, PET and MRI scans, at Marc's office for him to review Sunday night when he flies in from overseas, and a theatre booked for Kim's operation next week. At this stage, I have a formal meeting with Marc on Tuesday to confirm whether he can operate on the eye socket and/or the C3 tumour. It's amazing what you can accomplish when you have great support people and a reason to believe.

Initially, we thought Kim may have been suffering a side effect of the Opdivo immunology treatment called pseudo-progression. This is where tumours initially expand in size before the natural immune system kills the tumour, rendering the treatment a success. However, the conundrum is, owing to the position and its current effects on Kim's brain and eyesight, I can't take that risk. This treatment is just so new, with a limited amount of data available for professional oncologists to even make a hypothesis in many instances.

By virtue of 'Dr Sobb's' inquisitive nature, I'm constantly being told, when asking my litany of questions, that either they don't have enough data, they don't know or even 'We never thought about that.' I can't help but think that, whilst this therapy is certainly revolutionary, the pharmaceutical companies, in their haste to reclaim their investment, and the TGA, in their excitement at the prospect of this new treatment, may have acted in haste.

I am speculating, but from the perspective of someone who has spent many hours sifting through data and reports in search of conclusive evidence, there is still only a limited amount of timely data available when it comes to Opdivo and Keytruda (more on that later) immunology treatment. Don't get me wrong, as I said before, I'm sure in our lifetime we will see radiation and chemotherapy as ignorant and barbaric forms of treatment for cancer.

When we received the news of her eye, Kim was devastated. Kim has always taken such pride in the way she presents herself and the swelling of her eye has made her self-conscious. For me, the most upsetting moment was watching her attempt to read with a magnifying glass. I know how much solace she takes in being able to escape her situation by immersing herself in literature. However, Kim being Kim, and with an incredible and insurmountable reservoir of courage, she never complains to anyone.

When it came to supporting her men on Patrol One at North Cronulla, she simply donned her sunglasses and acted like nothing was wrong. She even went so far as to worry that she was holding me back. I said to her, 'I'll never let you fall behind.'

MY BUSINESS IS NOW NORTH

As courageous as Kim is, she's also hiding incredible fear. I explained that we can't allow cancer to define her, our relationship or our lives. What we are experiencing are nothing but bumps in the road, albeit serious ones. What's more important is the total journey and the experiences we have in that journey—those being our relationship, our family, our travels and the wonderful small things like swimming in the ocean together, walking with Reuben or sitting at the table with the family. These experiences define us, not the hurdles that cancer has brought. Idealistic? Maybe, but it is this mindset and spirituality that gives us hope. And hope combined with our faith is incredibly powerful.

I purposely haven't said much to the boys, and it's interesting how we can make silent contracts with one another. For obvious reasons, part of them doesn't want to know and I am happy to oblige. I tell them enough to appear that they know the intricacies of their mother's situation, but not enough to be knowledgeable of the possible realities. It is a way of me protecting them and them protecting themselves.

Oscar has his HSC coming up, Louis is attempting to redefine a new career in strength and conditioning with the NRL, and Jackson is starting his journey as a young manager. I know Louis senses something. It is not uncommon for him to call me three or four times a day just to ask where I am. Jackson, too, has his way through small acts, like coming home with his mother's favourite ice cream—the type she had cravings for while she was pregnant with him. Yep, ice-cream crunchy bars! The little things have never been so big.

I now plan for my upcoming meeting on Tuesday morning with our surgeon.

Monday 10 October 2016

I received a call this morning from our surgeon.

As I expected, he reviewed Kim's scans as soon as he flew in on Sunday night and we are scheduled for major brain surgery first thing Thursday morning. Kim is extremely anxious but is going about her business in her usual stoic way, preparing for a surgery that most people in their lifetime will never have to face.

As anxious as Kim and I are, make no mistake ... we are ready to fight.

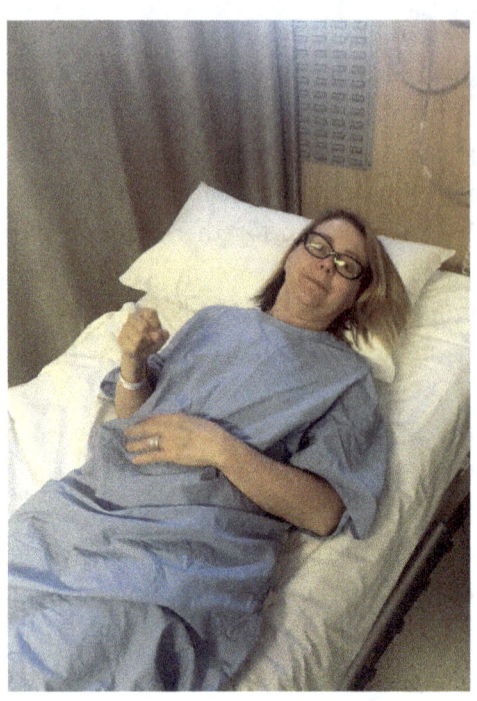

Thursday 13 October 2016
The Champ gives the traditional clenched fist salute as she heads into surgery this morning.

Now we fight.

I've just come out of a meeting with Dr Marc. He believes the surgery was a great success, albeit extremely complicated and a lot longer than expected. He explained that the tumour was extremely aggressive and had grown substantially since the last scan three days ago. This was evident by how much Kim's eyeball was protruding from the socket. If we hadn't operated, it would only have been a matter of weeks.

Kim is now in intensive care where the biggest thing in her recovery is ensuring there are no infections in the sinus or brain cavity.

I'll wait eight to ten days for the swelling to go down, then commence a mop-up radiation program. Yes, we will have the dreaded mask again! After we have completed the radiation, I will organise with Marc for further surgery to remove the tumour on C3.

I won't spell this all out to Kim as it is far too much for her to digest, but my aim for Christmas is that she is completely tumour-free and swimming out the back of North Cronulla with the members of Patrol One.

Friday 21 October 2016
I've decided to let the pictures tell the story.

One day before the operation:

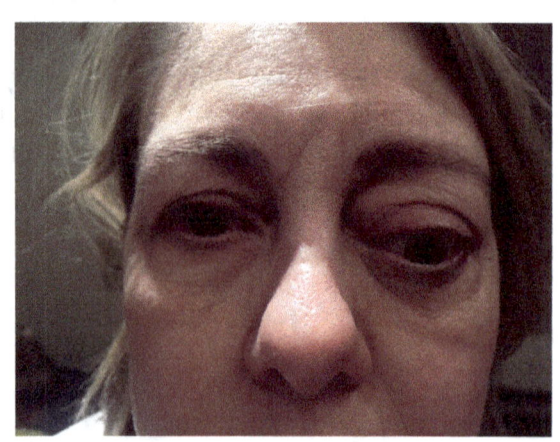

OCTOBER 2016—PSEUDO-PROGRESSION

One week after the operation:

Two days after the operation and supporting her beloved Patrol One at North Cronulla:

Today was bittersweet.

We were due to receive our Opdivo immunology treatment. However, as the nurse was about to fit the cannula in Kim's arm, the ward received a phone call from our oncologist. She said that owing to the risk of Kim's eye swelling again due to pseudo-progression from the Opdivo, she didn't want to risk any further swelling or damage to Kim's eye at this early post-operative stage.

Of course, 'Dr Sobb' attempted to argue the point and after a lengthy conversation over the phone with her, I thought better of it—or knew I had a succession plan anyway for further surgical work in the upcoming week!

The biopsy of the tissue removed showed it wasn't all tumour, but pseudo-progression swelling as well. This gives us some hope that Opdivo's one-out-of-five success rate may be working. However, time will tell.

Directly from this appointment, we went to see Dr Marc who turned to me with a wry grin when removing Kim's stitches.

'Sobbie, I should be a plastic surgeon. This looks great,' he said, with that great South African accent.

Kim does have some pain on the top of her skull because of a nerve ending that had to be moved during the procedure. However, Marc assures us this will return to normal. Kim also has some blurred vision. Marc explained this was caused by the tumour being attached to the globe of the eye and that it will take time for her sight to return to normal. If it doesn't, we will see an ophthalmologist.

I've already started pushing for Kim to be operated on next week to remove the tumour on C3, with radiation the following week around the eye and brain region where the last tumour was removed. The plan is then to recommence Opdivo.

My pledge to Kim and her family is to have her tumour-free for Christmas. I aim to keep that promise.

Reuben the Wonder Dog has been an incredible gift to Kim. In many cases around the world, surgery like this on the brain still consists of virtually splitting the skull completely down the centre. Even though Kim's was keyhole, it was still incredibly complex, traumatic and left her physically and emotionally exhausted. This is where having the unrequited love, devotion and loyalty of a German Shepherd like Reuben is priceless.

Jackson continues his academic journey—albeit a new experience for him! Louis and I enjoy our long silences together at the gym. And it was with great joy for his mother that Oscar received early entry to complete a Bachelor of Sports Management at the International College in Manly.

Wednesday 26 October 2016
We have just received confirmation that tomorrow Kim will receive further surgery to remove the regrowth of the cancer on her C3 vertebra. It will be almost two weeks since she had a major craniotomy, so this is testimony to the absolute courage and strength of one, Kimberly Sobb, my wife.

Three days after that surgery, she will commence ten cycles of intense radiation treatment on her left eye socket. And yes, she had to be fitted up for the mask again.

I discussed with our radiation oncologist, or should I say the good 'Dr Sobb' strongly suggested, that we also treat other highly suspicious areas that showed a high FDG uptake on her most recent PET scan. Our oncologist agreed, or should I say, could not be bothered arguing with me any further! To me, it seemed more efficient, streamlined and treatment-friendly for the patient.

We then wait two weeks for Kim to stop being an isotope! After that, I have scheduled Kim to recommence her immunotherapy of Opdivo intravenously every two weeks. A lot is going on and Kim and I have a lot to digest, but she simply takes it in her stride like a true champion. Sometimes, it is hard to ever believe we had a life without cancer, but I also know we have never felt closer.

October and November will be extremely challenging months for Kim and I in relation to the fight. We are determined, battle-hardened and fuelled by your support and our faith.

We shall overcome.

My business is now north.

Playlist:
Should I Fall Behind, Bruce Springsteen

November 2016—The Yellow Submarine

Monday 7 November 2016

A lot has happened in the last month: a craniotomy followed two weeks later by major surgery to remove a large and aggressive tumour on C3 and a tumour on the seventh rib.

It would be right to think after two major surgeries in a month that we would have a long and extended rest and recovery period. The reality is, we simply don't have that luxury. A recent PET scan showed some highly suspicious areas in Kim's pelvis again.

Last week, I held a planning session with our surgeon, Marc. Our aim is to conduct another syringe and cement procedure in the two areas we suspect in Kim's pelvis on or around Thursday 17 November at the Prince of Wales Hospital. This will coincide with finishing her final radiation program on her left eye socket and left seventh rib.

Following this, I will schedule planning sessions with our radiation oncologist and medical oncologist for further radiation on the pelvis area and our Opdivo treatment, respectively.

Treatment-wise, November will be tough for Kim. However, timelines and schedules take on a whole new mindset when you're dealing with this disease. I know both our chemo and radiation oncologists find me agonisingly frustrating to deal with, possibly magnified by the wonderfully close relationship I have with our surgeon, Marc, who has made himself available at any time.

The oncologists' mindset is to call the surgery we do 'radical', but from my perspective, it has saved Kim's life on more than one occasion. Remember the initial C3 vertebra that was impossible to operate on or even the most recent tumour growing from her eye socket into the brain?

While we could argue that whatever growth we've had could be explained as pseudo- progression—the initial positive signs of immunology working—its success rate is still only one in five. The guarantee I have when utilising Marc Coughlan's skills is that before the surgery the cancerous tumour is there. After the surgery, it's gone. Yes, there is some painful recovery in the days and weeks after, but nothing like those of radiation, or even chemotherapy, which at best can only guarantee the arrested development of the disease.

I am obsessed with having Kim tumour-free for Christmas.

Kim is exhausted, both physically and emotionally. At present, she carries a lot of pain in her ribs along with the healing scars on her head, neck and ribs.

The other morning, I woke up and jumped out of bed singing the Beatles' *Yellow Submarine*.

'What sane person jumps up in the morning and starts singing Yellow Submarine? Anthony Sobb, you are a lunatic!' she said, slowly rolling over.

It occurred to me that it was the first time in over two years that Kim had woken up and met the day with a smile. Who knew what the rest of the day would bring? More pain, anxiety and depression over being dealt these cards? Maybe further news that it had spread? Or perhaps those jagged ads reminding people of cancer? It didn't really matter. What mattered was she started the day with a smile and that made me happy.

With all the treatment being crammed into November, my plan is for December and January to be months of rest and recovery. As I have planned for her to take her Opdivo every two weeks, I scheduled a week at Noosa for the first week in December and then two weeks in Thailand at the beginning of January.

Apart from her treatment, I continue to manage her lifestyle recovery through high- antioxidant shakes using the goji berry superfood, along with preparing herbs three times a day and a nutritious diet. Sessions at the gym are a little less intense, however, I aim to change that in early December much to Kim's disappointment!

Brief walks along the beach at Cronulla certainly lift her spirits and I know she is looking forward to cheering on her silly old husband who is competing in surf boat rowing this season. I think she's secretly hoping for some major wipe-outs during big swells as payback for my gym sessions!

Kim's dark moments are dark, but she seems able to manage them better. She is tired and sore, but resilient and full of hope. She is my champion.

Oscar completed his HSC and the anxious little boy we were all so worried about when we left him at Joey's three years ago has returned home as this wonderful young man. Louis requested a longer transition period for us to get used to having Oscar back home, as they have started warring already.

However, Kim is greatly comforted to have all her boys under the same roof again. Jackson continues to commit himself to his studies and diligently applies himself to the responsibilities of being an operations manager. The home is a hive of activity and this circus, known as the Sobb family, keeps Kim's spirits buoyant.

No man, woman, child or family is an island. If anything, this situation reminds us of our need for humility, gratitude to others and faith—all of which I am still on a journey to learn more about.

Tuesday 22 November 2016
November continues to live up to the struggles and challenges we expected. Last week, she had the syringe and cementing of three tumours that had spread to her pelvis. To any healthy human, this would have been a mammoth ask. To somebody with half a left lung, only one major artery in the neck and depleted by numerous doses of chemotherapy and radiation, this verges on superhuman.

Kim approached the last surgery with great trepidation and awoke to explain, or should I say plead, 'I've had enough, Ant.'

Watching Kim suffer is perhaps one of the greatest tortures, however, I need to sober myself from these selfish thoughts to realise Kim's journey. She is a beautiful, healthy woman who's had life as she knew it taken away from her for no apparent reason.

These were supposed to be the best years of her life.

She had been healthy—physically and spiritually—yet here she finds herself: with pain, sorrow, what ifs, what for and, simply, why? I know my unbridled optimism often frustrates her. However, the irony is that Kim is my strength.

Recovery from this latest surgery came with some unrelated new issues. The worst is a post-radiation reaction, causing Kim's eyes and face to swell up with fluid. We quickly organised doses of the steroid, dexamethasone, but that only helped for a short period. Kim continually tells me how this disease has taken away not only her identity but also the way she looks. At the risk of sounding ridiculously corny, I think she has never looked more beautiful and has never been more defined as a person.

We meet with our radiation oncologist and chemo oncologist tomorrow, who will hopefully present some answers in relation to the fluid in her face. I also aim to bully my way through the doctors and ensure we start back on our immunology treatment of Opdivo. You may recall we commenced it, then had to discontinue it owing to the tumour in her eye. With no more scheduled radiation or surgery, my aim is to recommence it this Friday.

So, this is where Kim stands physically. This bruised and battered yet astonishingly beautiful and intelligent woman has a courage that fighters can only dream about. Emotionally, however, she is spent. Fortunately, we know now that the demons come to her door in the afternoon. I feel blessed to have work colleagues who know why, where and to whom I go to each afternoon.

Unfortunately, owing to the recent rigours of surgery, Kim has been far from able to keep up with her Spartan athletic gym program. We've tailored it now to a reasonable time on the treadmill, at a reasonable pace, and walks at dusk around the leafy streets of Lugarno, holding hands and talking about things that were and things that will be. The demons enter the door from time to time, and we deal with that through our union of strength.

While the success rate of Opdivo is approximately one in five, I hope I have prepared Kim to be in the best shape she can from a physical, emotional and tumour-less state.

We receive our next PET scan in January which will tell part of the story. However, with the lack of Opdivo data, it may take several months until we can categorically say if it has worked or not. When and if that time arrives, I will have a contingency, no matter what, and like Sisyphus, we will pick the boulder up and carry it to the top of the mountain.

We travel to Melbourne this weekend where I will conduct meetings with casino executives at Crown. However, the highlight for Kim will be attending the UFC event. I still can't get over how my wife can take such delight in attending a live combat event such as this. She hated when I stepped into the ring and even more so when her two elder sons fought. Somehow, I think she can identify with the ultimate battle. Perhaps that's why I call her 'the Champ'.

The boys are doing well and, to be honest, are not fully aware of the magnitude that surrounds them. That's a good thing. In blissful ignorance, they ask where their washing is or ask Kim to run errands for them, just as any son will ask their mother. It makes Kim feel good … frustrated at times, but needed and good.

Reuben the Wonder Dog wanders around the house from room to room with Kim as they chat with each other and agree on all matters. He certainly is a great listener and Kim certainly has a lot to say. The boys and I say he's taking one for the team. He pines like a baby when she is not around, and Louis says he is a disgrace to the German Shepherd breed for showing such emotion!

I certainly don't wish anyone to feel sad for us as I feel totally blessed to have one another in our family. This situation, in a cruel way, simply magnifies it.

It's hard to believe this will be the third Christmas we've had to share with this disease. I think of where Kim and the family have all come from, what we've all been through and dream and hope where we will all be in the future.

My business is now north.

December 2016—Absolute Denial

Thursday 1 December 2016

'They say the best-laid plans …'

As I write this email, Kim is in the Prince of Wales Hospital recovery ward after an unscheduled, or should I say semi-unscheduled, emergency operation to remove an aggressive and rapidly growing tumour painfully pressing against her sciatic nerve.

What I didn't mention in my last update was that immediately following Kim's last surgery, our surgeon Marc pulled me aside and informed me of the tumour he found whilst syringing and cementing Kim's pelvis. He explained it was in a difficult position to get to and dangerous to approach at that point in time. He told me to keep an eye out for any sciatic pain Kim may have.

Over the days after the last surgery, Kim began to complain about sciatic pain. I attempted to fob it off as post-surgery pain, knowing full well the reason for it. Finally, over the last couple of days, Kim found it extremely hard to even walk. I contacted Marc who, over the phone, organised a CT referral at my request. I knew Marc would need this as a planning scan. After reviewing the scan, he rang me yesterday, explaining it had grown rapidly and said he would make himself available to operate today.

Unfortunately, this is where my facade ended, and I told Kim the whole story. She immediately became emotional, knowing it meant further surgery. The demons came, we fought them and here I am now, writing to you as she recovers from what Marc said was a successful removal of the aggressive tumour.

I'll forward a more detailed update soon, but until then, please enjoy this recent photo of Kim with the centurion, best friend, number one buddy, best listener … Reuben the Wonder Dog!

Wednesday 14 December 2016

Unfortunately, the rough patch continues.

After Kim's most recent operation, I took her directly up to Noosa to convalesce and recuperate. The immediate relief from sciatic pain that we hoped would occur from removing the tumour did not eventuate. So now, not only is Kim dealing with the initial sciatica from the tumour, but also the flotsam and jetsam of pain and depression that comes post-operation.

In typical 'Dr Sobb' and corner-man fashion, I told Kim that all her pain was purely post-operative, and she would soon be on the mend. However, my years now of managing Kim medically, my late nights of self-education and my continued badgering of doctors for information and answers conveyed that something wasn't right.

While we were in Noosa, I stole away to the gym as a cover for a long, private conversation with our surgeon. He was ninety per cent sure it was post-surgery inflammation. However, this was at odds with days of pain and only just coming off the anti-inflammatory steroid, dexamethasone.

Organising a CT scan post-haste, as only 'Dr Sobb' can do, I added a multitude of enemies to my already long list in the medical profession. On

DECEMBER 2016—ABSOLUTE DENIAL

Monday night, during a work function Kim and I were attending, I received a call from Marc saying the tumour had regrown in that short period.

Ironically, at that event, Kim looked vibrant and beautiful, involving herself in political conversations, eloquently articulating her points. This was the Kim of old, I thought. Then, the phone call from Marc.

When we returned home that night, I had a teleconference with Marc at the actual eleventh hour.

'It is not a challenging procedure,' Marc informed me.

He believed he could remove the tumour. He commented that Kim was one of the most incredible physical specimens he had ever operated on, otherwise he wouldn't normally suggest a fifth operation in nearly five weeks. His real concern was Kim's mental state.

I asked to him to leave that up to me and said we would be ready for Marc to operate as soon as possible. We finished the lengthy teleconference with Marc saying, 'You guys are an inspiration and make all those years of study worthwhile.'

Then I walked upstairs to tell Kim the news she certainly didn't want to hear.

At first, there was immediate denial, and by that, I mean absolute denial.

She claimed I was joking. This turned into shock, anger and what I can only describe as the deepest, darkest hole of sorrow.

A fifth operation, more pain and more emotional depression from the general anaesthetic.

'You said the last operation was the last one!'

I felt like I had totally let her down.

Again, the demons came. They entered the house. We rallied. I attempted to give Kim a logical reason to believe, and the demons slowly dissipated. The faith Kim continues to show in me is disarming and humbling. I know for a fact it is not based on survival, but rather a long history of love and trust—two spirits who simply belong to one another.

So, tomorrow morning we go in for our fifth operation exactly fourteen days since the last. Kim certainly has great trepidation. I have trust and hope that within twenty-four hours of writing this email, Kim will be tumour-free again with the hope that our immunology treatment will continue successfully.

I haven't told the boys yet. We'll leave that to the very last moment—possibly as we walk out the door tomorrow morning—to give them as little time as possible to pontificate on the matter.

My promise is still to deliver my Kim to her family this Christmas, tumour-free. My aim is to keep that promise to her family, myself and, most importantly, to her. I have enough hope in my heart for both of us. I know, too, she has enough courage and strength for both of us.

Tomorrow morning, we go into the fire and face the beast again, down in the early rounds but coming home strong.

This is not bad news, but rather a setback that we shall overcome.

Friday 16 December 2016
Kim woke this morning for the first time in a long period without debilitating sciatic pain. Yes, she is still in a lot of pain, but it's post-operative and will pass in time.

I met with our surgeon, Marc, just before the surgery and in his wonderful South African accent, he pulled me aside and said, 'Well, what do you want to do, Ant?' No wonder I have a delusional identity crisis as 'Dr Sobb'!

I told him I think we need to go in hard. Kim was still feeling pain directly after the last operation, so it can't all be new tumours. He agreed. The surgery began and went for several hours.

Bruce Springsteen, as he has done through most of my life, kept me company with his autobiography until Marc's assistant surgeon, who has also become a friend, tapped me on the shoulder and withdrew me from Asbury Park, New Jersey.

He explained they had taken out massive amounts of tumour, including one that was attached to Kim's sciatic nerve. Can you imagine that? The Champ is one tough cookie. John explained that Marc went in search of places in and around the sacrum that in his thirty-five years as a doctor he had never been into as they combed Kim's body in search of tumours. They found significant amounts of tumour that had not been picked up in previous CT scans.

I've requested biopsies on all the tumours to see if we can track any pseudo-progression and measure any success of the immunology treatment. Marc sent us home as soon as he could. He understands that emotionally we need to be home, but also that owing to the five recent surgeries in nearly as many weeks, the susceptibility to infection while staying in hospital could be fatal.

So, as 2016 draws to a close, I ponder that perhaps Kim will celebrate this Christmas tumour-free. I reflect on the last two Christmases, which were a blur owing to Kim's illness. This motivates me to ensure Kim and the boys, including myself, make a conscious effort to truly reflect on the monumental importance of the ever present now and the gratitude it brings to what we should celebrate and pay homage to: our family, its great love, the reflection of the Christmas spirit, the gift and support of friends, and gratitude to God's graces.

While a subconscious part of my mind thinks the dawning of a new year will somehow bring a rewind, a restart, a clean slate, a repair, that's simply not the case. The reality is, 2016 will drift and morph into 2017. I will not fall asleep at the wheel. We will not capitulate in the fight. We shall overcome.

I wish you all a reflective Christmas.

My business is now north.

January 2017—No Retreat, No Surrender

Thursday 5 January 2017

Physically, for Kim, December and January have been tough. We now pick up the boulder and carry it back up the mountain, just like Sisyphus, for 2017.

After the operation just prior to Christmas, our fifth in nearly five weeks, we found additional complications. Whilst our surgeon, Marc, found numerous new tumours and removed them, the procedure was aggressive. I did tell Marc to 'go in hard'. This resulted in a new and intense sciatic pain down Kim's right leg.

To add fuel to the fire, I received a panic-stricken phone call from one of our oncologists who stated that Kim's haemoglobin levels were dangerously low. Remember, I'd hidden that Kim had been operated on so the oncologist would sign off on Kim receiving Opdivo.

Within twelve hours of this phone call, I had to organise for Kim to have a major blood transfusion along with a Vitamin B infusion. It's amazing what can be achieved when the stakes are high.

The positive was that after her second bag of blood, Kim felt significantly better. However, as the days moved on from Christmas to New Year, her sciatic pain became unbearable.

'Dr Sobb' did some extensive research on sciatica, discovering that the body's compression activities during nightly sleep inflame it. This results in extreme pain in the early hours of the morning. As the body decompresses during the day, there is some relief. However, further relief can be gained by specific stretching exercises and medication.

I got a hold of the medication—if I told you how, I would have to kill you!—and started Kim on a stretching regime specifically for sciatic pain at the Dog House gym. While this program did give some relief, the initial pain remained virtually unbearable for her. Each morning progressively became a little worse. Kim started each day emotionally spent and in tears of pain.

JANUARY 2017—NO RETREAT, NO SURRENDER

I contacted Marc who, even though on holidays with his family, sent me a prescription for a cortisone injection. Again, within twelve hours, I had organised for Kim to have the injection, which gave immediate, albeit short-term, relief.

Kim will also receive a CT scan on Friday which will enlighten us on the results of the last surgery, as well as options for dealing with her sciatica. We anticipate a more conclusive PET scan in February. I'll deal with the outcomes from that.

Emotionally, Kim, in most instances, is exceptionally strong. However, as I've said in the past, the demons do come and as you would expect, at one's most vulnerable time. But that's probably a time when Kim and I unite and are at our closest, so it's a dual effort. We're two partners literally locked arm in arm, backs against the wall and fighting. No retreat, no surrender.

Monday, we fly out to Thailand for eight days where Kim will eat, train and rest ... with maybe a little shopping! On our return, we embark on Opdivo immunology treatment every two weeks and five to ten cycles of radiation to her recently operated pelvic area to mop up any residual tumour cells from her recent surgeries. Reluctant as we are to recommence radiation treatment, we're resolved to it happening. I'm banking on our radiation oncologist not talking to our Opdivo oncologist so we can receive both treatments simultaneously. Lord knows why they are reluctant to do this, as I can't find anything but positive research into the two treatments working hand in hand. However, I will deal with this should it come to a head.

The last couple of Januarys began with great trepidation and 2017 is no different. What will the year hold? How will life unfold? For whom? And how will it all be brought about? I pray I will be able to accept the things I cannot change and have the courage to change the things I can. The rest is in God's hands. With that being said, we have hope in our hearts, and Kim, the boys and I have each other.

Monday 30 January 2017

Here is Kim enjoying the bar (with some lucky knucklehead at the Four Seasons at Koh Samui):

Only Kim could befriend a stray dog on a deserted island in the marine park off the coast of Thailand (the boys couldn't wait to show Reuben!):

JANUARY 2017—NO RETREAT, NO SURRENDER

Kim off the coast of Koh Samui:

As you can see from these photos, Kim responded well to her recent trip away in Koh Samui, not just physically, but also mentally and emotionally.

Only hours before we flew out, I scheduled a follow-up MRI scan, as the recent CT scan showed some concerning evidence that tumours had regrown in the lumbar region. Unbeknown to Kim, I organised for the results to be sent to me via email. The results, unfortunately, were conclusive. So, in between our daily training sessions at the hotel and whatever other activities or non-activities we had scheduled, I ducked out to make arrangements with doctors and surgeons for our return home.

I didn't want to burden Kim with any of it, particularly as she was responding so well to this change-in-scenery treatment.

So, tomorrow Kim returns to Prince of Wales Hospital for what will be her twelfth surgery. The legendary surgeon, Dr Coughlan, and I had some lengthy conversations while he was in Cape Town, and we were away. Again, he will remove any tumours he sees in the lumbar region and anything else he may find in Kim's C3, as she has been recently complaining about further pain in this area.

Marc and I spoke about how aggressive and fast-growing these tumours are, and yet Kim is physically in such good shape and training every day. One theory is that the rapid growth of the tumours could be pseudo-progression and a sign that the immunology treatment, Opdivo, is working.

Either way, both Marc and I agreed we simply can't take the risk, so surgery is our only option. Of course, with surgery, and bearing in mind this is her twelfth, comes all the flotsam and jetsam: the pain, the angst, the post-anaesthetic depression and so on.

Kim mentioned to a friend of ours the other day that she now sees going into surgery 'like a trip to the dentist'. Sometimes I take for granted Kim's courage and what she is going through, and has gone through, since her diagnosis in October 2014. Her plight, the way she has conducted herself, as well as looked after her boys, makes everything else seem so small.

Physically, Kim is in great shape. Her sciatic pain seems to have subsided considerably with the coming and going of pain in the C3 part of her neck. She trains with me at the Dog House every day. She dutifully consumes my high antioxidant shakes and herbal treatments three times a day, as prescribed by our Chinese herbal doctor.

The radiation treatment had to be postponed due to the surgery, so I'll organise five to ten cycles once Kim has recuperated. I've scheduled Kim for immunology treatment this Friday (yes, that's right, two days after surgery) so I'll ensure her haemoglobin levels are right by insisting Marc give her a blood infusion directly after surgery.

To put it in Marc's words (imagine the thick Afrikaans accent), 'She's an incredible human specimen, Ant. Whatever you guys are doing, keep doing it, because while I'm still standing, I'm committed to Kim and working with you guys.'

The recent summer heatwave has lured Kim back down to the beach. After much cajoling, kicking, screaming, whinging, whining, swearing and casting aspersions upon my parentage, I dragged her out through the breakers to the wide, peaceful ocean. There she floats on her back and gazes up to the sky, allowing the sun to warm her and the ocean to embrace her with this wonderful, soothing spirit. I can't describe it any other way. She returns to the shore a noticeably different person and has commented on how wonderfully invigorating the ocean makes her feel.

I have a few work trips coming up and Kim is looking forward to them. I'll sit in dining rooms dissecting menus, madly taking photos or notes on fit-outs or constantly leaving the table to look at other areas—kitchens, bathrooms and so on—all while Kim patiently sits at the table, occasionally shaking her head. It's the way we roll.

The boys continue their blissful ignorance about where Kim is really at. Kim and I both agree that's a good thing and the way we want it.

Oscar is learning to adapt to an adult life beyond Joey's as he prepares to commence his new adventure at the Manly International College of Management where he begins his degree in Sports Management. He'll live at one of the college's homes adjacent to the campus. All I can say is, God help his roommates. He wouldn't last a week with me based on the way he keeps his room. Kim and I are going to miss him when he moves out in March. There is something bittersweet about the end of a chapter and, of course, the beginning of a new one.

Louis and I continue our ritual of training together at the Dog House and patrolling together at North Cronulla. We have an unspoken language and commentary far more meaningful than anyone could give credit to. It's not more or less important than with the other two boys, simply different. Back in early December, he attended a job interview with the head of strength and conditioning for the South Sydney Rabbitohs (a Sydney-based National Rugby League team) and they offered him the job as a full-time staff member. He now works directly with their First-Grade team. It's an incredible opportunity for Louis as he is working with elite sports professionals. The current pre-season has kept him extremely busy. The prospect of travelling with the team this season is exciting, though he is on a steep learning curve. I think he recently provided the team with much entertainment when they requested that he spar with some of the players at a recent boxing session—that's another story for another time!

Jackson commenced a new job as the food and beverage manager of the large and well-regarded venue called Canterbury Hurlstone Park RSL—the exact same position I held twenty years ago! There is something quite historic and comforting about having worked there myself in the same role.

Reuben the Wonder Dog continues to be a blessing to Kim, and all of us, offering comfort and companionship.

As tomorrow's surgery looms closer and the countdown begins, Kim and I have surrendered to what has become a pre-surgery ritual and post-surgery repair. It's a path well-trodden despite wishing we never had to. Our greatest comfort is knowing we walk it together. It creates the ties that bind us.

My business is now north.

February 2017—Bruce and the Hope Estate

Friday 3 February 2017

It has been an incredibly hectic time.

At our request, Marc placed us second on his list last Tuesday morning as Kim likes to get these surgeries over and done with. Who can blame her? On her way to theatre, we said our usual goodbyes and had our usual ritual of a pumped fist to one another. After a brief kiss, I watched them wheel her away looking petrified.

I commenced my usual repertoire to occupy myself for what turned out to be the next six hours. I know every nook and cranny of the Prince of Wales Hospital like the back of my hand. I wander the floors, read a little, work from my iPad, badger my managers and annoy my PA.

I have a special car space I found in the hospital car park, which is almost like a cave. When I park there, under the cloak of darkness and anonymity, I will either sleep (sometimes cry), or listen to music. The hospital coffee shop knows me as 'Dr Tony', possibly because of how often I'm there and the way Kim addresses me. If they only knew!

Finally, Marc calls me, and we have our usual debrief. He explained that Kim haemorrhaged a lot. At one stage, they were worried they couldn't stop the bleeding. Eventually they did and whatever tumours were around the lumbar were again removed. I enquired about C3. He explained he didn't feel any need to intrude into this area surgically. We'll take that as good news.

Marc then gowned me up and took me into intensive care/recovery. Kim claimed she felt like she had been 'hit by a bus'. This is nothing new as Kim's early stages of recovery have never been good. Within the hour, as they move her to a ward, we organise a cup of tea. She slowly comes to, breaks her fast, and she miraculously becomes Kim again, almost like a flower opening. Yes, still in pain and uncomfortable, but incredible when you think of what she has been through in surgery. Even the nurses comment on how she recovers in a short time.

Much to Kim's disdain, I had already organised for her to stay overnight and I'm glad I did. It gives her extra time to recover under the watchful eye of the nursing team and enables her to receive some much-needed blood to make her eligible to accept her immunology treatment today.

The surgery achieved what we needed, which was to remove the ongoing tumours. However, as with all surgery, it comes at a cost. Kim's physical recovery is unbelievable and over the next two weeks I will continue to redress and look after her wounds.

It's possibly too soon to assess how Kim is emotionally. I can attest that she is exhausted and spent, so my aim is to create events and an atmosphere at home of wellbeing and positivity.

Monday 20 February 2017
In true, gritty Kim style, she has bounced back from her twelfth surgical procedure amazingly. Kim's focus and attention in following our detailed regime of diet, gym, natural herbs and rest has no doubt played a major role in recuperating from such a major surgery.

Our oncologist has scheduled a major full-body CT scan for 1 March. The results will be significant as they will determine whether the current immunology treatment of Opdivo is working. Should this not be the case, I've researched another immunology treatment, Keytruda, which has recently become available, and its data shows some significant results.

Unfortunately, we can't receive a PET scan. Due to the number of recent operations, she would literally light up like a Christmas tree because of inflammation rather than active cancer, giving us an incomplete view of her status. CT scans don't rely on FDG uptake and, while not as accurate as PET scans, they are far more valuable for surgeons. Our surgeon, Marc, obviously welcomed this.

I met with Marc last week for a planning meeting which revolved around concerns about Kim's sacrum bone fracturing because of the multiple rounds of surgery. Using Kim's latest CT scan, we will enter these images of her sacrum into a 3D printer to produce a prosthetic titanium sacrum for her. Our research indicates this has only ever been attempted once, albeit successfully, in China. Apart from strengthening an area of concern, the titanium prosthetic will cut the blood supply to tumours in this area, hence it has a two-pronged effect.

I know Kim is extremely concerned and apprehensive—who the hell wouldn't be? However, the outcomes of this bone fracturing and further spread of tumours outweigh this radical option of surgery. Marc is amazed at Kim's strength and resilience.

'Ant, Kim is an inspiration and miracle. I've never seen anybody quite like this,' he says in his broad Afrikaans accent.

The titanium prosthetic will take about a week to make after viewing her scans on 1 March. A further day or two for planning, and then it will be straight into the major surgery. It's hard to predict recovery time and rehabilitation as there is little or no precedent. I'll do as much research as possible on similar surgeries and, with Kim's courage and tenacity, the Champ will be ready to come out swinging for the next round.

Mentally and emotionally as strong as Kim is, she has dark times. The prospect of accompanying me on my work travels buoys her to look into the future. A big part of my role is to manoeuvre and create events and excitement. A simple suggestion like, 'Hey ... It's a beautiful night tonight! Let's have a family barbecue by the pool for dinner' can transform a mundane situation into a mini adventure, taking attention away from Kim's diagnosis. Even if it's just for one night, it's a respite and can fuel us with enough energy to carry us into the next day.

The recent Springsteen concerts were a classic example. As exhausting as it was for poor Kim because we attended four marathon concerts, she loved every minute with her boys (and Bruce!). I know at times I frustrate her with my unbridled enthusiasm and almost circus ringmaster-like behaviour at home. Yet, I know she loves me for the man I want to be, possibly not the man I am.

Here she is with the boys before we left on our road trip to Hope Estate for the Bruce Springsteen outdoor concert in the Hunter Valley:

FEBRUARY 2017 – BRUCE AND THE HOPE ESTATE

And then there is Reuben the Wonder Dog. No one spends more time with Kim than Reuben. No one can sit, stand or lie near Kim without him trying to get closer than them. His eyes never leave Kim. He wants nothing in return except that she allows him to love her. It's a relationship that's hard to articulate, yet one that is very real. He has given Kim peace of mind when she has been alone. If, for whatever reason, I haven't been there, he is happy to sit and listen.

So, the results of the next scan will lead to some major and radical treatment. Are we ready? I don't know. Does one ever know? No manual came with this new change in circumstances and events. I guess that's what makes it so frustrating, particularly if you're pragmatic. However, through all of this of late, I feel strangely overcome by gratitude: gratitude for the love of Kim, gratitude for the support of the workplace and friends, gratitude for the gift of my boys and gratitude that my faith will not let me down.

My business is now north.

March 2017—High-maintenance Patient Spouses

Monday 6 March 2017

I apologise for the delay in the update about Kim's scan last week. The good news is nothing has spread to the brain, or any other organs for that matter. As I mentioned before, PET scans are far more accurate. However, owing to her recent two weeks of intensive radiation, we had to settle for the less accurate CT scans. That being said, I'll grab and run with 'no tumours to the brain or organs' like a robber's dog!

The not-so-good news is a reoccurrence of tumour growth around the C3, plus a regrowth to her seventh rib and further tumours to her sacrum bone—it was only weeks ago that we operated and removed these.

Kim is experiencing pins and needles at the back of her head because of the tumours on C3 and some ongoing discomfort owing to the tumour in the ribs. Perhaps her most intense pain is in her legs caused by tumours on the sacrum. Despite taking special nerve pain medication before she sleeps, she still awakes in the early hours each morning with throbbing pains running through her legs. There is relief, however. When she does get up and move around, the pain slowly subsides to what is, in Kim's view, bearable.

Now, what to do …?

I've badgered and hassled our surgeon Marc to bring things forward and work around some trips Kim is looking forward to. If there were a medical practitioner's list of ridiculously high-maintenance patient spouses that should be avoided at all costs out there, I'm sure I'm on it.

I've planned with Marc for him to operate this Thursday to remove the reoccurring tumour on her C3 via a resection. At the same time, he'll drill into her seventh rib and cement. Fortunately, we can do both these procedures in the one operation because she will be facing down. There are many risks around haemorrhaging when having to turn a patient over during surgery. I'm hoping she will only have to stay overnight at a maximum.

The second operation will be far more major and radical and is scheduled for Thursday 30 March. This is where, through the latest technological breakthrough of 3D printing, we will insert a prosthetic titanium sacrum into Kim's lumbar region.

This has never been performed in Australia.

However, if Marc is any judge of a fit patient who could recover from such a surgery, our Champ Kim is the person to do it. I'm constantly amazed at her stoic attitude of putting one foot in front of the other and getting on with things, but truly humbled by the trust and faith she puts in me.

'Ant, you look after it and organise what needs to happen. I trust in whatever you say we should do,' she says.

If ever I needed an assurance of how much Kim loves me, there it is, right there. I can't ignore commentary such as this. It forges in steel the words those young twenty-year-olds said to one another over thirty years ago during our wedding ceremony at the St. Joseph's College Chapel. How life unfolds.

The next four weeks will be crucial, and certainly testing, in relation to Kim's treatment. However, I refuse to ever let this disease define or dictate to us. The bell's rung and it's time to come out and fight again.

Tuesday 14 March 2017

The operation last Thursday uncovered some small tumours on C3 which were removed again. Marc then searched from C1 all the way down to C6 and assured me Kim was clear. Unfortunately, at the neck of Kim's R7 rib, Marc had to drill into the bone, dig out and cement a tumour with a radius of around three centimetres. It doesn't sound much, but when you think of the size of Kim and her ribs, it's substantial. As a result, she awoke in considerable pain.

Recent scans have shown the tumours have already grown back in the lumbar and sacrum regions, so our next surgery is simply a path, though unwelcome, we must follow. Kim's ability to bounce back from operations such as this certainly isn't the same as it was twelve months ago. Perhaps it is also relevant to remember that this was her fourteenth surgical procedure in twenty-four months.

Usually eager to get out of the hospital as soon as possible, on this occasion she was happy to stay and recuperate further. This ended up being a blessing as at around 10.00 pm that night, she had a terrible turn with her blood pressure and staff had to act quickly.

Kim returned home the next day, drugged up, and within hours was at the Don Henley concert with her boys. What a champion!

On Friday afternoon, Kim joins me on a work trip to Singapore. Afterwards, I will fly her over to China to fulfil her lifelong dream of visiting the Great Wall of China, Tiananmen Square and the famous Terracotta Warriors of China. I purposely book-ended our return for 29 March, where the following day she is scheduled to return to hospital for the major surgery of replacing her sacrum bone with a prosthetic made from a 3D printer.

As we speak, they are planning the production of the prosthesis using MRI and CT scans. Marc, our surgeon, is heading a strategic planning team, as this will be the first time an operation like this is being attempted in Australia. 30 March is a scheduled date only and could change. However, it's the date we are aiming for.

As anyone would expect, even the stoic champion Kim is anxious, not only about the result, but also what to expect in the aftermath of the operation. There is little to no information, and we have no precedent to follow. It is very much a case of the unknown.

Throughout all of this, I've planned and negotiated surgeries, trips and so on, around her immunology treatment which follows a stringent time schedule of an intravenous drip feed in a registered chemo ward every fourteen days. In all honesty, when looking at how everything has unfolded, this Opdivo immunology treatment is possibly not working. However, further immunology treatment in the form of Keytruda is a contingency, and based on my investigations, a third, non-small, cell lung cancer-specific treatment is due to be released very soon.

Kim continues her weekly acupuncture, along with a high-antioxidant diet and an evening ritual of a hot footbath to aid circulation. She recommences training at the Dog House this afternoon at 3.00 pm with a session that will include cross trainer, rowing machine and core strength work less than a week since her last surgery.

The boys are aware of the magnitude of the upcoming surgery on 30 March and there is an unspoken anxiousness amongst the family. It's there in the small things, like each of us constantly aware of where the others are. We call one another daily and the boys seem to want to go out a lot less, preferring to spend more time at home.

Recently, in a moment of darkness and through tears, Kim told me she didn't want to live half a life. I explained to her that our lives would never be a half so long as we're together.

Friday 31 March 2017

Unfortunately, we've encountered a change of schedule for what was supposed to be Kim's radical surgery yesterday.

First, I have attached some photos from our most recent trip to China. Here is Kim in Shanghai:

Kim and I took a motorbike sightseeing trip through the old sector of Shanghai.

Kim and I visited the Terracotta Warriors dig site at Xian.

Kim fulfilled her dream of walking on the Great Wall of China (and it snowed).

Kim is at home in the cocktail bar in Beijing.

As many of you may know, Kim has a great passion for history and, as a natural academic, absorbed every moment of our time in China. Unfortunately, leading up to China she became quite ill in Singapore. I seriously considered terminating the trip, however, she came good once we arrived in Beijing. Our time in China was one museum and tour after another.

Kim was absolutely in her element, answering questions from the guide, and asking questions. I did everything I could to hide in anonymity to avoid being asked any questions. Of course, a la Sobb, I had no answers, and most of the time was not paying attention! If I don't see another museum, listen to another tour guide's lecture, visit an Empress Palace, look at a jade carving or hear the word concubine, it will never bother me! But I would do it all again for Kim. She absolutely loved it.

I purposely arranged for us to arrive home at midday on Wednesday so Kim could commence her radical surgery on Thursday morning. However, on Tuesday night, as we were about to board the plane from Shanghai to Sydney, our surgeon Marc called me. He enquired about Kim's wellbeing and mentioned some concerns around the timeline.

I explained to Marc that Kim was ready to go and we would like to proceed as per schedule. When we touched down in Sydney on Wednesday morning, a text came through from Marc asking me to call him urgently. Sensing something was wrong, I hid the conversation from Kim.

Marc explained he had formed a crack team of specialist surgeons who were all extremely excited about being involved in this ground-breaking surgery and amazed when Marc told them Kim's story. However, the team of medical engineers claimed they needed more time to prepare for the twenty-four-hour turnaround of producing the prosthetic sacrum bone. Marc explained we would have to wait three to four weeks as there was little room for error in a surgery like this.

'It's like a fight, Ant. You can't go in unprepared.'

Of course, I understood.

On explaining this to Kim, she completely deflated.

She had physically and mentally prepared for an extremely radical form of surgery, only to be told at the eleventh hour it was postponed. I could have laid down and cried with her as she wept a river. But I didn't have that luxury. That is not what Kim needed from me.

I tried to explain logically that the expert medical team Marc had put together wanted to 'get it right' and it was only three to four weeks. Kim lamented that she couldn't bear a torturous wait of three to four weeks. I completely understood her angst. How many times can you ask a fighter to get up off the canvas? How many more times is 'one more time'? Eventually, she found her centre of gravity, but hell, she has to battle one issue after another.

In a strange way, I welcome her resistance and, to a point, her angst. Elizabeth Kubler-Ross talks of acceptance, but neither Kim nor I are ready to accept the situation we find ourselves in as a fait accompli. There's too much love for one another and our family, too much more to learn and understand, too much humility to be gained and simply too much life still to be lived. So, if Kim is not at peace with this and her angst is refusal to be defined by this disease, then so be it.

On Monday, I will know the date for the upcoming surgery. The team of surgeons and medical engineers will remove her sacrum in the morning. Over the next twenty-four hours, the engineers will work, utilising a 3D printer and the original bone, to produce an identical prosthetic. The next day, Kim will have a second surgery where they will implant the prosthetic.

This will bring Kim to fourteen major surgeries, not counting numerous cycles of chemotherapy and dozens of cycles of radiation, in the past two-and-a-half years. If that's not a stoic, tenacious human, then please show me one. This journey and chapter in our life has given us an ocean of tears and moments of dark, dark despair, but it has also uncovered a deep sense of love, family and faith that I don't think we would have otherwise experienced. In a strange way, I feel blessed.

In the meantime, Jackson recommences his next semester at Notre Dame University where he will continue to fulfil his mother's dream of 'Please Lord, let one of my sons complete a degree.' His presence is a little scarce owing to work and relationship commitments, however, he more than makes up for it with the love and care he gives to everyone when he is at home. During a training session at the Dog House the other day, we came across an old poster on a promotional fight card that both Louis and Jackson were fighting on. All the other fighters, particularly Louis, were pictured shaping up like they would murder their grandmother for a dollar. However, there was Jackson, hands on his hips, with a beautiful heart-warming smile that would melt an angel's heart. Kim and I laughed together, arm in arm, and commented on his wonderful, gentle nature.

Oscar continues to adjust to life away from Joey's amidst the painfully military regime of 'Baron Anthony Von Sobb'. He laments that boarding school life at Joey's was a dream compared to the dictatorship and oppression of his father's household.

Louis was unceremoniously anointed to the professional sport of NRL when, just prior to kick-off of the opening round, he was warming up with the team of South Sydney Rabbitohs in front of a large group in the grandstand of Tiger supporters. The Tiger supporters began to scream expletives and profanities towards him that one would only hear in a shearer's quarters. He must have shown some reaction because his fellow strength and conditioning team member, David Furner (an ex-Raider forward who could throw them) turned to him.

'Hey, Louis, don't worry about it. If you fight one of them, you've gotta fight a million of them. Welcome to the NRL, son!'

I'm glad David said that to him because, knowing Louis, he probably wanted to fight all one million of them! Louis and I train together each day as usual and start our sparring in preparation for an upcoming fight this Friday. We still spend many hours on the beach patrolling, enjoying our long silences and taking comfort knowing we are there together. On the odd occasion, he'll just talk, and I'll simply listen—that is our way.

My next update will be about the outcome of Kim's next crucial surgery. While our faith is in the hands of God, we are committed to not capitulate.

My business is now north.

April 2017—Like Sisyphus, She Picked Up the Boulder

Thursday 20 April 2017
Yesterday was one of the darkest days Kim has experienced in our journey.

Oncologists seem to be so reticent about exposure to too much radiation from scans. I find this mindset quite contradictory, particularly when we want to empower ourselves with strategies on how and where to fight the disease. Hence, I turned to my good friend and surgeon Marc Coughlan.

'No problem, Ant. Just tell me what you want, and I'll write the referral,' he replied in his broad Afrikaans accent.

Hence, the day started with an extensive brain to lumbar CT scan, directly followed by four hours of intravenous treatment—a herculean task by anyone's standards.

Just prior to each immunology treatment, Kim must undergo a blood test and the most recent one diagnosed Kim with hypercalcemia, meaning her bones have begun to decalcify. This occurs for ten to thirty per cent of cancer patients when cancer has progressed into the bones. To deal with this, she needs to be hydrated with a saline solution for two hours before her immune treatment. The problem was that because of fasting for the scan, her already-hardened veins, due to hundreds of cannulas being inflicted on her body, were even more hardened. In hindsight, I should have known better.

It took numerous attempts on both arms to insert a cannula. By the time they had completed a successful one, Kim was in agony. By the time I arrived home later that afternoon, I found Kim upstairs in bed crying. I'd seen Kim cry before—I've seen many people cry before—but this was different. These were tears of deep, dark despair. I've never seen anybody with such fear in their eyes for their life. It frightened me to witness it. I gathered us both together, and we discussed hope.

Gradually, I coaxed her out of bed, then into her gym gear and then into the Dog House where, like Sisyphus, she picked up the boulder and started her training session.

Early this morning at around 3.00 am, unable to sleep, I went down to my office to research remedies and treatment for hypercalcemia. About thirty minutes into my self-education, I started to weep. It wasn't for me or the boys, but for Kim alone. I'd never seen fear in anyone's eyes like I saw in Kim's yesterday afternoon. The pain, the fear, the anxiety, the depression. Why Kim? As intelligent human beings, we deal with reason. I can't find any intelligent reason why Kim should suffer like this.

My mind drifted back to that first surgeon who, on explaining that the removal of Kim's C3 vertebra was impossible, said, 'I'm sorry. Bad things happen to good people all the time.'

At the time, that comment angered me. But on reflection, it occurred to me he was right. Bad things do happen to good people. In my family's immediate world, Kim is living proof. I still just haven't worked out why and probably never will.

Kim is courage, love, fear, beauty, determination, trust, loyalty, faith, pain, sadness, resilience, confusion, anger, frustration, peace and more love.

I anxiously await the results of the CT scan. Our radical surgery is now locked in for Thursday 18 May.

My business is now north.

May 2017—Two Hearts are Better than One

Wednesday 10 May 2017

The CT scan showed mixed results.

On a positive note, the cancer has not spread to any major organs. However, it continues to grow and regrow in Kim's bones. Regrowth has occurred in her seventh rib, the sacrum and C3. The C3 regrowth is the most concerning as the tumour is pressing against her spinal cord, which is giving her considerable pain at the base of her skull. There is also a new growth in C5.

As a result, we are going in for emergency surgery on Friday morning at the Prince of Wales. Marc will attempt to cut out the tumour from C3 growing into the spinal cord, as well as drill and cement tumours in the C5 and seventh rib bones.

The radical surgery to insert the 3D model of the prosthetic sacrum was delayed again because Marc still wasn't happy with the medical engineer's planning in relation to angles for the nerve entry into the sacrum.

'We have one chance to get this right, Ant, and these fuckers need to get it right.'

Sorry, Mum, if you're reading this, but that is what he said! And how could I disagree?

Initially, Kim was devastated as we had just returned from Bali, which we treated like a pre-fight camp. She lived on a diet of fresh fruit, trained every morning in the gym with me, then rested every afternoon and evening while I did my work. Even so, Kim now walks with a slight limp and is losing strength in her legs. As a result, she is keen to get this radical surgery done and dusted.

Marc and I had numerous late-night conversations while we were away, unbeknown to Kim. The sacrum has to wait, irrespective of the medical engineers, as Friday's surgery is far more urgent considering the growth into the spine. Marc is meeting with the engineers today and I expect him to give me a date on Friday for the radical prosthetic procedure.

Unfortunately, it appears our current immunology treatment has not been successful. Biopsy results have proven the secondary immunology treatment of Keytruda has only around a one in a hundred chance of showing positive results. Kim was devastated when we received this news on Tuesday, though I think I jolted her out of complete despair and into instant annoyance and anger with my unbridled enthusiasm.

'Well, who cares! We've got Marc Coughlan. One minute you're asleep on the table and the next minute you wake up from the anaesthetic and it's gone. No 'if' the treatment works and no waiting,' I declared.

Kim looked at me like a volcano ready to erupt.

'Are you kidding me?' she said.

Well, annoyance and anger with me have got to be better options than complete self-despair.

Of course, there are dark moments from the mental anguish and torture of the major radical surgery now being postponed for a fourth time. Most people would have capitulated. However, as Bruce Springsteen sings, 'Two hearts are better than one.'

Whenever Kim seems to slip into a dark place, God somehow gives me a little more strength. When I slip, possibly not so much into a dark place but more of an angry place, God gives Kim the strength to placate me, point out my shortcomings and enlighten me on accountability and humility.

It's strange how things work and what constitutes a good husband, a good wife or a good anyone when we're dealing with a situation of this magnitude. Most of us live most of our lives not having to deal with mortality. We simply drift from day to week to month, and then years without giving it any thought. But then, when you are forced to confront it, one can become obsessed with it, overthinking it and thus missing that invaluable ever present 'now'. If mindfulness taught Kim and I anything, it evoked this concept.

Thursday 25 May 2017

About an hour ago, I received the news Kim and I had been painstakingly waiting for over the last two months.

Next Thursday morning, on 1 June, at the Prince of Wales Hospital, our friend and surgeon Dr Marc confirmed he will undertake the radical surgery of removing Kim's sacrum, along with all the aggressive tumours in this area, and replacing it with a prosthetic. As I mentioned before, we only know of one other instance in the world where this took place and that was in China. My research reported it was successful, but there was little information pertaining to the actual surgery and recovery.

Marc has decided that rather than create a prosthetic from the 3D printer, he will utilise the original sacrum bone once removed and have the medical engineers use it as a cast for the prosthetic. Once made, he will then insert the prosthetic.

The two-month wait has taken its toll both physically and emotionally. The angst of having the surgery postponed then rescheduled multiple times has magnified a rollercoaster of emotions.

From a physical perspective, it is not a matter of if we move forward with the operation, we just must. In a matter of weeks, Kim has gone from being a gym junkie and semi-professional-level athlete to not being able to walk without the aid of a walking stick. Louis and I have developed a tailor-made program very different from her original one as she is losing the strength in her legs at an incredible rate.

Walking up steps has become a major problem, and she can only just bear her own body weight. The purpose of the surgery is to remove the large masses of tumour around her sacrum, as well as the sacrum itself, thus returning the strength to her muscles and relieving nerve pain.

Marc doesn't believe Kim will be in hospital for an extended period after the operation. The aim is for her to return home as soon as possible to reduce the risk of infection. To put things into perspective, this will still be Kim's fourteenth major surgery in approximately twenty-four months.

I continue to prepare Kim's Chinese herbal treatment three times a day as well as antioxidant shakes. We both believe these have been a major factor in aiding in her immune system for recovery after surgeries. If I can offer any advice at all for dealing with this illness, it is the value of diet, physical training and a positive mindset.

With the new immunology treatment of Keytruda offering only a one-in-a-hundred chance of success, we have decided to stay with the Opdivo immunology treatment as we are not prepared to capitulate to it not working. Although tumours have spread and regrown in C3, C5 and the seventh rib, which were resected in surgery two weeks ago, they still haven't spread to any of the major organs. Our hope is this may be due to the Opdivo treatment. Call it a mixture of science and hope, but if that's what gets us through and keeps Kim buoyant, then so be it.

For such a beautiful, independent and intelligent woman to undergo such a debilitating disease, it is inspirational to see Kim come this far. The 'black dog' has come more often, and it breaks my heart to see her that way. Such is her love and trust for me, that when I take her hand and guide us out of the darkness, she follows. It is humbling. Her love and trust give me strength.

In a strange twist, my devotion to her comes, unfortunately, from a selfish place. I can't imagine my life without her. The movie *Into the Wild* put it so eloquently: the meaning and value of life is only experienced when you can share it with another. Keeping it only for yourself renders it worthless.

While we met this latest news of the rescheduled surgery with some excitement, there is also much reticence and trepidation. I don't want to go into any detail about what could go wrong as I don't think it serves a purpose. However, it weighs heavily on Kim's mind. It's yet another yoke she carries and yet another miracle of the strength and determination of this woman.

With all this happening in her life, the flotsam and jetsam of her men still take on monumental importance: the tidiness of Oscar's room and relationship advice, the tidiness of Louis' room and ensuring that he doesn't diet and train too hard, the tidiness of Jackson's room and making sure he is always immaculately dressed for work. All this is compounded with just being there, body and soul, for her husband, whether cheering at the beach finish line at surf life-saving carnivals or cheering together at Joey's rugby games. Sometimes it is just patiently sitting opposite him at a dinner table pretending to listen as he rambles like a savant, dissecting server service operandi, menu design and decor. She simply belongs to me and I to her.

Here she is enjoying her Joey's rugby with Oscar and my Uncle Barry. It was a beautiful Saturday afternoon at Scots where the Joey Boys punched way above their weight and won.

Here is Kim supporting her North Cronulla boys at last week's IRB Surf Life Saving Carnival at Mollymook.

The boys sense something big is happening. Kim's physical disabilities are so apparent and hard to ignore. While not an open discussion, they certainly display an acute awareness as evidenced by the random hugs and kisses they give her or going out of their way to make her day-to-day chores easier. I accommodate them and play the game of giving them enough information to fuel and pacify their conscience, but not enough to make them anxious and give them despair. They don't need more. It serves no purpose. Kim and I just want to be their mum and dad.

Oscar is coming to terms with life outside Joey's and the responsibilities that come with adulthood. He's passing his exams, only just, but in Sobb terms, a pass is a pass thanks to their father's DNA.

Louis and I still spend many hours each week training. We have brief moments where we talk of matters of great importance, but there is little small talk. He approaches his role with the strength and conditioning team at Souths diligently, and from what I can observe and the feedback I have received, he is considered a valuable team member and contributor. His lack of small talk and regard for silence is appreciated at the club.

Jackson's high-octane approach to life continues to burn like a supernova. Burning the candle at both ends, he has immersed himself in the food and beverage operations at Canterbury Hurlstone Park RSL, as well as in his studies for his MBA. However, neither is more important than ensuring all is well with the family. If Jackson is anchored to anything, it is to his immediate family, and for that I am grateful.

While we were away in Bali, the boys either spoilt Reuben rotten or treated him like Boo Radley (see *To Kill a Mockingbird*). When Kim arrived home, he sulked for all of five minutes, then wouldn't leave her side. They continue to potter around the house together like 'Chip 'n Dale' except Kim does all the talking and Reuben does all the listening.

Through all this, the family dynamics have not changed. Kim is the brunt of many of our jokes and equally the rose who the boys and I all love, protect and defend. No-one is a protected species or immune to being brought into line. Sulking in any way, shape or form is totally prohibited. We are politically incorrect, make totally inappropriate jibes at one another and at the same time are fearlessly loyal and protective of one another. When the 'black dog' comes, Kim and I ensure the boys are never aware of it and, most of the time, the 'Sobb circus' continues to roll. Go figure!

Thursday's fight is a major turning point on this journey and a path we have no choice but to follow. We fear not the fight, nor the battle ahead of us. I continually reassure Kim of the hopelessness that was presented to us two years ago prior to our initial radical surgery on C3. I explain to her that since we were told to 'get your affairs in order', we have watched our boys develop in their careers, shared numerous trips overseas, spent hours on patrol at North Cronulla together, attended rugby games and surf carnivals together, and simply bathed in each other's company. I tell her we shall do it all again after this surgery on Thursday. Amen.

The bell tolls and we fight again.

May our business continue north.

Playlist:
Two Hearts, Bruce Springsteen

June 2017—The Kim Sobb Resistance

Thursday 1 June 2017

The surgical team headed by Marc only just finished after an eight-hour radical surgery.

Kim is in the ICU. Unfortunately, they won't let me see her.

I am currently waiting to have a debrief meeting with Marc who will let me know Kim's status and the success of the surgery.

Monday 5 June 2017

Last Thursday began with Kim and I leaving home at 5.00 am after what was an extremely restless and anxious night. Ever the anal and pragmatic organiser, I ensured we had everything packed the night before to ensure the morning was as seamless as possible. I realised any small bump in the road or concern would take on monumental magnitude owing to our nervous anticipation of the morning's upcoming surgery.

In darkness and silence, we made our way down the M5 motorway towards the hospital. Kim broke the silence only once, explaining she wanted to go back home. I reminded her we had faced such a situation before, two years ago, and this was no different.

'My darling, we will get through this, and we will continue our life with one another.'

We admitted Kim at the Prince of Wales Hospital around 6.00 am.

As Kim waited to be taken into pre-theatre, she became quite emotional, explaining she wished this nightmare would end and that she just wanted to go home.

Inside, my heart broke. How could you blame her for asking, 'How did I arrive here at this place?'

We held hands. I kissed her on the cheek and promised I would see her on the other side.

The orderly wheeled her away and our eyes never left each other's until the pre-op doors broke our line of sight.

Shortly afterwards, Marc came and saw me in the waiting room.

'Are you worried, Ant?' he asked in his broad Afrikaans accent.

'No,' I said, then I gave him a Saint Anthony medallion that was given to me years ago by a very close friend.

Its once silver coating and sharp edges were now black and dulled by my constant and methodical rubbing. It normally sat on my desk, and I often instinctively reached for it in deep moments of contemplation. The physical action quenched the physical anxiety, but I guess it was more of an emotional comfort. My namesake, St. Anthony, the patron saint of lost things, is the one who will never give up, the one who never loses faith, the one who will never turn his back.

Marc explained that his mother often did the same thing when he was a young boy back in South Africa.

'Ant, I'd go on these trips and find that my mother secretly planted Saint Christopher medals in my rucksack!'

If the moment wasn't so serious, it would have been funny, but it further connected us. He told me I needed to be somewhere he could contact me quickly if the need arose. This meant that my makeshift bed in the car at my favourite secluded car space was not an option. At around 7.45 am, I scouted the floors of the Prince of Wales and found a secluded lounge where I set up camp and simply waited ... and waited ...

Kind-hearted nurses walked past me, asking if I was waiting for anyone. I must have looked like a sad, lost, stray dog waiting for its master. The truth be known, I probably was.

At around 2.45 pm, I received a text from Marc's assistant surgeon explaining the surgery was finished and they would be in touch. This immediately sent alarm bells. The standard protocol was that Marc came and saw me, gown and all, straight after the surgery to give me an immediate debrief.

A lot of things passed through my mind at that moment. Kim and I didn't fear death. What we did fear was not being together.

An excruciatingly long forty-five minutes passed before my now good mate, approached me with his broad smile.

'Ant, it was absolutely amazing! I went into places of the human anatomy that in my entire surgical life I've never ventured into or seen before. We cut out all the tumours we could see around the lumbar and sacrum region. I then took out the sacrum, made an identical mould out of a cement putty and replaced it.'

Marc also informed me that during the procedure, Kim went into a critical haemorrhage. Fortunately, we had brought a highly reputable vascular surgeon onto the team who stepped in to address the critical blood loss. Marc also informed me that famous surgeon Dr Charlie Teo came on board as he was interested in the procedure Marc was about to embark on.

There we have it! The first time in Australia and, to our knowledge, the second time in the world, and the Champ came through. The Champ came through! Not only because of her incredible courage and tenacity, but also because of the love and grace of God guiding Marc's hand and the love and support that embraced her from people such as yourselves.

Unfortunately, we will be back in the saddle of surgery later next month when we remove tumours that have reoccurred in C3 and the new one in the right seventh rib. Marc said it was too dangerous to attempt these during this surgery. He also commented, 'Shit, Ant, don't you ever stop!'

That was Thursday morning and Kim came home late Sunday morning. The large scar on her stomach is quite painful. Getting in and out of bed or rising from a chair is done slowly and gingerly.

However, the scars will heal, and the pain will dissipate. Last week, she was walking with a walking stick. However, even at this early stage of recovery, Kim can walk bearing her own weight without any trouble.

I will now step up my role as wound nurse and dietician. My aim in approximately two weeks is to wear the gym coach hat again and recommence our sessions back at the Dog House which paid such great dividends in leading us to where we are at this point.

Tuesday 20 June 2017

It has now been three weeks since Kim's most recent radical surgery.

Here she is out for dinner, approximately one week after the operation.

She had her first session back at the Dog House also one week after the surgery, on the treadmill and doing light weights.

'Mate, the woman is a machine!' messaged Dr Marc Coughlan back eloquently when he heard.

Her recuperation from the actual surgery, given the circumstances, is progressing well. Her physical rehabilitation in relation to the strength returning to her legs and general weight-bearing remains unclear. With little or no precedent or benchmark to follow, it is hard to measure. Kim has returned to using a walking stick, though I keep her moving at the Dog House.

At a recent pre-operation camp prior to our last major surgery, I stole Kim away for two nights to a hotel on the Gold Coast. With the weather still being so beautiful, and after about half an hour of convincing from 'Dr Sobb', I had her walking laps around the pool. She commented on how much relief it gave her. With this in mind, I began further investigation into hydrotherapy and physiotherapy, found a location and spoke to the physios where Kim will now commence another form of treatment.

Tomorrow we are scheduled to meet with our radiation oncologist where it will be my intention to badger, bully and simply wear down the doctor to allow Kim further radiation treatment for new tumours on C5 and the left and right seventh ribs. I will not leave that office until the oncologist has signed off on further treatment for Kim.

Whilst I had scheduled some further surgery later this month with Marc, I've currently put it on hold pending Kim's emotional and physical wellbeing. We continue with our immunology treatment every fortnight, as well as our three-times-a-day preparation of specialised Chinese herbs.

Emotionally, 'Churchill's black dog' does return. I'm not sure whether that's from the copious amounts of anaesthetic or the simple flotsam and jetsam that come with the disease and the energy we spent on fighting it. Either way, it is a reality and depletes the quality of life and its 'present-ness'.

This is where the importance of creating events comes in. Our IRB surf carnivals are held in the winter off-season and at regional beaches up and down the coast of NSW. These create a perfect catalyst to get away for weekends where Kim can leave 'Kim, the patient' in Sydney and return to 'Kim, the loyal supporter of North Cronulla'.

Here she supports her aging old husband and fit young son in wonderful regional beach carnivals. She can cheer her son who has proudly made the NSW team, and be the loving, condoling wife when I run up the beach dead last.

'Ant, that was a great sprint up the beach to finish!' she'll say.

With all she has to bear, along with the fatiguing, pained legs from walking up and down the beach, all she wants to do is comfort her silly old husband.

I am a lucky man!

On July 23, I am fortunate to take Kim on my annual work trip to LA and Vegas. Here we will tag on Canada and a much-anticipated return to her place of birth. These events keep her buoyant. While I spend much of my energies creating them, we are both aware and wary of the percolating 'black dog' that simmers just under the surface. Mindfulness, meditation and mindset keep that dog at bay and on the leash.

I have been contacted by an LA documentary and film-maker, now based in Australia, who wishes to make a documentary on Kim's fight, journey and the work associated with Marc Coughlan. Kim's most recent radical surgery was filmed and the initial interviews with Kim, along with Reuben the Wonder Dog, began this week.

Of course, this became great ammunition for the boys and I to tease Kim, particularly about her so-called comfortable and leisurely apparel that she claimed to be wearing when interviewed. The boys and I called her everything from the world's greatest ham to Australia's version of Zsa Zsa Gabor. It was fun and for a moment, it reminded us of how things used to be. I'm not sure where this will all end up, but somehow Kim and I feel an obligation to the people coming after us to let them know of the power of hope, love, faith and the will to continue to fight.

Thursday 22 June 2017
I marched into the radiation oncologist's office heavily armed and with Kim. He asked why we were there and what he could do for us. I bluntly told him we wanted treatment and rattled off exactly where we wanted it. Like most of our other doctors, he reached into his usual armoury of, 'We are going to need scans and reports, so we can't start immediately.'

I proceeded to open my infamous Rain Man wheelie bag and produced the three most recent reports along with scans. These I obtained from my underground medical team working for the 'Kim Sobb Resistance'!

The result? We commence ten sessions of radiation starting next Tuesday to Kim's left and right seventh rib, her C5 vertebrae and, at this stage, around her lumbar region.

However, before we receive the radiation, we needed to proceed immediately to the radiation ward to do pre-scanning and imaging. This involves tattooing to ensure the radiation spots are accurate. Unfortunately, I had miscalculated (by one vertebra!) that part of this setup work includes a fitting of the dreaded mask. For anybody even the slightest bit claustrophobic, this is an unbelievably torturous thirty-minute event. Immediately upon beginning the process, I could feel Kim's anxiety. Most people find it a herculean task to get through this once. This will be Kim's third fitting.

The staff at the centre know us well and gave me the flexibility of being with Kim except for the radiation periods. I stand by Kim's radiation machine as they fix her head and mask to the table. She communicates with me by squeezing my hand.

Together, we have developed a strategy to help her through these moments where I talk in a low monotone voice, almost like a mantra, and describe places for us to metaphorically escape to, while gently and rhythmically stroking her arm. I describe to her the wonderful, warm desert air of Red Rock and the cooling sensation of water on her skin as we float weightlessly under the Nevada sun.

Apart from becoming incredibly courageous, Kim has also developed an incredible discipline where together we can steal ourselves away during moments of treatment. Sometimes she stumbles and I know this by the way she squeezes my fingers and the heavy onset of breathing. With this, I stroke her arm a little stronger to bring her back to that comfortable place.

This time, I pondered how I despised this disease and what it does to individuals. Strangely enough, it also acts as a catalyst to remind Kim and I how much we love one another, the wonderful support and friends that we have, and this incredible resilience to fight and overcome. The bell rings for the next round and radiation treatment starts again Tuesday morning.

My business is now north.

Playlist:
With Every Wish, Bruce Springsteen

July 2017—Hunting Invisible Game

Tuesday 4 July 2017

In the four weeks since Kim's radical surgery, much of the extreme swelling in her abdomen has subsided. Kim now fits back into her favourite outfits, giving peace to the boys and me from her constant (and mistaken) lamenting of 'I've put on too much weight!'

The major scar on her abdomen is healing well. I think I have become quite proficient in treating and dressing major post-operative wounds. From a tumour perspective, the surgery was a success. However, Kim is still in constant pain and experiencing weight-bearing issues. She has trouble walking distances without the aid of a walking stick.

I'm hoping much of the trauma around her nerves from the operation will dissipate, but no one really knows. As a result, on top of her normal pain medication, she currently lives on anywhere from twelve Panadol tablets upwards a day, simply to help her deal with the extreme pain in her legs.

From a treatment perspective, we are onto our second week of radiation. Unfortunately, we've had to stop our immunology treatment as our oncologists don't want to run radiation and immunology treatment concurrently. She continues her ritual of Chinese herbs and super-antioxidant shakes that I prepare for her each day, as well as weekly acupuncture.

The new regime of hydrotherapy that 'Dr Sobb' organised for her has become a hot topic for comic relief in our family. Kim is the baby of her class, being the only patient under eighty years of age. Her new friends save her places in the pool and fuss around her at lunchtime. Some of the older men even try to show off their feats of strength in front of her, all great opportunities for the boys and I to tease her! However, all in all, she is finding great relief in the weightlessness of this therapy. Again, it's a constant reminder to us of the importance of physical activity when dealing with the disease and its treatment.

'Churchill's black dog' returns from time to time. Even though we are more experienced in the signs of it, it is still crippling. Again, events take on monumental importance and I attempt to make an event out of anything, so much so, that Reuben the Wonder Dog will soon have a young sister Lily to look after, in the form of a giant apricot English Mastiff. She was born last Thursday, so we will bring her home in around eight weeks. Kim is excited, but anxious. Just what we needed … another big dog and gatekeeper to Kim!

The off-season surf life-saving carnivals up and down the coast of NSW have been a welcome distraction. Last weekend, Kim followed her North Cronulla up to the State Titles at South West Rocks. Here, Louis was presented with his NSW team regalia, her husband stumbled at the water entry for the Quarter Finals and the carnival was stopped for an hour as a two-and-a-half-metre great white shark was spotted circling the patient pickup area and buoys approximately 150 metres offshore!

In two weekends, Kim looks forward to flying to Coolangatta to support her men and the team of North Cronulla for the Australian Surf Life Saving Championships.

The following week, I fly her off to the United States and Canada. Kim is really excited about this trip. I'll have my usual meetings with casino executives and investigate restaurant layouts and fit-outs while Kim soaks up the Nevada Desert sun, reads a book and gently immerses herself in the anonymity of being Kim Sobb—not a cancer patient.

The boys are all doing well and their coping mechanisms of only wanting to know just enough and not too much keeps the Sobb family circus rolling.

Reuben the Wonder Dog continues to flip out whenever Kim pulls her luggage bags out to pack for a trip. He knows she is going somewhere. Little does he know he has much to cope with ahead of him as the breeders inform us that Lily will be bigger than him at three months of age! I think we should have called Lily 'Rasputia' from one of Eddie Murphy's characters in Norbit.

When we return from our trip, we will decide whether we need to surgically resect the tumours on the left and right ribs. Whatever direction we decide on after that will be based on a further full-body PET scan.

Despite the debilitating effects of this disease, Kim continues to not only look after me, but give me strength. God's grace looks after the rest.

Friday 7 July 2017

In the last forty-eight hours, several things have occurred.

On a positive note, our radiation oncologist informed us that Kim will not have to wear the claustrophobic and debilitating mask during this current radiation treatment. He believes the scans claiming a tumour on C5 were misread. Herein lies the frustration and subjectivity of being a patient, along with independence and empowerment being taken away—Kim had to put up with a terrifying half-hour ordeal to mould the mask ready for treatment.

A further tumour on C3 is still growing but cannot take any more radiation. We also can't treat the recent area where the sacrum was removed because of its proximity to the spinal cord. Hence, the regrowth of tumours in this region is possible. What we are treating are the left and right seventh ribs.

After a recent lengthy conference with Marc, he explained how happy he was with the stability and outcome of the operation on the overall sacrum region. Unfortunately, he also informed me that Kim now has cancer growing in the bone of the acetabulum, more commonly known as the hip socket.

He explained that whilst not ideal, he felt confident that his newly developed system of syringing out the tumour that was eating into the bone and filling the cavity with hot, liquid, fast-drying cement would be a relatively simple procedure.

Upon informing Kim of this information, she was devastated. Add onto this the severe pain and her crippling attempts to walk, I cannot blame her. I confided again with Marc and suggested he write me a referral for a cortisone injection. At the very least, it will give Kim some respite for a limited period while we are away. He agreed and this will occur in the upcoming week.

Marc and I have scheduled a lengthy meeting on our return to review the full-body scan and strategically map out the surgical resection plan. We will attempt to give Kim's mind and body the least amount of resistance and optimum chance to fight the cancer. So, despite her excitement at the prospect of us going away, we will have much to deal with on our return.

Attempting to deal with this guerrilla disease is like hunting invisible game. Kim is becoming sick and tired. Again, who can blame her? I know my unbridled enthusiasm at times frustrates her. But, to her absolute credit, after becoming angry or frustrated with me she simply says, 'I really do need your positive attitude sometimes, Ant, no matter how ridiculously optimistic it is.'

Comments like that are all I need to keep me going, no matter how hard it gets. I often remind her of the ten months they gave us to get her 'affairs in order' in October 2014. I tell her that no one gave us a chance, but we refused to listen to them, and took matters into our own hands.

'Look where we are now,' I say.

We have a future to look forward to and too much love for one another to give up now. So, with this change in the game, we take a new tack, a new direction and a new strategy into the fight. Possibly a little wearier, but make no mistake, we have the same resolve to fight the good fight. Together.

Our business is now north.

Playlist:
Hunter of Invisible Game, Bruce Springsteen

August 2017—Returning Home

Monday 14 August 2017

Well, Kim is back from her tour of 'the home country'.

Here she is sitting back and enjoying the Toronto summer and waterside.

AUGUST 2017—RETURNING HOME

One of the highlights was the Niagara Falls.

The Champ looked as beautiful as ever at a Montreal French restaurant.

Kim is never more at home than when she is travelling. During my work-leg in Vegas, Kim bathed in the Nevada Desert heat which gave her some relief. From there, we travelled to Canada, visiting Toronto, Niagara and Montreal.

I could sense the deep emotion from Kim, particularly when we were in Toronto. Jokingly she said to me, 'Ant, I feel I'm returning home.' Deep down, I knew there was some truth in it.

Unfortunately, despite her brave face in the photos, Kim experienced some incredible pain running down her left shoulder and arm, along with her limp. Just prior to leaving Sydney, a friend organised a second and third opinion on our last CT scan in relation to C5. Not surprisingly, the scan had been misinterpreted, and there was a large tumour growing on C5. As frustrating as this news was, it enabled me to prepare.

Hence, when Kim started experiencing the pain while we were away, I knew the cause and nature of it. Prior to going away, I booked theatre time and Marc Coughlan for resection of the tumours on C5, both the left and right seventh rib and a resection and cementing on her left hip bone. This is scheduled for three days' time. For Kim and I, it can't come quick enough, owing to the intense pain she is experiencing.

With that being said, we did experience somewhat of a miracle whilst we were away. On 2 August at Niagara Falls, we celebrated our thirty-first wedding anniversary. For some unknown reason, for the first time in nearly four years, Kim experienced a completely pain-free day. It was amazing.

That night I lay awake (as I do most nights) and my mind turned to that young couple thirty-one years ago, standing at the St. Joseph's College altar. Unaware of the life that lay before them and certainly not contemplating the situation we find ourselves in today, they only knew instinctively they wanted to spend the rest of their lives together. I pondered on that into the early hours of the morning; our life together and how it has unfolded—and felt blessed. Until the morning came, I felt content to watch Kim sleep and feel her breathe.

As the trip moved into its later stages, finishing in Montreal, the intensity of Kim's pain grew. Not having my medical and support team and being away from home made it incredibly hard for me to help Kim manage the pain. My short-term solution was to increase her pain medication. While this gave some slight relief, it caused counter-symptoms and complications.

One afternoon in Montreal, I left her curled up on the bed in excruciating agony so I could make a mercy dash to a pharmacy where I had to explain my situation with Kim in my most basic 'kitchen French' to the pharmacist on duty. Fortunately, her humanity came through and she supplied me with some special medication which relieved Kim of the counter-symptoms of her pain medication.

Comprehending extensive and acute pain is something, fortunately, that most people never have to deal with in their life. We think of pain as a present or short-term moment. I find it hard to grasp the sheer courage of Kim, and anyone else in her situation, contemplating years of extreme pain with little or no relief. Respite is found only in the solitude of broken hours of sleep.

With everything said and done, Kim had a wonderful experience while we were away. She is now cautiously looking forward to relief from the tumour resections with Thursday's operation.

To keep the events coming, Kim eagerly awaits the arrival of her new pup Lily, the giant English Mastiff. Fully grown, she will weigh over ninety kilograms. Kim rarely does anything in halves! Lily is the pup at the front of this photo.

The boys really missed their mother and displayed wonderful affection when we returned home. This included about half a ton of dirty washing. I strangely understood her bittersweet complaining about this. This labour of love gave her purpose, reminding her of the simple and small things that bind and tie a family.

For me with the boys, it was similar. Jackson and Oscar initially rejoiced in the entropy during the absence of their militant father. Louis, of course, recessed into his own world with regimented training and diet. By the time we got back, it was a little like Lord of the Flies with the boys in dire need of someone to bark commands and bring back order. Well, that's my deluded take on it, anyway!

So, here we are. Kim receives a full CT scan today, meaning Marc will have something very current to work on during Thursday's operation. I'm not quite sure what the rest of the scans will show, though I have an idea. Either way, they will determine our next tack.

Kim continues to be an incredibly beautiful human being and an exceptional woman displaying courage that many of us can only dream about. She loves the Sobb men unconditionally and the Sobb men, in turn, rely on her like oxygen for life.

The bell has rung and it's time to leave the stool and engage in the combat.

Friday 18 August 2017
This was approximately Kim's nineteenth major surgery—hence we were cursed to know intimately what lay ahead. The night before, I bumbled around like Rain Man preparing and packing, making up my makeshift bed in the back of the car and ensuring the house and the boys would all be organised in our absence.

Kim, on the other hand, verged on being rebellious, refusing to pack until the eleventh hour almost as a sign of defiance. We were classified 'no food' from midnight, followed by water only, then 'nil by mouth' from 5.00 am, with arrival at the hospital at 8.00 am. Kim's pain at this point was acute. I counted back and set my alarm for 4.00 am so I could wake her and administer pain relief, knowing she would receive nothing until the anaesthetist's injection at approximately 10.00 am.

The one-hour drive to the hospital felt like an eternity. I broke the silence with my attempts to keep Kim positive by reminding her of the success we experienced from other resections. She literally gave one-word answers. I totally understood the mental torture she was going through. Each time she wakes from major surgeries such as this, they progressively become more traumatic.

The moment we turned into the hospital, she burst into tears, telling me she couldn't go through this again. I held her hand and reminded her we were in this together. We simply put one foot in front of the other. We checked into pre-admissions at around 7.30 am and then waited ... and waited.

As we waited, the pain returned. Realising I couldn't give Kim anything, I looked for ways to take her mind off it. I had purposely brought my iPad and began to go through the hundreds of pictures I had recently taken on our trip away. It worked well for a while—until the last picture.

Then, when it became almost unbearable, the Champ herself pulled out the Ace card and began to tell me her set of rules and guidelines for when she was gone. This included everything from guidelines to dating, age-appropriateness and when and if girlfriends could be introduced to Reuben and Lily! It certainly helped pass the time as I quizzed her for further clarification. We laughed until we cried.

Thankfully, at around 10.30 am, they wheeled her away. We gave our traditional last kiss to one another, raised fists and for approximately the nineteenth time said we loved each other as I finished with, 'I'll see you on the other side.'

Our eyes didn't leave each other until the swinging hospital theatre doors closed. I waited for a moment, took a deep breath and went with my trusted wheelie bag full of Kim's medical files in search of the quietest corner of the hospital for some respite from the rest of the world.

Owing to the severity of this surgery, I needed to stay within phone contact distance. Due to the concrete of the car park, my car 'bedroom' was not an option. It was a matter of sitting and waiting.

You can think about a lot of things when you're in a situation like this and have a lot of time on your hands, and I did. As per usual, a multitude of questions, with little to no answers, led me back to the present.

Finally, after approximately three hours, my great mate and surgeon Marc found me and in his broad Afrikaans accent exclaimed, 'Ant, how do you manage to find these places?'

He explained they had done a lot of work, particularly around the ribs, hips and again around the sacrum and iliac regions.

'What about C5?' I questioned.

To my surprise, he explained they were going in for a second surgical session with Kim to do her upper body, including C5. He was just giving the surgical team a five-minute break and a change in theatre. He quickly skolled a can of Coke, scoffed a ham sandwich and said, 'I've got to go back in there now, Ant. We're doing our best.'

Finally, at around 5.00 pm, I got the text from Marc that they had just finished and to meet him up at his office. At the meeting, he explained it was a far bigger procedure than they had anticipated. The multiple cycles of radiation had turned the tumours quite fibrous and made them difficult to resect. Nonetheless, he had taken out a substantial amount of the tumours.

He also commented on his concerns surrounding Kim's left hip as Kim walks with an exaggerated limp nowadays. He explained he had organised an orthopaedic surgeon to look at her with the possibility of putting in a metal screw to help stabilise it, thus stopping a potential fracture.

'Ant, she is truly amazing. I can honestly say I've never operated on anyone quite like her. Just her sheer strength and resilience are unbelievable. The surgical team and I can't believe how strong her immune system is. To have not one single infection after so many major surgeries is unheard of,' he exclaimed in his broad Afrikaans accent.

I eventually bullied my way into the recovery ward. A friend of mine always said, 'Walk like you belong and no one will ever question you.' When I saw Kim, she became quite emotional. Apparently, she had been asking for me for some time. The moment she saw me, and we held each other's hands, her anxiousness left her.

From there, we quickly moved to the intensive care unit. This unit is virtually my home ground owing to the number of times Kim and I have been there. I've made friends with some of the nursing staff and many enemies with the unit's doctors. Moments after being admitted, I re-commenced my warring with the doctors, insisting on a PCA (an intravenous patient self- administering pain-relief button with our post-op pain-relief drug of choice, fentanyl).

The doctors have long been unimpressed by my knowledge of pain-relief treatment, and so began the power plays. But a phone call to Marc, and Kim's PCA was installed immediately. It frustrates me that things come down to this. Neither Kim nor any other patients should ever need to experience unnecessary acute pain. I am sure my path will cross again with my nemesis doctors in the ICU unit.

I spoke to Kim this morning and, though still in much pain, it was not as bad as yesterday. I tell her that every day things will get a little better. I tell her she will join me this summer on patrol at North Cronulla beach. She will lie on the sand and bathe in the summer sun. I'll take her out the back where she will float in the ocean looking up at the sky. We will travel to India in the new year, and, of course, she will need to look after the Wonder Dog and newly arrived Lily.

That is where we are.

AUGUST 2017—RETURNING HOME

Thursday 24 August 2017

Kim stayed three days post-operation at the Prince of Wales. She was in acute pain and there were some real concerns about the leakage of spinal fluid from the numerous large incisions made in her back. These were done to enable Marc to resect as much tumour as possible from different locations in her body. They started just below the hairline on her neck, then followed a trail all the way to her lower back.

During our stay at the hospital, Marc organised for an orthopaedic surgeon to see Kim. The ever anxious, yet pragmatic 'Dr Sobb' and his wheelie bag supplied him with the latest appropriate CT scans immediately. He went away for an hour and returned, giving us 'the news' that Kim needed to have a complete hip replacement, as the risk of hip fracture was critical.

Kim, still suffering from physical and emotional post-surgery trauma, was gutted. This was just the kind of news you don't need to hear while attempting to recover from your nineteenth major surgery.

'Ant, I can't live my life like this anymore. I know I'm afraid to die, but I just can't live like this. I'm done,' she explained.

'OK then, we can give up tomorrow, just not today,' I simply said, not wanting to argue or antagonise her.

And that became my mantra to her in the ensuing days when the pain became great.

'We can give up tomorrow, just not today.'

So, the days turned into a week and the wounds were lovingly cared for by 'Nurse Sobb'. (Picture Curly Joe from The Three Stooges in a nurse's uniform with red lipstick and false eyelashes!)

The orthopaedic surgeon explained it would be a week in hospital post-surgery, followed by a week in a specialised rehabilitation hospital. The outcome was intended to avert the inevitable fractured hip, which could be fatal. Equally important was instant pain relief from that region. As Kim now walks with an exaggerated limp and a walking stick with chronic pain in this region, it was a promising incentive to move forward with this surgery.

Kim has her bone scan and x-ray of this region next Tuesday. An appointment with the orthopaedic surgeon follows that afternoon where we will schedule an immediate date for the hip replacement. I've also organised for Marc to work in tandem with the orthopaedic surgeon to cut out any further tumours once the hip bone has been taken out.

It will be Kim's twentieth major surgery.

'Nurse 'Curly Joe' Sobb' continues to redress and lovingly care for her wounds, and we have developed a ritual each morning when the pain is at its most critical. This includes pre-organised medication waiting by the bedside, a hot shower to increase the core body temperature and lubricate the joints, followed by a hot breakfast with her favourite coffee, the ABC News already on and Reuben the Wonder Dog awaiting her arrival at the kitchen table. It all sounds so basic and simple, but the reality is it comforts her, and that is how we start each day.

Of course, I had to source the best possible walking stick, and I certainly have paid the price. Recently at the local grocery store, we meandered down the aisles while Kim prodded me with the stick, pointing at items to procure like I was some K-9 retriever. Eventually, I unceremoniously grabbed my highly researched walking stick from her clutches and in no uncertain terms told her where I would put it should she continue to behave like a diva and treat me like Lassie! We both looked at each other and burst into hysterics. As I've said before, the little things have never been so big.

The boys continue to handle our situation in semi-ignorance, and I oblige them. There is no need for them to be upset if I can help it. With South Sydney's early exit from the NRL competition, Louis is planning a trip with his mates to the Americas and Canada, returning just before Christmas Day. I think the escape will do him good. Jackson continues to lose himself in work, though is now spending a little more time at the Dog House. I'm encouraged and happy he is seeking balance in his life.

While Oscar (or 'Little Buddy' as he is known to me) can legally consume alcohol and vote, he is still just that: my 'Little Buddy'. Kim and I both comment on how young he still is. We are happy we kept him that way. He will have many years ahead of him to carry the burdens that come with responsibility, maturity and adulthood.

Reuben the Wonder Dog will not leave Kim's side (and I mean literally). So, it is with great trepidation we await the arrival of the giant Lily in two weeks.

Wednesday 30 August 2017

Just a short update about the outcome with our new orthopaedic surgeon.

During our meeting, he reviewed the CT, x-ray and bone density scans that the good 'Dr Sobb' had organised that morning. After reviewing them, he explained that orthopaedic surgeons have a point-scoring matrix relating to the chances of a critical incident occurring such as fractures or breaks, with twelve being the highest. He explained to Kim that she scored around eleven. So, he said we had to act immediately.

As a result, Kim will go to the Prince of Wales for a total hip replacement this coming Monday. Unfortunately, our poor new orthopaedic surgeon had not yet acquainted himself with the persona of 'Dr Sobb'. With pre-organised questions on my tablet, I dived straight into them!

Further to being a total hip replacement on the right side, and owing to the erosion of the bone, the false socket will be cemented in to create further stability.

A regular hip replacement surgery has a duration of approximately one hour. This particular version will see Kim on the table for two hours. This is nothing compared to her last six-hour surgery just thirteen days ago! She should wake to little or no pain in the hip region—a completely new situation for Kim—as well as immediate mobility in this area. She will recover in hospital for six to seven days.

The only pain Kim will feel is when weight-bearing, like attempting to walk, for several weeks. It is suggested that she doesn't have to go to rehabilitation, though. So, Kim, welcome back to the Dog House with your worst nightmare trainer ... yours truly!

The bell tolls again and we are encouraged to have something within our grasp to fight for.

Our business is now north (without a walking stick!).

Playlist:
Tunnel of Love, Bruce Springsteen

September 2017—Only Give Up Tomorrow

Tuesday 5 September 2017
The week leading up to the hip operation, unfortunately, ended up being some of the darkest we have experienced.

The impact of the last surgery on C5 less than fourteen days ago, and the instability of this region, began to give Kim acute pain down her left shoulder and arm. The pain in her right hip also became far more acute, making walking nearly impossible even with the aid of a walking stick. At one stage, the depths were so dark, the pain so acute, the weeping so inconsolable, she cried to me, 'Ant, I just want to be with my father.'

Kim's father died suddenly when she was fifteen years of age.

What must a person be feeling to say something like this? How do you answer somebody who cries a question like this? At that moment, I thought, 'What are we doing here? Why are we here? What has Kim done to deserve this? This was not how we planned our life to be.' Situations like this happen to friends of friends. They're topics at a dinner table when people are having cathartic moments of gratitude. I didn't want us to be a dinner topic.

The millisecond moment passed as I began to give Kim a verbal audit on all we had to be grateful for. From things as simple as her wonderful dog Reuben, through to how fortunate we are to have the great medical support we do through Marc, our three great sons, the wonderful trips we have ahead of us, the upcoming surgery to relieve her hip pain, and finishing with the love we have for one another. Then, as we had done many times before, I metaphorically took her by the hand and gently led us out of the darkness.

Immediately, I decided to do whatever I could to empower ourselves and ensure Kim was in as little pain as possible by utilising pharmaceuticals, at least until she had recuperated from the upcoming hip replacement surgery. Yes, it was a short-term strategy—and possibly not ideal—but I simply couldn't have her going through a situation like this again. Not if I could help it, anyway.

So, in the week leading up to the surgery, our strategies included not only an increase in these potent drugs, but equally important, military-like timing and pragmatic preparation to ensure constant pain relief. Once I had worked out the dosages and the specific types (we had approximately five different varieties of pain-relief prescriptions to take), I mapped out a timetable.

After some initial trial and error, the schedule ran morning, noon and night, including setting my alarm for around 3.00 am which acted as a bridge through the night. 'Nurse 'Curly Joe' Sobb' was not a pretty sight during those 3.00 am calls!

However, increasingly noticeable was Kim's limp and her dramatic decline in mobility.

The morning of the pre-op was almost a rerun of the nineteen previous surgeries Kim has experienced. She dug in her heels, leaving everything to the last minute—a sign of her defiance and refusal to accept the disease's demands. You've got to love her tenacity and fighting spirit!

On the other hand, 'Rain Man Sobb' bumbled around at a million miles an hour, implementing plans from the night before and, much to the anger of Kim, got us to the hospital half an hour early at 9.30 am. Then came the waiting ... and more waiting!

Kim was 'nil by mouth' from 5.30 am, so I had rescheduled her pain-relief medication alarm for on the dot of 5.30 am. However, by around midday, Kim was in almost unbearable pain as the medication had completely worn off. 'Dr Sobb' reacquainted himself with his friends and foes—which he has all over the Prince of Wales Hospital—and eventually made them give Kim some pain relief. I even added some of my own that I had snuck in. Marc Coughlan, if you're reading this, please forgive me!

As I counted down the minutes with Kim until the pain relief kicked in, we again went through my iPad photos from the recent trip, our wonderful friends in Vegas, the miracle at Niagara Falls for our thirty-first wedding anniversary, and Kim's trip back to the homeland of Canada. Relief finally kicked in, and again we waited.

Finally, at around 1.30 pm, the wardsman came to give us the call-up, and we completed our usual ritual of a kiss, a pumped fist and a 'see you on the other side'. As usual, I stood there for the longest time while they wheeled her out the door.

I received the call at approximately 5.00 pm from our young Irish orthopaedic surgeon. He informed me that Kim's hip was already fractured when they opened her up. No wonder she was in so much pain and couldn't walk! This must have occurred in the last week without us even knowing it.

He said he found a good part of the pelvis and anchored and cemented the artificial hip with two giant screws. He was extremely happy with the outcome of the procedure.

'I know you guys like to leave the hospital early, but she is going to need to stay here for a little while,' he went on to say. Our reputation precedes us!

Kim woke feeling virtually no pain in the hip region, as promised. The only pain was down her left shoulder and arm due to instability with the nerve endings from the previous surgery. 'Dr Sobb' thought it best to take the Henry Kissinger approach rather than the Stalin approach to requesting self-administered, opiate-based pain relief.

The nurses, who now know us by name, responded quickly, and Kim was soon comfortable again. She has her own room, her Kindle and I've organised ample photos on her phone of Lily, the boys and our holidays for her to reminisce upon. At this point, she should be home by the weekend and walking out of the hospital without any assistance, as opposed to hobbling in with a walking stick.

The weekend holds a homecoming full of love from all her boys: Jackson, Louis, Oscar, Reuben (the Wonder Dog) and me. An added extra will be the arrival of Lily and that Kim will proudly, and unassisted, walk back in through the front door that she could barely walk out of a week ago.

Training camp will commence immediately at the Dog House where Louis and I have already drafted up a program and split the shifts. As dark as things got, we kept the promise to 'only give up tomorrow, never today'.

To give you a break from my self-indulgence of Springsteen, I leave you with one of Kim's favourite poems.

How Do I Love Thee?

How do I love thee? Let me count the ways.
I love thee to the depth and breadth and height
My soul can reach, when feeling out of sight
For the ends of being and ideal grace.
I love thee to the level of every day's
Most quiet need, by sun and candle-light.
I love thee freely, as men strive for right;
I love thee purely, as they turn from praise.
I love thee with a passion put to use
In my old griefs, and with my childhood's faith.
I love thee with a love I seemed to lose
With my lost saints. I love thee with the breath,
Smiles, tears, of all my life; and, if God choose,
I shall but love thee better after death.

Elizabeth Barrett Browning

Thursday 14 September 2017

After two long weeks post-surgery at the Prince of Wales, nicknamed now by Kim and I as 'Prisoner of War', Kim was transported by ambulance to the rehabilitation hospital, Waratah House at Hurstville.

The stories of grandparents, great uncles and other older patients who had received hip replacements with miraculous recoveries quickly subsided into brutal reality thanks to our orthopaedic surgeon.

'Guys, this was not a regular hip replacement. In fact, I was doing things to Kim's hip I've never had to do before. It was incredibly complicated and intrusive. It will take a long time to heal.'

Then, like all things in Kim's and my battle through this illness, it happened. And it came from the incredible amounts of pain relief and pharmaceuticals Kim had to take post-surgery: her digestive system shut down.

Following the intrusive nature of the surgery and some of the lymph nodes being severed, the body's natural swamplands also opened. Kim's leg filled with fluid and ballooned to nearly double its size. It was not quite the recovery we had expected. But, in true Champ style, she battled on.

Don't get me wrong. Often, I arrived at her hospital room to find her in bed crying to herself. But during those two weeks post-surgery, we brought her system back into balance, the pain under control, and went from bedridden to a walking frame, then walking frame to crutches.

With post-surgery behind us, we now start the next chapter of rehabilitation. Much to Louis' and my delight—and being unable to get our hands on her at the Dog House—Kim has an extremely busy rehab program commencing each morning and going well into the afternoon.

The physio claims it will be approximately six weeks until full recovery, '... but after those six weeks, you will be dancing.' Well, not with yours truly who has two left feet and is best known for the 'cigarette stomp'!

Using a fight analogy, it was a long, hard, grinding round and one in which our opponent was much stronger than we expected. However, the bell rang and we're still on our feet. Our aim is to climb from the stool and meet the next round bouncing on our toes, rather than limping.

Our love for one another has never been stronger and we will continue to 'give up tomorrow, just not today'.

'Fight one more round. When your feet are so tired that you have to shuffle back to the centre of the ring, fight one more round. When your arms are so tired that you can hardly lift your hands to come on guard, fight one more round. When your nose is bleeding and your eyes are black and you are so tired that you wish that your opponent would crack you one on the jaw and put you to sleep, fight one more round—remembering that the man who always fights one more round is never whipped.'

James
'Gentleman Jim' Corbett—
Former World Heavyweight Champion

SEPTEMBER 2017—ONLY GIVE UP TOMORROW

Thursday 21 September 2017
Here is Kim meeting Lily Girl for the first time during day leave from the rehab hospital.

Here are Reuben the Wonder Dog and Lily Girl (at ten weeks).

Four weeks ago, Kim hobbled into the Prince of Wales Hospital with a fractured hip. Tomorrow afternoon, she walks proudly out of the rehab hospital with the assistance of a cane. It just shows this incredible woman's courage.

Rehab included morning gym sessions and afternoon hydro-pool sessions. Kim, of course, was the spring chicken with her new pals. The physiotherapists found great amusement when Louis and I attended her hydro-pool sessions and demanded she 'lift her knees higher' and 'do one more lap'. Little does she know what fate awaits her at the Dog House!

The rehab hospital was such a welcome change from the Prince of Wales. With the newer amenities, better staff ratios and better food, Kim found a semblance of peace and balance. While still needing a regime of pharmaceuticals to control the pain in her hip, she is certainly better than before its replacement.

Managing the household in her nearly four-week absence brought its challenges. The early morning production of attempting to separate and feed two big dogs was just that ... a production! Housekeeping, laundry, feeding the boys, and then the daily evening dinner routine for the dogs was nothing short of a military blur. We got through, just, and can't wait for Kim to come home.

Next weekend brings the dreaded anniversary of October. It was October 2014 that Kim rang me with those words that forever changed our lives.

'Ant, it's not good news. I've been diagnosed with stage 4 lung cancer.'

In the initial days amid the confusion, we were told surgery was not an option though immediate chemotherapy and radiation could be organised. With a hushed, reverent voice, I was told to 'get Kim's affairs in order' and give her copious amounts of the opiate, Endone, and dissipate into the blissful abyss.

Then the bell rang!

We took our four cycles of the highly toxic cisplatin. I even pissed off our then oncologist and demanded two more cycles for no other reason than I knew Kim was strong enough to take it.

We had literally dozens of cycles of radiation, including two with the dreaded mask.

We found a like-minded surgeon in the great South African Dr Marc Coughlan.

We had a major preparation surgery that clamped one of her major arteries in her neck.

We removed the third vertebrae and replaced it with a prosthetic.

Kim then had a left lobectomy where her left lung was removed.

More radiation.

Various operations drilled and syringed cancer from her bones and replaced it with cement.

We were told by our then oncologist that Kim would not live to see Oscar's school graduation in September 2016.

We found a new oncologist.

A craniotomy removed a tumour growing into her brain from behind her left eye.

More radiation.

Various surgeries to resect tumours from her pelvis.

Not allowed any more radiation.

We commenced immunology treatment using Opdivo.

Removal of the sacrum bone and replacement with a prosthetic.

Further resections of the tumour growing on her C5 vertebrae.

Cracked pelvis, then the removal of her hip, replaced with a prosthetic.

Opdivo immunology didn't seem to be working, so I bullied the oncologist into trialling Keytruda immunology.

All that has brought us forward to now, October 2017, three years since being diagnosed stage 4.

However, it is remiss of me not to mention some of the important things that happened during those three years.

We laughed. We laughed a lot.

We wept an ocean of tears.

We held each other.

We led each other hand-in-hand out of the darkness of the 'black dog'.

Looking at each other was the last thing we did prior to every surgery.

The first thing we saw in every recovery was each other.

We supported one another.
We were parents.
We cheered from the sideline.
We sat across from each other on dinner dates.
We travelled the world.
We found a new appreciation for one another and our boys that we never knew existed.
Our faith was questioned.
Our faith grew.
The little things were never so big.
We dutifully attended surf life-saving carnivals.
We sometimes fought, but always made up.
We appreciated every day and pined for each other when we were separated.
At times, we felt blessed, yet at other times, cursed.
We held hands all the time, somehow, even when Kim was on crutches.
We spent hours together as a family training at the Dog House. Even when she could do very little, Kim always did something.
We lived life on our terms and kept our business north.

Our oncologist recently commented that only between one per cent to seven per cent of stage 4, non-small cell lung cancer patients contain the cancer only to the bones. It was surprising to the doctor that her learned colleague—'Dr Sobb' aka 'Nurse Curly Joe'—was already aware of this data. The oncologist was possibly not attuned to the great power of faith, hope and the sheer courage and tenacity of Kimberly Irene-Frances Sobb.

Thank you for your wonderful support. Despite Kim's great strength, we couldn't have got through this alone. I now tell Kim there is much to do.

Her loyal manservant and protector, Reuben the Wonder Dog, needs her.
Lily Girl needs her.
Her boys, Jackson, Louis and Oscar, need her.
And I certainly can't live without her.
There is a summer to be spent watching her hopeless husband and masculine son patrol with North Cronulla.
There is a trip to India to see the Taj Mahal and witness the great Ganges River.
Most of all, there's too much unfinished business of simply growing old together.
My business is now north.

October 2017—It Always Seems Impossible

Thursday 19 October 2017

The last few weeks have been a rollercoaster in all aspects: physical wellbeing, rehabilitation and emotional pain.

Rehab was a lot slower than we anticipated. However, as we made progress with her right prosthetic, Kim's left leg dramatically lost strength and became increasingly painful, until even walking with assistance became nearly impossible.

With this fresh pain increasing and the loss of strength, coupled with starting an un-trialled immunology treatment, I requested Marc write us a referral for a full-body CT scan.

The scans unveiled large tumours growing close to Kim's C4 vertebrae and around the sciatic nerve on the left side of her pelvis, which are causing the incredible pain and loss of strength in her leg.

Kim's immobility was one thing, albeit frustrating. However, the acute pain was debilitating, both physically and emotionally. I had one incredible 'barney' with our oncologist who subtly accused me of attempting to 'stockpile' and 'doctor shop' pharmaceutical pain relief.

'If you're accusing me of doctor shopping and stockpiling pain relief for Kim, then call it what you will. My question is, where is everybody at 3.00 am when I have to carry Kim from the bed to the bathroom crying with pain, or shower and dress her each morning crying in pain? Where are you all then? I'm a resourceful man. I will do whatever it takes to ensure Kim is never in any unnecessary pain. If that means being accused of doctor shopping and pain-relief stockpiling, then so be it,' I replied.

There was a long pause.

To our oncologist's credit, she gave me her mobile number, assured me we now had twenty-four-seven access to her and guaranteed me numerous contingencies of pain relief for Kim. Around the same time, she reviewed the scans I had requested through Marc and admitted Kim immediately to hospital where she is now receiving shots of morphine every two hours, along with further pharmaceutical pain relief every other hour.

From Kim's and my outlook and perspective on pain management, this certainly isn't ideal. However, it is necessary to ensure Kim is stable. A critical incident could paralyse Kim owing to the location of the tumours adjacent to her spine. Being pain-free in a stable environment is where we need to be right now until surgery next Thursday.

I met with Marc this morning at 6.45 am to review Kim's scans and set a plan for next Thursday's surgery. Whilst not experiencing any pain in or around C4, the tumour there is growing perilously close to the spine and eating into the fourth vertebrae.

'Ant, if we don't do something about this, it will collapse by December.'

As a result, Marc will take out the disintegrated C4 vertebrae, replace it with a further prosthetic and attempt to resect as much tumour in the area as possible.

The second critical part of the surgery will involve flipping Kim onto her stomach. This is always a dangerous move during surgery due to the risk of haemorrhaging. Then he will attempt to resect as much tumour as possible from her left sciatic nerve, hopefully giving strength back to the left leg and giving Kim instant pain relief.

'Ant, you guys give me the inspiration to want to fight as a surgeon.'

This surgery takes place next Thursday at the Prince of Wales.

Physically and emotionally, Kim has been through the absolute wringer. I honestly don't know where she gets the wherewithal. I can't help but think it comes from our deep love for one another and the need to be connected. She is spent. Our aim is for this surgery to create a new chapter, not dissimilar to three years ago when Marc operated on what was considered an inoperable tumour on C3.

I remind Kim of all we have done and experienced together in the three years that followed.

> Masses, graduations and wonderful Saturday afternoon games at Joey's.
> Saturday night dinners.
> Wonderful overseas travels.
> The boys.
> The dogs.
> The flotsam and jetsam of life.

These memories fuel and encourage Kim until next Thursday's surgery.

The boys are all doing well and are attempting, in their mother's absence and in their own strange ways, to help me maintain the household, although there are times when I wish they wouldn't! Lily Girl, our eight-week-old giant English Mastiff, has been an absolute breath of fresh air. She is the apple of the family's eye, along with Reuben the Wonder Dog. Kim absolutely adores her (thank God!).

The anticipation of some upcoming trips has also buoyed Kim. She has always wanted to visit India, and we are fortunate enough to have the wonderful world-renowned chef, Christine Mansfield, personally organise our itinerary and trip. Kim is thrilled. This is planned for early February.

I'd be lying if I didn't say the situation at the present time is anything but extremely difficult. But we have hope in the form of support from friends and family. Hope in the form of an incredible friend and surgeon in Marc Coughlan. Hope in the form of our deep love for one another and hope given to us by our faith.

Friday 27 October 2017

In the week leading up to the operation, we admitted Kim to Waratah Private Hospital in Hurstville. She had become almost totally immobile, losing the strength in both her legs, and needed round-the-clock morphine pain relief.

As much as it pained both of us to be separated, it simply had to be. As time passed, her acute pain became better managed. Her anxiety grew though, as the strength left in her legs diminished daily. In addition, she experienced increasing pain in her right groin, adjacent to her new prosthetic hip.

'Let's just put one foot in front of the other and manage it one day at a time,' I continued to say.

I reminded Kim that each day was a day closer to the surgery and that with surgery came new hope. 'Dr Sobb' negotiated, or as others would say, badgered, annoyed, pestered, cajoled, bribed, bullied and demanded Kim's patient transfer from Waratah Private Hospital and admittance to the Prince of Wales Hospital. Honestly, I'm sure it would have been bloody easier to transport the Pope from Rome to Sydney! As the great Nelson Mandela once said, 'It always seems impossible, until it's done.'

With that, Kim arrived at POW ('Prisoner of War'/the Prince of Wales) and we both began to mentally prepare for Thursday morning.

During my pre-surgery meeting with Marc, we agreed on entry through the neck and a prosthetic C4 or C5, pending what he saw when he got in there.

The plan was to cut out any further tumours and trim the tumour around the vertebral artery. After this, the team would flip Kim onto her stomach and enter her lower back to resect tumours on the left side of the pelvis and trim the tumour growing on her sciatic nerve.

Between this meeting and the surgery, I met with the orthopaedic surgeon who inserted Kim's prosthetic hip. We reviewed the x-rays, and I explained to him about Kim's increased pain in the right groin region. He explained that the hip was fine in relation to the prosthesis and the pain Kim was experiencing was because of new tumours.

We are now fighting the cancer on a new front.

Marc contacted me early Thursday morning, as he usually does. We went over the game plan one more time and I explained to him we also needed to look at Kim's right groin.

'No problem, Ant,' he said.

We finished the conversation with him asking me to pray that God guided his hand.

'I know the Big Man is in your corner. Don't lose your nerve. Go hard, brother,' I replied.

Kim received her four-hourly morphine injection early in the morning, so we experienced little of the normal pre-surgery pain and anxiety. Marc scheduled her as 'first cab off the rank', thus ensuring he was fresh and had no time constraints. I set up camp in my usual position, greeting and reacquainting myself with the few staffers who know me, and staring down the nemesis of staff I have annoyed over my years of being Kim's 'doctor', husband, security guard and partner in life.

The surgery took four hours. During that time, Marc and his team worked like trojan intellects. I know Kim and her body unconsciously worked like a champion fighter with them.

I watched *Into the Wild* for the fourth time and reminded myself that true happiness can only be experienced when it's shared. Situations like the one Kim and I find ourselves in force us to contemplate many of the subjects and situations we often ignored pre-cancer. I've come to believe that sometimes it's not about the answers. In fact, sometimes there simply is no answer. But that shouldn't stop us from asking the question and considering why. We ignore too much, are too ungrateful and appreciate too little.

'Ant, all went well. Meet me outside theatre now,' said the text from Marc.

The giant South African whose hand God had just guided was a real sight. Apart from that broad Afrikaans accent, he is a big man who walks with a swagger. He has a cheeky grin that would light up a room, but an awe about him that says tread carefully or risk waking the sleeping elephant.

'Hey, Doc Sobb,' he said, 'Everything went really well.'

He calls me that in jest, but I wear it as a badge of honour.

'If this was Nicole, I would do exactly the same thing, mate,' he has often said to me, referencing his own wife.

During our debrief, he explained he had put in a prosthetic C5.

Kim basically has a new and prosthetic neck. He cut out the tumours he found around the immediate region and trimmed the tumour on her artery. Attempting to resect this could have ruptured the artery, meaning Kim would have haemorrhaged to death on the table. Remember that we had to clamp and remove Kim's other vertebral artery when we put in the prosthetic C3 three years ago.

Marc also confirmed that he cleaned out numerous tumours and bone fragments around her pelvic region on both the left and right side, as well as trimming the tumour growing on Kim's left sciatica.

He went on to explain that he had never done work like this on any one individual patient, and he certainly wasn't aware of any others.

We hugged.

'I've got to get back into theatre, Ant. There's another patient waiting on the table for me,' he said as he skolled what remained of his piccolo coffee.

As he walked away at break-neck speed, I shouted out my request for preferred post-surgery pain relief for Kim.

'Don't worry, Doc Sobb. I've got it!' he screamed back.

What a man!

A few hours passed before they allowed me into the intensive care unit, and it was now late afternoon. When I got to Kim's bed, she had been crying to the nurses for some time, asking where I was.

Once I got there, she gripped my hand like a vice and immediately ripped into me.

'Where have you been?'

She then lectured me on a range of topics, in between consciousness and unconsciousness. Topics ranged from the movie *Into the Wild*—yes, go figure the coincidence—Lisa Wilkinson, Bruce Springsteen on Broadway, my recently shaved head and why Oscar had to repeat the subjects of accounting and statistics!

Then back for another round of, 'Where the hell have you been, Ant?'

Yes, Kim is a handful when coming off the anaesthetic post-surgery. As the hours unfolded, she became a little more lucid. With this came some anxiety and post-surgery realisation of what her body had gone through. She became emotional.

'Soon we will start our new chapter,' I explained as she held my hand.

The intensive care unit has a ratio of one patient to one nurse who sits posted at a desk at the foot of each patient's bed. Initially, the nurse politely asked me to move from time to time while she diligently carried out her duties on Kim. This moved to polite chatter about visiting hours, which were now long over. It then escalated to a blatant, 'It's time to go, sir.'

I begrudgingly took the hint and 'Dr Sobb' tottered off into the shadows of the 'Prisoner of War' car park and, from there, to home, where hungry boys, dogs and housekeeping matters awaited.

I will go back to 'Prisoner of War' where I expect Kim to move out of the ICU and into a regular room sometime today. I'll try to hustle her out of hospital on Sunday with the aid of my partner and doctor in crime, Marc Coughlan.

The past two weeks have been intense and for those close to me, both socially and in the workplace, your support and patience has overwhelmed me.

As you would expect, I am thinking about the future and planning.

My business is now north.

Playlist:

Our wedding video soundtrack: *The Power of Love*, Frankie Goes to Hollywood

November 2017—Only Half of Anything

Wednesday 1 November 2017

Last Friday, I headed directly to the intensive care unit to find Kim in severe pain with two acute pain relief systems entering her via cannula. One was morphine and the other was phencyclidine. Not long after my arrival, they moved Kim out of intensive care and into a private room.

Around this time, Kim became anxious and agitated. She complained to me about not lying straight and falling through the bed. I took little notice. However, fifteen minutes later, whilst I was out in the corridor topping up her iced water, I heard her screaming for help.

I rushed back into the room and saw Kim turned on her side, desperately gripping the rails of the bed, screaming for me not to let her fall. From Kim's perspective, she was precariously hanging onto the ledge of an incredibly high cliff.

She was having a psychotic episode.

The nurses rushed in, fully aware of what was happening. They madly stuffed pillows behind her back to give her the feeling of support and instructed me to explain to her that she was hallucinating. The way Kim gripped my hand and the absolute look of fear in her eyes told me she truly believed where she was. The nurses cut the cannula delivering the phencyclidine and slowly, after about twenty minutes, Kim became lucid. I contacted Marc directly afterwards.

'Ant, do you know what they call that stuff on the street? It's PCP. Angel Dust. No wonder she was tripping out.'

With that episode over, we now had to deal with Kim's burning pain in her legs. We found that if I massaged ice bags into the backs of her legs, it numbed the nerve endings and gave her relief. So, this is what we did for the next forty-eight hours.

By Monday morning, we had the pain managed, albeit through pharmaceuticals and icepacks. However, I could tell Kim was incredibly anxious. I contacted Marc.

'Mate, we've got to break out of here now,' I said.

By 1.30 pm, Kim and I drove out of the gates of the Prince of Wales Hospital, possibly prematurely, but we were heading home. Home to the boys, home to the dogs, home to where the food tastes better, where our bed was warmer and a place where Kim physically and mentally felt sheltered.

To get around the house, Kim has two mobile walkers, one for upstairs and one for downstairs. I also purchased a wheelchair for when we venture out of the house. Her mobility is extremely limited. However, at least her pain is managed and, more importantly, we are together and at home.

I take her out on her first venture tonight, albeit in a wheelchair. It breaks my heart to see her not only physically, but emotionally broken. I remind her she is a beautiful, intelligent and strong woman and that she should never refute the value she brings to our relationship and our family.

I've scheduled Saturday for a return to training at the Dog House where we start the rehabilitation and rebuilding program. I have great confidence not just in her physical attributes, but also in her courage and mental tenacity.

I also have much to gain. Without Kim, I'm only half of anything.

So, we are back at home, back in the fight. We've taken a few shots, lost a few rounds, but between the two of us, we have much left in the tank and much to fight for.

Wednesday 15 November 2017
We've just returned from a work trip I had in New York to gather information and resources from their art galleries. In hindsight, the timing of the trip, so close to her last major intrusive surgery, proved almost disastrous.

After the long-haul flight, Kim became completely wheelchair-bound. Whilst we had brought along a wheelchair and crutches, upon stepping off the plane, Kim lost all strength in her legs, rendering the crutches useless. We may have been close before this trip, but before we arrived back home this time, we went through some of the greatest hurdles we've ever encountered on this journey. With almost complete loss of her mobility, the acute pain also rose. Managing her medication became paramount.

We planned to be in New York for a week but we had to cut it short, though we had a couple of windows of great joy. We were fortunate enough to spend an afternoon at the world-famous Solomon R. Guggenheim Museum. It is an art gallery Kim had longed to see for many years.

While she was in awe of Monet's and Picasso's incredible art, I was madly taking photos of presentations, finishes, and lighting. I purposely medicated her so she was virtually pain-free for the duration of the gallery tour. As I wheeled her through the venue, she pointed out distinctive features, attempting to give the knucklehead pushing the wheelchair some cultural education.

I also took advantage of being in New York by taking Kim to see my beloved Bruce Springsteen in his latest intimate show, Springsteen on Broadway. We sat in the dark together, hand in hand, like we were the only two people in the theatre, listening to his stories of life, love and music. At one part of the show, he recited the Our Father prayer. Our hands squeezed a little tighter as we glanced at each other. Nothing more needed to be said. The whole mood changed in a New York minute.

In the taxi on the way home, I received a call from Jackson. From the tone of his voice, something was very wrong. He informed me that our latest, beautiful addition to the family, Lily, who had brought us so much joy, had collapsed and died. Kim immediately knew something wasn't right. I informed her an issue had arisen at work. I simply couldn't tell her. Wheelchair-bound and in so much pain, I couldn't do it to her.

In the ensuing twenty-four hours, Kim's pain became unbearable. Even the incredibly strong opiates weren't giving her any relief. Finally, after sitting her in a chair under a hot shower, I contacted my incredible partner-in-crime and PA, Julie.

'Jules, you've got to get us home now,' I said.

That was at approximately 11.00pm. We were on the 6.00 pm flight home the following day. It didn't help that throughout the flight Kim kept mentioning that she couldn't wait to see Lily and Reuben. I felt like such a traitor. Selfishly, I contemplated telling her but was thankfully sober to the fact that I only wanted to share my grief.

The moment we got home, I sat her down and told her. I'm sure you can guess the reaction. That wonderful little four-legged bundle of joy who gave Kim so much release had been taken away from us. I don't know what's worse ... watching someone you love slowly evaporate from your arms, or the crushing blow of instant loss.

The doctors can't chart where we should be right now in relation to Kim's mobility. The surgery she undertook is so radical and unique, there is little data to guide us. I tell Kim that if they don't know, then somewhere within that void of ignorance lies hope. We live in that hope. We embrace that hope.

We will train like we've never trained before in the Dog House and start our own rehabilitation program.

'I'll follow you wherever you want me to go, Ant,' she said like the champion that she is.

So, we arrived home yesterday morning, and by the afternoon I begrudgingly had her in her swimmers. In incredible pain, I carried her down to our pool where she began to walk laps with me in the cold but buoyant waters. Today, we start our first session back at the Dog House. I will commence it by telling her our next chapter starts today, right here in this gym.

'When we are no longer able to change a situation, we are challenged to change ourselves.

Between stimulus and response there is a space. In that space is our power to choose our response. In our response lies our growth and our freedom.

Everything can be taken from a man but one thing: the last of the human freedoms—to choose one's attitude in any given set of circumstances, to choose one's own way.

What is to give light must endure burning.

I grasped the meaning of the greatest secret that human poetry and human thought and belief have to impart: The salvation of man is through love and in love.

Those who have a 'why' to live, can bear with almost any 'how'.

Each man is questioned by life; and he can only answer to life by answering for his own life; to life he can only respond by being responsible.

Live as if you were living a second time, and as though you had acted wrongly the first time.

I recommend that the Statue of Liberty be supplemented by a Statue of Responsibility on the west coast.

Ever more people today have the means to live, but no meaning to live for.'

Viktor Frankl

Friday 17 November 2017

Due to Kim's increasingly acute pain, I organised an immediate CT scan of her pelvis.

The results showed Kim has now fractured her left hip.

No more weight-bearing.

Trip to Noosa beach cancelled.

Dog House training stopped.

Awaiting response from our orthopaedic surgeon regarding possible surgery.

Monday 20 November 2017

The legendary boxing referee, Judge Mills Lane, once said, 'There is no job undignified if it's done with dignity,' and this has been Kim's approach all along.

The transition into a wheelchair for someone with such grace was devastating for Kim, but she's done it with dignity. And, like the battle-hardened Champ that she is, she deems it just another tough round along with all the others we've had to fight during this journey. However, through all her courage and strength, Kim is incredibly fragile right now. She is constantly auditing her life.

Why did this happen?

How did this happen?

Why me?

Did I do something to deserve this?

All questions without answers, yet all questions anyone in this situation can't help but demand answers for.

It's this horrible, constant circle with no ending. Yet, through all of this, she continues to put one foot in front of the other and dons her happy, brave face while continually apologising.

Last night while dressing her, I lapsed momentarily and got frustrated about not being able to put her favourite shoes on before we went out.

'I'm sorry for all of this, Ant. It must be so hard for you,' she said in true Kim form.

Embarrassed, I apologised for my selfish attitude.

'Kim, losing you would be like losing the rain,' I replied.

Whilst emotionally anxious and fragile, she is also in incredible pain because of the fractured hip. She needs to take a lot of medication at very specific times to ensure the pain stays tolerable.

The fracture on Kim's non-prosthetic hip is extreme, right through the ilium. I received the news directly from the radiologist centre after I put Kim through a rigorous session at the Dog House. In hindsight, I could have killed her. It's a frightening thought, but I also can't ignore the sheer courage and determination of Kim to go through a session like that.

The daily ergonomics and basic human kinesiology, while not an issue for me to assist with, are causing Kim unbearable pain. The risk of a total break could prove fatal. As a result, I spoke to our oncologist yesterday who agreed the best place for Kim right now, while in this holding pattern until surgery, is hospital.

So, this afternoon, we will admit her to Waratah Private Hospital in Hurstville. This is her preferred hospital because of its facilities, proximity to home and, of course, for old 'gutso' (as I sometimes affectionately call her), the food is good. You'd be surprised how important small things like food become when you're in hospital for extended periods.

Just this morning, I received a text from Marc Coughlan who had been negotiating with our orthopaedic surgeon about the fractured hip.

'Ant, he doesn't want to take on the pelvic stuff. However, I believe I can help. Let's talk tonight,' the text read.

So again, our great mate, the swaggering South African, is prepared to ride shotgun on our next dangerous mission. We're teleconferencing late tonight. My hope is to confirm surgery at North Gosford Private Hospital which has the computers and technical hardware Marc needs to perform such highly complicated surgery. I then have to organise the 'Popemobile', aka patient transfer.

During all of this, Louis is trekking through Canada. Owing to our closeness and the situation with Kim, he rings or texts constantly. I tell him this is his 'into the wild' adventure, and not to be distracted emotionally. I reassure him we will all be here when he returns the week before Christmas. Even so, I miss his silent presence and company.

The beautifully frustrating Jackson tests my tolerance one minute and warms Kim's and my hearts the next. He has stepped up to the mark, particularly during this very tough recent period in our family's life.

The NRL World Cup has been a godsend as it's kept Oscar distracted and away from his mother's situation. Yet, he is always the first to jump up and help me carry Kim's wheelchair up and down the stairs.

Losing Lily was crushing to the family, particularly Reuben. He has become even more protective and clingy to Kim if that's possible. Just look at the photo!

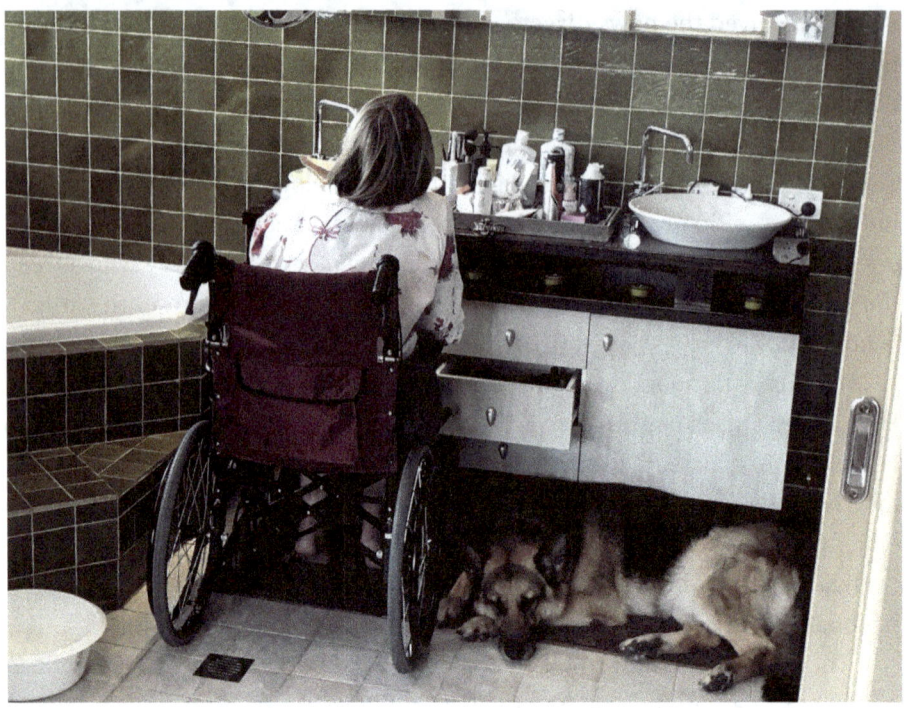

He must be on top of, or directly next to, Kim all the time. Somehow, dogs just know.

The good news is my legendary PA, Julie—'the bloodhound'—searched country-wide and found a litter of English Mastiff puppies. The two sisters and their mother can be seen in the following photo.

Our new Lily flies into Sydney this Sunday from Western Australia to join the ranks of the 'Sobb circus'.

We continue to put one foot in front of the other. Kim has the courage and I have the 'why'. I'm simply not ready to lose the rain!

Monday 27 November 2017

As we have become accustomed, things didn't pan out as we hoped.

Having numerous surgical procedures can drive the body into haemoglobin overload causing dangerous clots, so while Kim was in hospital last week, our oncologist gave her an ultrasound to check for blood clots. The results showed a foot-long clot in her leg just below her knee. Panic followed because Kim only has one fully working lung and if the clot moves to her chest, she could end up with a pulmonary shutdown.

They immediately injected Kim with a blood thinner, and she's been receiving two injections a day since then. We organised an emergency procedure to insert a filter into Kim's veins just below the lung to stop the clot from spreading further.

Clots this size take anywhere from six to eight weeks to clear. However, as we've learnt previously, medication treating one thing can hinder another. The blood-thinning agent used to reduce the clotting could cause serious haemorrhage issues for Kim's upcoming surgery.

Marc has agreed to perform the surgery on Kim tomorrow at North Gosford Private where he will utilise computer technology to insert a large screw diagonally through Kim's pelvis to create stability in the fracture.

Our plan is to have a couple of days' recovery in Gosford Hospital, then re-admit Kim to Waratah Private Hospital for intensive rehabilitation. We hope that Kim will regain the strength in her legs so she can lose the wheelchair. Again, time will tell as no-one is sure what the outcome will be. There is little to no precedent for patients who have journeyed down this path in these circumstances.

I keep Kim positive, reminding her that summer is here, and she will soon feel the warm white sands of Cronulla on the soles of her feet. She will soak and float in the cooling oceans of North Cronulla beach. In our alternate life, we loved, yet possibly took for granted, these simple pleasures. They have now become a major driving force to climb off the stool to fight one more round.

Kim is quite anxious, but again I remind her we have much to fight for.

My business is now north (to Gosford and onwards!).

December 2017—This Must Be the Place

Monday 4 December 2017

Last Tuesday's operation was scheduled for the afternoon. Marc purposely placed us last on the list to ensure he had no time constraints, then drilled an eight-inch screw vertically through Kim's fractured left hip region.

After eight-and-a-half hours in the waiting room, the lock-up nurse approached me as I sat alone and suggested I go home and have a good night's sleep. They had explained that I could see Kim in the morning, but not post-surgery. I begrudgingly shuffled out the door and headed to my Norman Bates-style accommodation, conveniently located close to the hospital. There, I sat alone and ate North Gosford's excuse for a pizza.

Early the next morning, I met with Marc to organise and fast-track our escape route back to Waratah Private Hospital in Sydney. By 10.00 am, we were on the freeway, Kim gingerly sitting on two large hospital pillows I had borrowed accidentally-on-purpose.

During this experience, absolutely nothing has come easy to Kim. Perhaps that's why I nicknamed her 'the Champ'. This chapter in our journey is no different.

It's now nearly a week since the operation. The initial intense pain has subsided (to a point), however, the wound will not heal. The blood thinners we are using to clear the one-foot clot in her leg are also stopping her blood from coagulating, which is affecting the healing process. So, for the last four days, she has been carrying around a machine which has a vessel to store the drained fluids of the open wound. We realise we need it, but it acts as a constant metaphor and reminder which we could certainly do without.

In usual Champ style, the physio has her up on the high walker doing laps of the ward, morning and afternoon. Of course, 'Dr Sobb' (or 'Nurse Curly Joe' should you wish) adds his extra two bob with further laps when I visit.

This week, we hope she progresses to the smaller walker, then to crutches by Friday. Hopefully, with the wound beginning to heal, she'll return home next weekend. Recently, Kim has had to spend an extensive and exhausting amount of time in hospital and away from home. Most people never have to experience such numerous, lengthy and extensive stays in hospital. As courageous as she is, many times I've arrived unannounced and found her weeping alone in bed.

After those visits, I often sit alone in the car and weep for her. We are currently having the house retrofitted to accommodate her—much to her disgust—though her pragmatic side realises it must be done.

The imbecilic three stooges, aka the Sobb boys, are quite excited about the construction of an electric chair to take her up the two flights of stairs to our bedroom. Reuben the Wonder Dog, in the meantime, pines for Kim. Each morning when we let him in, he heads straight to Kim's side of the bed in our bedroom where he is used to greeting her. He'll sniff there for a while, then plonk himself down, the great lump that he is. He lets out a huge sigh of breath and waits for her. It's the same routine every day.

Lily, our new pup, arrives from Perth tomorrow and the family is excited at the prospect of this new addition. She will only enhance the dynamics of our family.

Tuesday 12 December 2017

Last Saturday at around 10.30 am, I walked into Kim's room at Waratah Hospital to find her completely dressed, standing with her walker, bags packed beside her.

'Get me home, Ant,' were her first words.

'Champ, we'll be off like a robber's dog,' I obliged, and that's pretty much where the romantic scene ended!

An hour later, we were still there as dithering, officious staff demanded signatures on endless amounts of paperwork disclaiming us from their duty of care. Kim exclaimed that 'Doc Sobb' had taken more stitches out of her body than possibly any other doctor and nobody packs a pressure bandage like 'Nurse Curly Joe' (aka yours truly!).

We raced home like two young lovers stealing away into the night. For a moment, we felt liberated. It's hard to explain, but for that vacuum in time it was just Kim and I. No cancer, no doctors, no pain, no fear.

'Kim, we've made it. You're home,' I said, pulling into the driveway.

She burst into tears.

Moments later, Kim was met by her loyal guardian, Reuben the Wonder Dog, and we introduced her to our beautiful new addition, Lily.

Kim's arrival at home has been challenging, particularly with mobility, as we have a three-storey house. Pain management has also been difficult. Kim is still convalescing from three major surgeries in three months, and this doesn't include the numerous doses of radiation received from CT and MRI scans.

The following day, Sunday, brought us to our first session back at the Dog House. With it came much pain and a few tears, but she never stopped throughout the one hour of excruciating agony. Two weeks since the surgery, her wound is still open and weeping. I diligently redress the pressure bandages daily and even had to take one of the remaining stitches out myself as instructed by my learned colleague Dr Marc Coughlan!

DECEMBER 2017—THIS MUST BE THE PLACE

We've had great support from friends such as Kim's hairdresser who comes in once a week to gently attend to Kim's hair. We also have our family physio, who over the years has treated surf life-saving, boxing and various other gym injuries of all the Sobb family. He visits Kim at home twice a week, giving her incredible relief as she begins to recondition her muscles and joints.

Here at home, I also have better control over her high-protein and high-antioxidant diet, as well as the religious preparation three times a day of her Chinese herbs. If I can get her wound to coagulate, we'll take advantage of the summer months and commence pool rehab exercises at home.

Our short-term strategy is for Kim to stand by me on patrol, just like she did in the old days. Our midterm goal is travelling through India in February, at worst on crutches. Again, the little things have never been so big.

As a family, we can't wait to be together again for Christmas. It has always been an extremely special time in our family's lives. We have a long tradition of sitting together on Christmas Eve while Kim has a glass of champagne and I prepare my very secret recipe of spicy Oysters Kilpatrick. Nothing could be so simple, yet nothing more complete.

The Sobb Christmas lights, on the other hand, are legendary amongst family and friends for our strategy of 'more is better'. They represent peace on Earth, goodwill to all men and the birth of a new King.

So, our aim is to have Kim home by next weekend, met by her four boys, loyal Wonder Dog, little Lily and a house full of Christmas spirit.

Louis returns from his adventure 'into the wild' on 21 December. We talk every morning and I remind him not to waste a moment because there are no replays in life. I tell him our time alongside one another at the Dog House resumes on his return.

Oscar, meanwhile, is beginning to respect the essence of time.

'Dad, I can't believe it was a year ago since I finished at Joey's.'

Jackson remains the wonderful, smiling, larger than life, apple of his mother's eye.

Things are far from perfect, yet we all feel such incredible gratitude for what we have, who we have and our love for each other.

'Feed the people. Stay alive. Merry Christmas!' as Bruce Watson from Big Country said during Band Aid.

Thursday 14 December 2017

The situation is relentless, as too is Kim's courage.

In hospital, staff tend to focus on one singular matter, which on our last stay was Kim's wound and rehabilitation. The whole picture can sometimes get lost. On Sunday, the day after I brought Kim home, I noticed her neckline looked completely out of proportion. Her C5 vertebra was clearly outlined beneath her skin. Around the same time, Kim complained of neck pain, along with severe and acute headaches when she woke each morning.

By 11.00 am on Monday morning, I'd asked Marc to text me a referral and contacted a senior member of the imaging centre for a complete CT scan on Kim's neck.

On Tuesday afternoon, Marc called me, explaining that Kim's C5 vertebrae had collapsed, and she needed to be in a Miami J neck brace immediately. Any form of neck hyperextension would be catastrophic.

'Ant, I need to operate on her now,' he went on to explain.

Catastrophic!

'We've just lived the last three years of our lives catastrophically,' I thought to myself. I organised the neck brace immediately and we head back up to North Gosford Private Hospital for emergency surgery early next week.

Kim became teary as I explained the latest catastrophe to her.

'Ant, if you say we need to do it, then let's just do it,' she replied with unbelievable composure.

For someone to have such incredible faith in me is unbelievably humbling. I can wear it as a badge of honour, but there are times, too, when it is the hardest burden to bear. I write these updates for many reasons. Some are obvious and others are not. However, one thing borne from them is that I want to make a testimony, a statement and something to evidence the incredible courage and selflessness of Kim.

She apologises for putting me through this and is always so grateful for what I do. Simply put, mine is the absolute easiest job as it's borne from love. Her courage and fight are borne from complete selflessness. Everything she does is not for herself or her own self-preservation, but for me and the boys.

In the meantime, I keep her neck stable and attempt to maintain our usual 'dailies', or what remains of our somewhat normal life. I explain to her that this operation is our ticket to standing on the beach of North Cronulla together again and feeling the waters of the great Ganges River in February.

Friday 22 December 2017

I wasn't quite transparent in the last update about Kim in relation to this twenty-fourth surgical procedure. I see my role as Kim's partner and trainer to not only prepare her but also protect her. I played down the length and complication of this surgery.

I knew Kim's fasting period would be lengthy. Anyone who knows Kim knows she turns into the Hulk if not fed at least three square meals a day. So, after dinner the night before, I ensured I pumped her with large portions of my specially prepared protein and antioxidant drink, along with about a dozen Anzac biscuits to keep her sugar levels up.

We drove up to Gosford on the Wednesday morning, fighting the ridiculous Christmas Sydney traffic, but calmed by the voice of Bruce Springsteen as we listened to his audio from the book, *Born to Run*. I may have never read a book in my life, but I've listened to this one a dozen times!

We arrived in Gosford at around 11.30 am. Surprisingly, they admitted her immediately into surgery, where the anaesthetist passed comment to Kim and I that it was only a short operation.

Separately from Kim, and not knowing my modus operandi, he then went into a complete blurb about the complexities and lengthy duration of the procedure. He told me I could see Kim later that night in the ICU unit at around 7.00 pm.

The impending seven-hour wait felt more like seven days. Marc texted me during his breaks with one-sentence updates. I wandered the hospital, becoming acquainted with every square metre of the property and those who inhabited it.

Finally, knowing Marc had completed the surgery at around 6.00 pm after booking the entire afternoon surgical theatre just for Kim, I broke into the ICU unit. During my seven-hour wait, I had purposely stood by the door to learn the security code access.

Once in, I was fortunate to bump into Marc's assistant surgeon who gave me a complete post-op update. He explained they had resected large amounts of tumour around the C5 and manipulated it back into the spine using four screws and a plate.

'Mate, your wife is a living legend amongst the orthopaedic community. She is just incredible,' he commented.

Without exception, whenever Kim and I reunite after any of the surgeries, she becomes emotional. After the initial long embrace and emotional outpouring, she pushed me away.

'Why did they say it was only going to be a short, simple surgery?' she asked me to explain.

There was a long dark pause, a vacuum between us, then a collective burst into laughter because we both knew why. Considering it all, Kim was in great shape physically and emotionally, though that would change as the anaesthetic wore off.

I kept her buoyant by speaking of the sea and North Cronulla, the Dog House, the flavours of India and the Ganges River. By 9.00 pm, the ICU nurses hinted that I best leave Kim to sleep.

I made my way back to the 'Bates Motel' where I ate a takeaway red curry with my fingers. Yep, the Bates Motel doesn't have any cutlery! I didn't care. I was exhausted, but Kim had made it through the surgery. She was in good spirits, and I had plenty to be grateful for. My Kim was still on her feet when the bell rang for this round.

The following day, Marc teed up all the staff to bypass most of their protocols to ensure we got home as soon as possible. I had scripts for all the medication I asked for and they gave me access to whatever and as much as I wanted in relation to wound dressings. 'Ol' Doc Sobb' and 'Nurse Curly Joe' were like children in a candy store!

We loaded up the car, I surrounded Kim with cushions, and we stole away through the Gosford roads to *This Must Be the Place* (one of Kim's favourite Talking Heads songs), aka home.

Kim was still in quite some pain and remains so today. It will take time until the wounds heal and the swelling subsides, but we will make it to the next chapter.

She will feel the sand between her toes and float in the soothing sea waters out the back of North Cronulla with her personal lifesaver. She will taste the flavours of India, see the beauty of the Taj Mahal and witness the great Ganges, not in a wheelchair, but standing and bearing her own weight, without a neck brace.

Saturday 30 December 2017

Today we kept the promise to feel the sand of North Cronulla under her feet and dip in its cool, refreshing water.

The Champ is also a handy surf lifesaver's assistant.

We now head towards India.
Our business is now north.

Playlist:
This Must Be the Place, Talking Heads

January 2018—Her Courage to Get Busy Living

Tuesday 30 January 2018

Marc and I met early this morning before his suites opened to patients. This allowed us the privacy and the time to discuss and review Kim's scans. He meticulously laid them out, asking me questions about Kim's symptoms and general health. He explained options and strategies to me and graciously humoured me by seeking my opinion. He also spoke again of Kim's courage and resilience and how she alone has completely changed his views on strategies when treating patients.

'Ant, Kim has taught me so much. I feel an incredible debt of gratitude to her. She is an amazing woman.'

I could only nod in agreement.

We also spoke at length of the dogma in the medical profession, particularly the mindset around diseases such as cancer. While similar-minded people attract their own cohorts, the danger is always the insular mindset one can develop if you don't take the time to consider 'but what if'.

I told him the story of the great Muhammad Ali saying to the press, 'A man who views the world the same at fifty as he did at twenty has wasted thirty years of his life.'

Marc expanded that wonderfully wiry grin.

'You're so fucking right, Ant. These guys [in the medical profession] just don't see it,' he said in his most Afrikaans accent.

The outcome is that we head up to Gosford Private Hospital early next week for our twenty-fifth surgery where Marc will resect a tumour on Kim's L5 to reduce the sciatic pain in her left leg.

We also noticed some regrowth in her left orbit where we had our craniotomy, so during the same procedure, if possible, we will cut out the regrowth of the tumour there. Marc was excited about Kim recommencing her hydrotherapy and believes it will greatly aid in strengthening her right leg.

JANUARY 2018—HER COURAGE TO GET BUSY LIVING

She is looking forward to joining me in Melbourne this week for a few days while I attend some meetings at the casino. I fuel her courage to get busy living by bringing forward and mapping out my upcoming work trips.

My business is now north.

Ellis Boyd 'Red' Redding: 'Hope is a dangerous thing. Hope can drive a man insane.'

Andy Dufresne: 'Hope is a good thing. Maybe even the best of things, and no good thing ever dies.'

—*The Shawshank Redemption*

February 2018—Oven Mitts

Monday 2 February 2018

Kim's craniotomy and the resection of a tumour from her L5 have been rescheduled for Tuesday 13 February. Her mobility is decreasing, and her left eye is showing signs of the tumour's growth. However, that didn't stop the Champ from joining me down in Melbourne, looking as beautiful as ever.

I'm confident next week's outcome will give much-needed pain relief from her sciatica, as her knuckles have become blistered from attempting to support her bodyweight when sitting.

I also have a teleconference this afternoon with our radiation oncologist, where I'll try pushing for some further radiation post-surgery to both regions. It means the dreaded mask again if we proceed—this will be her third. However, I know our love for one another will give us both the wherewithal.

So, Tuesday we fight.

Tuesday 20 February 2018

Marc placed us third on the list behind two fairly simple procedures, leaving the rest of his theatre time for Kim. So, with a 7.30 am check-in, we strategically planned to leave for Gosford late on Monday night, giving us the least amount of time in the terribly depressing and dilapidated 'Bates Motel' in Gosford.

After a restless night, I had Kim up at 5.30 am. As instructed by our anaesthetist, I went about force-feeding Kim half a litre of Gatorade and placing oven mitts on her hands. Due to the hundreds of cannulas Kim has had painstakingly inserted, plus the copious amounts of chemicals and treatment, finding suitable veins to administer the anaesthetic has become nearly impossible. The Gatorade and mitts did the trick, despite Kim telling me she hated Gatorade and looked ridiculous arriving at the hospital wearing oven mitts—you've got to laugh! (The Gatorade hydrates the body, and the oven mitts warm the body, swelling the veins for easier cannula access).

Once we arrived, they took Kim into pre-theatre almost immediately.

We went through the usual ritual of our farewells; kiss on the cheek, a long-paused hug and me telling her I'll see her on the other side.

I did my usual walk, following the wardsman and her bed right to the door, waiting until I saw the very last of her bed enter a place I could not follow her.

The surgery was three operations in one. The first was a craniotomy to remove the regrowth of a former tumour from inside her left eye socket which had the potential to grow into her brain. They then flipped Kim over, removing large multiple tumours growing on her left seventh rib. From there, they made another surgical incision to remove numerous tumours around her pelvis, particularly one located on her L5 which was causing acute sciatic pain.

Normally, Marc only attempts one of these at a time. However, Marc knows our situation, and more importantly, he has an intimate knowledge of the Champ's heroism and ability to fight.

Once I saw the last of Kim's bed disappear, I had to wait.

During those four hours, I had a lot of time to ponder. The Yin and the Yang. The wish, the curse. The good, the bad. The big, the small. I pondered the river of tears this disease and situation has caused our family. And yet, during our pre-cancer life, when Kim and I thought we understood the love and appreciation of one another, we really didn't. It wasn't until after the diagnosis and this journey did our love and appreciation for one another truly come to light and show its blessed face. Maybe without this disease, we would never have transcended to this point. I guess we will never know. We just have to appreciate that this was a wish or a gift that came with the curse.

Kim woke from the surgery and spent three uncomfortable—yet much needed—nights up at Gosford. I made the long, five-hour return car trips from home and work to the hospital.

By Friday lunchtime, I had the Champ home, still quite sore. Emotionally, she needed to drink from the cup that only our home, the boys, our bed, the dogs and my food can give her.

Creating events is not only an important part of taking Kim's mind off things—they also remind her that this disease will never take everything from us. So, Saturday night for many years has always been our dinner date night. I was determined that this Saturday night, the night after she left hospital from a major surgery, was going to be no different.

I possibly haven't yet articulated to you another of my newly acquired skills, besides doctoring and nursing—female wardrobe assistance. I can tell you the importance of a camisole when wearing a fine dress, the importance of not wearing a black bra under a sheer top, the difference between a halter neck dress and one that sits just off the shoulders, and, of course, one never wears a plunging back dress without a strapless bra. In fact, I would go so far as to say that if the whole CEO thing goes pear-shaped, I could hold down my own as a wardrobe assistant to any female diva. Though, in the early days, it did come at the cost of numerous pieces of clothing being hurled back at me with Kim muttering the simple word, 'No!'

So, on Saturday night, Kim rattled off what she wanted to wear. I, like a loyal Collie dog, rustled into her wardrobe to fetch and retrieve the requested outfit and accessories for our night. The following photo shows the result: a beautiful woman sharing a date night with her husband on a Saturday night, sipping on a glass of rosé champagne.

FEBRUARY 2018—OVEN MITTS

At home, Kim still needs a walker to move about the house and a wheelchair should we venture out. The eye and rib wounds are healing well. However, the lower back wound still requires me to redress it twice a day. The blood-thinning injections I give her nightly owing to her large blood clot still hinder the coagulation and healing of this wound.

In the upcoming weeks, we recommence ten cycles of radiation into the eye and rib area, though we can no longer receive any further treatment to the pelvis. We are seeking further opinions through an oncologist at the Chris O'Brien Lifehouse, a specialist cancer hospital, about the possibility of further chemotherapy.

Kim is still on massive amounts of pain-killing opiates. While this is not ideal, it has become a fact of life in managing her pain. Each day, Kim becomes a little stronger from the surgery. Where this leads to or ends up, no one really knows. All we do know is we refuse to capitulate.

My business is now north.

Playlist:
Badlands, Bruce Springsteen
I Wish I Were Blind, Bruce Springsteen

March 2018—The Delicate Art of Lymphatic Massage

Tuesday 20 March 2018
Let's start with Lily at only five months old (!) watching TV with Kim and Louis. We continue our tradition of having dinner together every Sunday.

It has been one month to the day since Kim had her twenty-fifth major surgery. The wounds for the craniotomy above her left eye and the seventh rib in the centre of her back have nearly healed. However, the wound on her lower back from the tumour resection of the pelvis continues to bleed steadily. It still needs to be changed at least three times a day using surgical-grade bandages. Kim's body is unable to heal her wounds due to her body's immune system being virtually non-existent. The copious amounts of radiation and chemotherapy have brought this on. After being Kim's post-op nurse for twenty-five surgeries, I've become efficient with dressings, in particular, compression bandages. However, three months is too long under any circumstances, and it has also halted the prospect of radiation treatment to these areas. So, I began my education into how I can best control and accelerate Kim's healing. I realised I needed to dramatically increase Kim's protein levels, hydration intake and BMI (body mass index). Kim's BMI is currently nineteen, which is extremely low.

Kim is also dealing with the damage to her lymph nodes from the various surgeries. Substantial amounts of lymphatic fluid have moved into her feet, causing massive swelling. Another educational session resulted in the purchase of compression stockings and learning the delicate art of lymphatic massage, which aids in draining the fluid. Kim and I work as a team three times a day with Kim doing the upper body massage, and 'Nurse Curly Joe' (yours truly) doing her legs.

Recently, we changed to a new oncologist located at the Chris O'Brien Lifehouse. This hospital is dedicated to treating cancer patients and we are both impressed with the facility and the attitude of the staff. It's so apparent that they 'get' what the patients and carers are going through. Kim finds it confronting, as many very ill patients are there. As you would understand, she still struggles with thoughts of 'I shouldn't be here' and 'What am I doing here?'. I simply sit in the waiting rooms and scrutinise everybody, trying to piece together their story, usually finishing with a prayer to wish them well and give them strength.

The professor's first strategy was to organise for a sample of Kim's tumour to be sent over to America for mutation testing. The results will give us options for different chemotherapies to help treat and slow down the disease. Apart from Marc's surgery, Kim has received no treatment for the cancer since September last year. The oncologist also commented that he couldn't believe a patient diagnosed with this type of cancer for this period had not had it spread to any organs. I can't help thinking that maybe our options of radical surgery with Marc, embracing Chinese herbal medicine and the hours and hours of training at the Dog House might have something to do with it.

I'm hoping within the next three weeks Kim's wounds have healed enough for her to receive her final treatments of radiation. Unfortunately, this also includes the dreaded mask, but the Champ has been in that dark place before and I know together we can get through it again.

Kim and I usually start our days at around 4.00 am each morning with the first regime of pain opiates followed by a complete dressing change. A listless lie down for a few hours follows, then I get Kim up again and dressed. Next, I take her downstairs to Lily, Reuben the Wonder Dog, ABC News and a hot nutritious breakfast. Regimes like this are so important and give her stability given that every day is a challenge.

I return home from work in the afternoon as we now know that is when the 'black dog' lurks at the entrance to Kim's door. I quickly re-dress her and it's off to the Dog House for a session that Louis and I have put together, usually to the background of Bruce Springsteen music. From the Dog House, it's home for an early dinner, evening pain medication and some TV with the boys, Reuben and Lily. Then it all starts again the following morning at 4.00

am. It's not ideal, but it works. It's amazing what people can cope with when the need arises.

From a mobility perspective, Kim still cannot walk unassisted. Around the house, she uses a walking frame. Whenever we venture outside, we utilise the wheelchair.

As expected, Kim is emotional and fragile at times. The longevity of this illness, the surgeries and the treatments have all taken their toll. Yet every morning, she gets up with me. Every day, she goes to the gym with me. And when it's time to receive her treatment, she turns up with me.

Don't get me wrong, we have some absolute 'clangers' along the way. She rightly tells me I don't understand what it's like, and that she is sick and tired of my perpetual glass-half-full speeches. She also points out that living with a manic ADHD control freak is exhausting at times. All these points (once I have calmed down from my own anger) are completely valid.

To keep Kim emotionally strong, I'll make an event out of anything. Something as simple as preparing a special meal at night or bringing her favourite ice-cream home—salted caramel no less—always brings a smile to her beautiful face.

What makes it all bearable is that we have each other. Without each other, we are nothing. Incomplete. A puzzle without a piece. Somehow, being together gives us the purpose and strength to withstand the burden that is hardest to bear. Kim and I ensure we tell each other this every day.

Meanwhile, for Oscar, the world has begun to turn again as the NRL season commences. Now with a steady girlfriend, he is learning the demands of those who should be obeyed! He is still relatively naïve—or perhaps chooses to be—in relation to Kim. At times, this can be a little frustrating.

'Wow, Mum, the house looks really messy since you've been sick!'

Or …

'Mum, can you take my washing out of the washing machine?'

I think his cluelessness, whilst frustrating, is a sign that Kim and I have successfully sheltered him from the reality of our situation.

Louis is his quiet, reserved self. We talk to each other daily on the phone and both keep one eye on Kim whilst at the Dog House training together. He still has his moments, though. Whilst walking into the tunnel after South Sydney's recent loss to Penrith, an aggressive Penrith fan hurled abuse at Louis, casting aspersions upon his handsome good looks. Just as Louis was about to dish out a little of his own old-school retaliation, a hand reached over from behind, grabbed him on the shoulder and with a matter-of-fact, fatherly-like tone said, 'Don't you even think about it, Louie.' It was the infamous South Sydney Football Manager, Shane Richardson.

Number one son, Jackson, is very special to Kim. However, he can sometimes try even Kim's patience, such as losing his driver's license several times.

'Who needs to wear a seat belt?'

'Why shouldn't I be able to drive and use my phone at the same time?'

'I was running late for work.'

'That old bag in front of me didn't use her blinker.'

... You get the drift!

Combine this with him wanting to constantly drive Kim in her wheelchair when we go out for our Sunday dinners, and you have a recipe for disaster. Despite this, his sentiment and heart are true.

My business is now north.

> *'Unable to perceive the shape of you,*
> *I find you all around me.*
> *Your presence fills my eyes with your love.*
> *It humbles my heart.*
> *For you are everywhere.'*
>
> — Likely by Hakim Sanai,
> translated and quoted in the film, *The Shape of Water.*

May 2018—We Had Our Rituals

Friday 4 May 2018

My apologies for the delay in Kim's latest update. Things have been quite hectic, particularly in relation to Kim's treatment.

Yesterday marked the tenth and last fraction of our most recent radiation which included the dreaded mask. Her left eye socket and left seventh rib, along with the pelvic region, are now completely maxed out for radiation, so it's bittersweet. Each morning, Kim bravely wheeled into the radiation treatment area where the staff gently lay her on the table and delicately locked the mask onto her head. It never got any easier. Yet, Kim stoically confronted it each day, never complaining, simply getting on with the job.

We had our rituals, and the staff were extremely respectful and patient with us. I'd lay my hand on her chest and talk her through some breathing exercises. For a few moments, we visualised the wonderful waters of our villa in Bali, taking her mind back to where she could smell the ocean, see the views and remember the way the water felt on her body. I'd then quickly dash out as the doors were closing and treatment would begin.

Apart from the side effects of radiation, Kim continues to experience longer-term issues such as the wound from her operation six months ago refusing to heal. I continue to change her surgical-grade bandages three times a day, however, it is frustrating for Kim as at times the less than perfect 'Nurse Curly Joe's' dressings have leaked, causing blood to spill and stain clothing. After lengthy discussions, Marc Coughlan suggested we look at hyperbaric treatment to get oxygen to the wound to assist in its healing.

Initially, the treatment centre was reluctant to review Kim's case as they usually only deal with high-performance athletes. However, 'Dr Sobb' can be convincing and after several phone calls and emails, I've organised a consultation for next Tuesday with the possibility of treatment on Tuesday afternoon. I think the office manager of the centre got sick of me and

MAY 2018 — WE HAD OUR RITUALS

capitulated! Treatment involves Kim sitting in a sealed chamber the size of a home theatre, in a lounge chair where she can read while the room is pressurised with oxygen. There are little to no side effects, apart from Kim's body being imbued with oxygen. Marc and I aren't sure if it's going to work, but the Champ, in true form, is up for giving it a go.

I can tell she is fatigued, verging on exhausted, yet she still fronts up day in and day out.

'What's next, Ant? Are we training this afternoon, Ant?'

I simply don't know how she does it. It is her that gives me strength.

During a recent trip to Bali, Kim had this unbelievable surge of wellbeing. The weather, the beauty of the island and the spirituality of the Hindu people created this metaphorical elixir.

'Ant, I just feel so good here,' were some incredible words I'd not heard in a long time.

MY BUSINESS IS NOW NORTH

We had an incident during the trip where I became frustrated with the resort management because I had specifically booked a certain villa for Kim and I. As I became more frustrated and impatient, the Anthony I'm embarrassed about—and attempt to hide—began to surface. During this, Kim reached out, held my hand and said she understood why I had wanted that particular villa. She knew it would take us back to the times before she was diagnosed with cancer.

'It's OK, Ant. I know why you're doing it, but it doesn't matter. We're here together and that's all that counts.'

With that, the storm subsided and the Anthony I despise retreated. Yet again, the patient became the carer, the follower became the leader.

Other than that, the trip to Bali was incredible. I went about my work, meeting with executive chefs and food and beverage managers. From time to time, this included being told 'this is a staff only area, sir' and getting escorted out of kitchens. Kim sat in the villa, patiently reading books in the sun and receiving herbal treatments from the wonderfully gentle women of Bali. She was physically, emotionally and spiritually uplifted.

Since getting back, and still unable to walk without the aid of a walker, she attends the Dog House with me and does a special exercise regime Louis and I have developed for her. The three of us lock the door of the Dog House, turn up the music, and go about our workouts, leaving the world outside. It's a sacred time and place for the three of us.

Sunday week, we head off to the U.S. for my annual trip to Vegas. First, we'll spend four days in Mexico City. Kim is so excited, being the adventurer she is. I've organised a private tour guide each day and Kim has a list the length of her arm of sites she has investigated. It warms my heart to see her so excited.

This will also be special as I've organised for the boys to meet us in Vegas. When they were much younger, we all used to go on these trips, so it's somewhat of a family holiday reunion. The boys are equally excited about us all being together again in the city where we now have many close friends. I will set Kim up in the morning in a shady spot by the pool complete with Kindle and sunglasses with the boys on 'Kim duty' as I go about my meetings.

Despite our family's closeness, as the boys grow older, they are leading independent lives. This trip is a wonderful excuse and conduit for them to revert to the way things used to be, when life was much less complicated and they were more innocent. I draw a wry grin, anticipating having to referee some of the fights and arguments that will come forth when Louis and Oscar share a room, just as they did all those years ago.

Travelling and seeing new places is not only a wonderful distraction for Kim but also reminds her of a reason to believe. A reminder that our life has still so much more to offer us. A reminder of what the doctors said we couldn't do and are now, nearly four years later, still doing. A reminder that we can be in control of our destiny should we decide not to surrender and capitulate.

Even at home, Kim and I still keep our dinner dates each weekend. Even though she attends them in her wheelchair, she begins the night as she did before the diagnosis and treatment—with a glass of champagne. The evenings may be shorter and her appetite not as big, but this is unimportant. What is important is the ritual we continue together.

We are having a full-body CT scan next Thursday and this will determine how we proceed.

My business is now north.

Playlist:
I'll Work for Your Love, Bruce Springsteen

Monday 21 May 2018

While in Mexico City Airport, heading to the departure gates and on route to meet up with the boys, Kim collapsed into unconsciousness. I worked on her as best I could on the floor of the terminal, but she died in my arms. I'm sorry. I couldn't save her.

I have no more business.

Ant

May 2018—The Journey Has Ended

Thursday 24 May 2018

I feel a sense of commitment to finish these updates the way I started them.

Perhaps I simply need some form of closure.

Maybe it's a little of both.

The first two days in LA were good, although a little difficult with Kim being wheelchair-bound. She loved to travel. She loved the flotsam and jetsam that go with it. The packing, the anticipation, the excitement—it all made her feel alive.

We checked out a couple of 'hip' LA eateries and I pushed her around the shopfronts of Rodeo Drive. From there, we flew to Mexico City, and that's where our trouble began.

Almost immediately on landing, Kim experienced breathing difficulties. On our first morning, I woke around 4.00 am to frightening gurgling sounds from her. I turned on the light and found her frothing at the mouth and semi-conscious. I attempted to bring her back to lucidity and FaceTimed my legendary friend, Dr Marc Coughlan, who did a consultation via phone on the spot.

After much discussion, we worked out the high altitude, combined with Kim operating on only one lung, was having a huge, negative effect on her respiratory system. I contacted the concierge to request an Oxy-Viva oxygen kit, but, of course, they didn't have one. Instead, I organised for half a dozen oxygen cylinders from an emergency medical centre to be delivered to our room. Hooking her up to oxygen made a major difference, so much so the absolute champion she is wanted to keep going.

We visited all the major sites and ruins over the next four days. It was difficult, in fact, more than difficult, to push Kim in her wheelchair while carrying around a portable oxygen tank, yet she never complained once. The art galleries and historical ruins were sustenance enough to make what would be impossible for others, possible for her.

But, by our fifth and final day, we'd both had enough. What kept us going was the anticipation of meeting the boys in Vegas and the change in altitude bringing respiratory relief. The night before we left, I purchased a gas compressor so we could travel on the plane where gas cylinders are not allowed.

That night, I also bribed a doctor to write a referral, sight unseen, for Kim. I gave him her diagnosis, practically dictating the referral whilst standing in the hotel lobby as Kim slept upstairs. I had no idea how important this document would become in the ensuing twenty-four hours.

Come morning, we got ready to leave, but as we transferred to the portable oxygen compressor, Kim began to go downhill. On the way to the airport, I constantly had to wake her up and remind her they wouldn't let us travel unless she was lucid.

'Don't worry, Ant's here. He'll make it happen,' she said jokingly. She even had the wry humour to recite a quote from *Mad Max 2*—'You wanna get out of here? You talk to me.'

But it was like an Indiana Jones situation. We were racing to get out of there. After a brief stop in the lounge, I could see she was deteriorating even further. Finally, we got the boarding call.

As we were heading to the gate, Kim lost consciousness. I don't wish to articulate the moments that followed. I don't think it serves a purpose. I'm still attempting to deal with it myself, still experiencing multiple flashbacks. I don't wish that burden upon you, too. With Kim passing away at the terminal, so began a litany of other issues. Again, ones I won't burden you with.

The trip home with Kim's ashes was lonely and surreal. It has been thirty-three years since I travelled alone on a plane. As the hours counted down till landing at Sydney Airport, my anxiety rose. It wasn't the relief one usually feels as the clock ticks down over such a long flight. Rather, it was the tension and anxiety at the thought of leaving Sydney a week ago with Kim, only to return without her.

It was devastating.

Arriving home, the boys were incredibly anxious to see me. It wasn't easy. It breaks my heart to see Reuben continue to wander from room to room in search of her. He doesn't seem to comprehend that I have returned home without Kim. And now, I am organising the funeral service.

The journey has ended.

The following photo is the last one taken of Kim and I together. Little were we to know that almost exactly forty-eight hours later, Kim would pass away.

Take a close look at the photo. Don't be distracted by the wheelchair or distortion of Kim. Look deeply into the backdrop. It's a beautiful day. We are at the ancient Aztec ruins in Mexico. Now, look at the forefront. We're still holding hands. We appear happy. If you could look deeply into our eyes through the sunglasses, you would see that we are still very much in love.

The final bell has rung. The fight is over. It's time to rest now, Champ. You fought the good fight, left nothing in the tank. You fought with great courage and never fell to your knees. You didn't quit on the stool; you were always on the front foot. As the legendary boxing trainer Johnny Lewis once said, 'The winner of a fight is not always the man with his hand raised.'

I think you're right, Johnny.

Ant: 'Kim, will I ever find you again?'

Kim: 'Of course, Ant, just keep heading north.'

Part Three:

Unravelling

That Moment

18 May 2018 was Kim's and my last night in Mexico City before we were due to meet up with our middle and youngest sons, Louis and Oscar, in Las Vegas. The boys were in transit from Sydney, and we were anxious and excited at the prospect of catching up with them—and of leaving Mexico as soon as possible.

During our five-day stay in Mexico, Kim's health deteriorated dramatically. Ignorantly, I had not anticipated the adverse effects of the extreme altitude of Mexico on Kim's body. She only operated on one lung following a lobectomy three years earlier. Magnify this with the late stages of cancer, the flotsam and jetsam of radiation, chemotherapy and twenty-five major surgeries, and her body was simply preparing to die.

Two evenings earlier, I woke in the middle of the night to a frightening gurgling and snoring sound. When I turned the light on, I discovered Kim was frothing from the mouth. In my attempt to wake her, I discovered she was not slumbering but in a state of unconsciousness. Instinctively, I gently shook her, called her name and told her to wake up in some attempt to make her lucid. Much to my relief, Kim came to.

It was the early hours of the morning, so I rolled the dice on a FaceTime call to our good friend and surgeon, Marc Coughlan.

'Ant, she needs oxygen! Now!' Marc explained during the brief consultation.

With that, I contacted the hotel management and requested their Oxy-Viva. Even though this was a Four Seasons Hotel, you must remember this was Mexico. Of course they didn't have one. Yet, it's funny how innovative and driven you can become when the stakes are so high.

I started ringing twenty-four-hour medical services intent on purchasing oxygen cylinders. With a substantial bribe to the concierge and extortionate prices for the oxygen gas, half a dozen commercial oxygen gas cylinders with masks got delivered to our hotel room in less than sixty minutes. Administering the oxygen to Kim gave her instant relief. It soon became apparent that she needed the oxygen to stay alive.

THAT MOMENT

Fast-forward now to the evening of 18 May. It was our last night before we headed out to meet the boys in Vegas. Kim, as she had been for the last two months, was completely wheelchair-bound and needed a constant supply of pure oxygen.

To celebrate our reunion with the boys, I suggested we go down to the hotel lobby's famous Tequila Bar. Kim looked at me and uttered a word I have hardly ever heard her say to me.

'No.'

* * * * *

A few days after Kim's initial diagnosis, I unexpectedly came home early and found her quietly weeping alone upstairs in our bedroom. It broke my heart. I knelt beside her and quietly hugged her.

There was no need for talk. We both knew what this was all about.

Eventually, she moved away from my embrace and through her tears explained she couldn't do this without me.

'Ant, I will do whatever you tell me to do. I need you to take over. I just don't know what to do.'

At that moment, a switch flicked, a new identity was made, a new person, a new role and a new purpose in life. And so began Kim's compliment by me saying 'Yes', sometimes begrudgingly, when I pushed her to the Dog House to train, or when she needed to take her herbs and high-protein drink, but always 'Yes'.

* * * * *

So now, unbeknownst to me that it was our last night together on this Earth, Kim uttered the word 'No'.

In hindsight, I am ashamed of myself. I became angry and explained I would go by myself and left her there on the bed.

I made my way down the elevator to the bar where I ordered a glass of the most expensive tequila on the menu. Theatrically, and with great pride, the waiter ceremoniously poured this extremely rare tequila. He left the table, unimpressed with my lack of enthusiasm. I simply stared at that glass of tequila for what seemed like an eternity.

My anger turned, and I was overcome by shame and guilt. I left the table and the tequila and headed straight back to the room. I entered and found Kim where I left her on the bed. I stood at the foot of the bed for what seemed like the longest time, staring at her.

'What are you looking at, Ant?' Kim asked in a genuinely inquisitive tone.

'I think you look beautiful,' I replied.

Kim explained I must be blind.

I walked over to the bed, dropped to my knees, placed my head on her lap and burst into uncontrollable tears. I told her I was sorry and that I was a selfish person and had let her down. She gently stroked my head, assuring me that wasn't the case.

Now, I can't help but see the irony that here was Kim dying, soothing me.

I slept very little that night, determined to make up for my temporary lapse in judgment in looking after Kim.

When morning came, Kim had further deteriorated. She was weak, semi-conscious and couldn't breathe without the oxygen. Armed with a breathing machine compatible to take on a plane and that doctor's certificate, which I had obtained with a major bribe, we made our way to the airport.

'Darling, you're going to have to try to remain lucid or they will not let you on the plane,' I said as Kim drifted in and out of consciousness.

'If you wanna get out of here, you've gotta talk to Ant,' she wryly replied, paraphrasing from the movie *Mad Max 2*.

And, for the last time in her life, she made me smile.

At the airport, I shooed off well-meaning people wishing to give assistance.

Kim asked to go to the bathroom before we boarded our flight, though she was falling in and out of unconsciousness every couple of minutes. Redressing her afterwards, she was like a rag doll.

My aim was to get us to the boarding gate for our flight. Heart thumping, I knew everything wasn't right.

Out of the bathrooms and onto the concourse of the airport, Kim's limp body slid out of the wheelchair and onto the cold hard linoleum floor. I knelt by her, and it dawned on me like a tremendous punch to the gut.

Kim was dying. I looked into her eyes.

'Don't you fucking die on me, don't you fucking die on me!' I screamed.

In her eyes, I saw fear. Not acceptance. Not peace. But fear. Fear of death.

'Ant, get me out of here,' she was saying to me.

I started CPR. First the breaths, then the pumps.

Nothing.

People stepped around us or stared.

I felt an arm push me aside. A voice screamed in English, 'We are doctors.'

Like a numb zombie and on my knees, I moved aside.

After an eternity, they turned to me and explained they were sorry. Kim was dead. I curled up next to her, took her hand and placed it on my cheek. I don't know how long I lay there for. Seconds. Minutes.

A crowd gathered but, in my mind, it was just Kim and I.

A Mexican official, along with the two doctors, pulled me off Kim. Translating, the doctors explained that Kim's body needed to be taken to the morgue for a full medical autopsy which would take approximately a month. They also explained their plane was about to leave and the official would not let them go.

I explained there was no need for an autopsy nor for them to be detained. I produced the bribed medical certificate from the doctor (that I had dictated to him in the hotel lobby the night before), which stated that Kim was terminally ill and diagnosed with stage 4 lung cancer. The official begrudgingly allowed the doctors to leave.

With the American doctors gone, I was alone with the Mexican Airport officials. In their broken English, they explained I needed to remove all Kim's jewellery before they transported her body.

I gently removed her rings from hands withered by disease and the toxicity of chemo and radiation, then lay back down next to her body. I watched crowds of people walk past us. Some stepped over us, others turned their heads, and some made the sign of the cross.

I had this incredible sense of being alone, of lying next to something or someone I deeply loved who no longer existed.

It was like falling into an abyss.

An insensitive tug on my arm interrupted my dark numbness.

'We have to go now,' a man with a heavy Mexican accent said.

I watched them unceremoniously place my wife, the person I had looked after so intimately, on a stretcher.

By now, I had been assigned two new officials. Their general demeanour created instant mistrust. Still numb with shock, I focused on maintaining a mental attack posture.

Kim had often spoken about her wish to be cremated. The officials, almost gleefully, informed me it would be at least a one-month waiting period. I know Mexico is a big country, but do that many people die and wish to be cremated each day for there to be a one-month waiting period? It didn't take me long to work out their motive.

'How much will it cost? It needs to happen immediately,' I replied.

'10,000 US dollars,' was their succinct reply, their answer a little too swift and well-rehearsed.

There was a brief pause.

'And you will need to pay cash upfront …,' they finished.

I agreed.

We walked to their car where they said they would take me to the nearest ATM.

Their transport was double-parked at the nearest exit. It was a station wagon with half the rear seat laid flat, leaving just enough room for one person to sit in the back.

They politely opened the back door for me where I obliged and sat down.

Turning to my left, Kim's face stared back at me.

These men had the audacity to place me in the hearse carrying my wife's dead body. If I had been semi-numb before, I now became totally numb.

This was a dream.

It wasn't real.

I felt nothing.

Everything slowed down.

We must have driven for twenty minutes, eventually stopping at an outlet still within the airport.

'There's an ATM here. I'll come with you,' said the driver, turning to me.

At the ATM, I discovered the withdrawal limit was 5,000 US dollars.

I communicated this to the driver standing too close, well within my personal space. What did he think? That I was going to make a run for it?

'That's ok. Ten-minute drive to another,' he replied.

We returned to the station wagon where the officials, Kim and I took that silent ten-minute drive, and completed that blood money deal.

From there, we went to an airport administration office where they handed me to another official to complete paperwork. The station wagon took off, and I never saw Kim again.

By now, it must have been afternoon siesta time because I sat in that office alone for what seemed hours. Eventually, with the aid of an intern who spoke English, I completed the necessary forms, and that was that.

Kimberly Irene-Francis Sobb officially no longer existed on this Earth, by the order of Mexican government officials.

The intern drove me back to the same hotel I only left a few hours ago with Kim. During my time waiting in the administration office, I had sent a short 'Kim Update' explaining Kim's passing. I also made one of the hardest phone calls I've ever had to make. It was to my son, Louis, who was in transit at LA Airport with our youngest son, Oscar. They were waiting for a connection to Las Vegas, where they were looking forward to being reunited with their mother and father.

They were totally unaware of what had occurred. I switched out of my zombie-like numbness into a moment of clarity. I needed to be on point for this phone call.

When I got through to Louis, they were both at a diner in the LA Airport. I asked him to leave the table, away from his younger brother, and go somewhere quiet. Louis being Louis never questioned my request. When he was in a secure and private location, I started the conversation.

'Louis, you need to listen to me very carefully. Do you understand?'

'Yes, Dad,' Louis dutifully replied.

I explained the heartbreaking news that his mother had died and that he needed to return to Sydney. He would also need to explain the situation to his younger brother.

Back in my hotel room, the reality sank in. I felt physically ill. My phone rang, and it was my great friend, Bo Bernhard, who resides in Las Vegas. Bo is a professor at the University of Nevada and a long-term family friend who had championed Kim and I during these challenging times.

'Sobbie, I'm so sorry. Are you ok? Where are you?'

I explained I was currently in a hotel room.

'Are you alone?' he then enquired, to which I answered yes.

'I'm on my way,' he said.

I explained it wasn't necessary. I couldn't ask that of him.

'You don't have to, my friend. I'm currently walking to the flight gate to board a plane to Mexico City,' he replied.

It truly was a case of 'cometh the hour, cometh the man'.

Bo arrived and within hours, armed with the gift of speaking fluent Spanish, he ensured Kim's ashes would be delivered to me the following day.

I then made the long trip back to Sydney.

This time, Kim wasn't sitting beside me like normal. Instead, she was in a wooden box with a crucifix, and delicately positioned on my lap.

Travelling South

While travelling home with Kim's ashes, I had a moment of connection with her.

I was back in the busy Mexico City Airport, hugging Kim's urn of ashes like they were my life's breath. Despite what people say, few people in Mexico speak English. It was pandemonium and I couldn't find anyone to explain the directions to my gate. It was this location where, days before, I had watched and felt Kim take her final breath and leave this world, leave me, and go to a place I could not follow.

Rewind back one week and Kim was putting up with one of my ridiculous random conversations. I had dredged up and begun discussing a cheesy Australian martial art movie starring George Lazenby and a pathetic Bruce Lee imitation called Jimmy Wang Yu. I then YouTubed and played her the official trailer song, Sky High, by a British band called Jigsaw from 1975. We laughed and laughed and sang the song together. Now remember, this is an obscure pop song from a cheesy Australian martial art movie back in 1975.

Fast-forward to 2018, Mexico City, with a grieving widower clutching his wife's ashes, disorientated and anxious.

'Where are you? Why did you have to leave?' I actually whispered into the wooden urn.

With that, I heard the *Sky High* song by Jigsaw over the speakers in Mexico City Airport.

I kid you not.

I smiled, patted the urn and somehow my angst at being disorientated washed away.

* * * * *

The boys handled it in their own ways.

Oscar initially didn't seem to grasp what had occurred. I think it was too surreal for him. That's not necessarily a bad thing, but when the reality set in, it was important I be there for him. I watched him closely. He may have been slightly oblivious, but he was still quite fragile.

Jackson, owing to his closeness to Kim, was emotionally shattered. He was in the depths of despair as I continued to console him. I told him that in the week leading up to his mother's death, she constantly spoke of how proud she was of him. For a time, he was a work-in-progress, but he's grown emotionally stronger.

Louis and I remained extremely close. He shared with me his insatiable anger at having his mother robbed from him and my soulmate robbed from me. By virtue of his physical status and skills, I needed to monitor him. I reminded him that nothing will bring his mother back and certain individuals, despite how much they antagonise and annoy him, cannot and should not be blamed or pay the price for our loss.

Reuben simply couldn't understand how I could leave with Kim but return without her. He was lost and agitated. He walked from room to room, looking for her. If visitors or strangers rang the doorbell, he became angry and vicious. Again, something I had to watch extremely closely.

* * * * *

The first thing I did after arriving home was remove anything that reminded me of the cancer.

Within hours, I rid our household of wheelchairs, walkers, walking sticks, ramps and any other accessory used by handicapped people such as Kim. I removed the stair-climber within three days.

I completely cleaned out Kim's extensive wardrobe, accessories and shoes within two days of arriving home. Over the last eight to ten months, I'd become Kim's page. To most men, including me until eight months ago, our partner's clothes are just that: our partner's clothes. However, I now had an intimate connection with those clothes. I knew which piece went with each accessory in what was an extensive wardrobe. I knew Kim's favourites, and I knew what she liked to wear on certain days to certain places.

Seeing her walk-in wardrobe full of these memories broke my heart. So, I cleared it out. The irony was, once I saw it empty, I felt I had lost something, even though I kept a few items of clothing that I just couldn't let go. I'm struggling with the loss of Kim. We lived a co-dependent life—be that right or wrong.

She needed me to look after her and I needed a purpose in life, which was to look after her. Those who knew us well knew that occurred and that it developed long before she was diagnosed with cancer. We simply did everything together. We pined for one another whenever we were separated and physically had to be touching or holding hands at any given time. Between leaving for work and returning home, we talked to each other four or five times a day. That's the way we were. I don't expect everyone to understand it, and in classic, best-practice marriages in this politically correct world, it may have been perceived as wrong, but we never cared.

Kim had needs, and I had needs, and together we fulfilled them. I feel this inexplicable urge to be with her and I feel that wherever she is, she needs me, too. It's sad, and it's lonely. I feel broken and incomplete. I fill my days by trying to keep the house and the boys upbeat as I attempt to reorientate my work-life. It won't be easy, but I have an incredibly loyal and close work team around me. I am deeply indebted to them.

My business is now north.

The Grief

We are now several years since Kim, tragically, on the floor of Mexico City's Airport, left to that place where I couldn't follow her.

Adjusting the boys' and my lives while dealing with the grief has been overwhelming. As per my nature, and not dissimilar in my knowledge quest to help Kim fight the cancer, I became messianic in my search to understand grief.

I gorged myself on TEDx speeches about grief and researched papers written by 'experts'. I even delved into one of my favourite pastimes, cinema. Go see the movie *Collateral Beauty*.

In the end, I turned to the only way I knew to make sense of things that made no sense. And that was to write. To empty my thoughts on paper seems the only way to give me some form of respite both consciously and subconsciously. I thank you for allowing me to share this self-indulgence.

What I've come to know about grief

Grief is a personal thing. You can't buy, sell, borrow or lend it. It is yours, and yours to carry every step of the way. Should you be fortunate enough—as I have been—good friends will walk alongside you on that path, but they can never carry it for you. Some will feel you should share it with them or feel you should share theirs, but I've learnt that's impossible.

There are stayers, and there are goers. Some stay for a while and then go when it becomes too hard. There are few surprises about who in your life does what. It is what it is.

Many people, though not all, both close and otherwise, can unintentionally be less than understanding. Others can be incredibly brave and courageous. I have observed people purposely attempt to avoid me—or is that my paranoia?

'Oh, Anthony, I was hoping it wasn't you. I just don't know what to say to you,' one exclaimed when I approached, then rushed off, leaving me standing at our local shopping centre.

On the other hand, I have witnessed great courage when people have made the decisive action to approach me and explain how sorry they were. I've always made it a point to thank them for their courage.

Unfortunately, numerous moments occur where people try to validate, justify and compare their grief with yours—friend, work friend, best friend, cousin, brother, sister, mother, aunty, nephew, or whatever the relationship. This angered me. It turned the loss of my wife into some form of competition or self-promotion. I found it selfish and thoughtless.

The pain of grief is physical. It is not depression. It is not a mental illness. Yes, it causes great emotional turbulence, but it is physical, too. One moment, your partner of thirty-three years is there, the next moment, they are gone. The bed you shared is empty. Their toothbrush is no longer on the vanity. Their clothes have been erased from your wardrobe. You will never hear their voice call your name again and the clips you've recorded before they left to the netherworld are clung to and played over and over again in some vain form of sorcery to summon them back to you.

The pain never goes away. You simply become accustomed to bearing it. The tears are endless, and while they come and go—in my case, when I'm alone at the Dog House gym—the pain is constant. Despite distractions, it is constant.

The way you cry in deep grief is different to any other form of tears. The sounds even caught my own attention, at times so desperate, coming from somewhere so deep inside. It is a deep, desperate wailing.

I want recognition, not pity, just an affirmation that Kim existed, lived a good life, was an incredible partner, loving mother and beautiful human being. I want affirmation of the horrible injustice and suffering she experienced.

The small things have never been so big. Receiving my new Medicare card without Kim's name on it. Cancelling my ancillary credit card (that had Kim's name on it). Ticking the box that says 'widower' or receiving mail addressed to Kim. They all take on monumental significance as moments of loss.

The cinema is a great haven and place to hide. Whilst possibly not ideal, it serves a purpose with its darkness and anonymity. In contrast, dining alone is like dining on stage with a white, hot spotlight—ironic, considering Kim's and my favourite pastime was dining out together.

You become confused because the timeline formula for the death of your partner has been totally ignored. For instance, a parent recognises the distinct possibility that in the 'circle of life' they will die before their children. Children, too, believe they will most probably outlive their parents. When I met Kim, my life truly began, so I believed logically that our lives would end relatively close to one another. Cruelly, not so.

You consciously do insane gestures or actions like texting your lost one to tell them you're missing them or begging them to come home. You keep their phone charged just in case they call or return. Crazy, I know! Or you keep pieces of their clothing just so you can smell their scent again.

Despite all the right advice given in good faith, it is painstakingly hard to carry on. In my case, I had this insatiable need to be in the netherworld where my partner is. This is a struggle you deal with every morning you wake up. It is unrelenting.

The big bang moment

It wasn't so much a 'big bang' moment, but rather a gradual 'slap in the face' moment where I realised my loved one, Kim, was never coming back.

I removed my wedding ring after thirty-three years. This ring was blessed at the altar, witnessed by my closest family and friends, the band placed on my finger by the very person I am grieving for. I removed it stubbornly, clumsily and unceremoniously.

You would think there could be glimpses of slight relief with the possibility of moving on, but unfortunately there's not. I am now not only floundering in a deep sea of grief but also bumping into islands of anger. Anger, even with Kim.

'How could you leave me?'

Anger with the world and the injustice of Kim's life being tragically taken so early. Anger at why her final years were filled with so much pain and why her final moments of life were so frightening.

Despite what Dr Elizabeth Kubler-Ross states in her book *On Death and Dying*, Kim did not accept death. She feared it. I looked into her eyes the seconds before she died, the moment when she knew she was dying, and she certainly did not want to die.

You do not forget those moments or looks. They haunt you.

180 degrees

The 180 degrees slowly creeps up. It's a slow burn. It is a gradual awareness and place. I hated and despaired of it, but it is a self-preservation mechanism.

Those images and clips of Kim that I watched and pined over for hours on end, whilst cruelly torturing myself, began to be watched less and less.

It is not that I'm forgetting my soul partner—quite the opposite.

I simply cannot take any more of the pain. I became angry and frustrated with myself and everyone else in this world, including Kim, and at the injustice and insanity of needing to see this evidence of Kim, along with the inverted pain it brings. So, I protected myself by watching them less and less.

With this, not only comes anger, but guilt.

My despair and sadness became simple punctuation points of deep, elongated anger.

I am angry with everyone and everything.

I'm certainly lucid enough to realise that the common denominator is me. Hell, the whole world can't be wrong! And so, my anger is magnified with the frustration and dissatisfaction that the majority of this issue is me.

The rhetoric of 'life is unfair', 'you drew the short straw' and 'that's fate', amongst others, is bullshit.

What about 'Karma'?

What about 'What goes around comes around'?

What about 'Simple, plain justice!'

All of Kim's suffering and pain, the sheer tragedy was for what?

Nothing.

In the end, it all just boils down to injustice, and that angers me.

It angers me that the doctor Kim despised, who, at one of our most vulnerable points, from behind the safety of his desk, looked at us both and said, 'I'm sorry I can't help you. Bad things happen to good people all the time,' is probably right.

What fuels my anger is that people move on—as they should—but I can't.

I cannot seem to let go of looking after Kim, even when she's gone. Some militant, combatant persona has pledged loyalty to 'the cause of Kim'. As our credo tells me, I cannot, and will not ever, give up on Kim. To do so would be the ultimate act of cowardice and disloyalty. And so, the anger burns, consuming me and almost always harming those closest to me. It is self-destructive, but in some cruel, sick way, I am drawn to it.

The other night, I woke myself up. My own crying interrupted my usual shallow slumber and escape from a life without Kim. I was crying and holding on to Kim's nightie. Attempting to explain my grief to others reminds me of when friends from a different culture pass the comment, 'We don't have a word for that in our language.' That is how I feel when attempting to articulate and explain the depths of grief I feel with the loss of Kim. I, too, struggle to articulate it in such a way that others would understand.

Maybe they are not meant to understand.

Maybe I shouldn't be attempting to articulate it—inviting them into my darkness.

On reflection, it's possibly selfish and destructive, as it is not their grief to carry, nor mine to share.

Christmas and New Year

When writing this in January 2020, two major turning points occurred. The first was I could no longer say 'my wife passed away last year'. Strangely, it was something I held onto because it made it feel more recent and somehow kept Kim closer to me. The reality is the source of my understanding of real love died in 2018. Now it's 2020. Time ruthlessly, without memory, consciousness or emotion, marches forward.

The second occurrence was the second Christmas without Kim.

Christmas was the time that my family, before Kim's death, absolutely cherished and loved. I have exchanged the memories of what I loved about Christmas for anxiety about marking the number of Christmases without Kim. This year it's two, next year it's three, then five, ten and so on.

My fear is that Kim will just drift away—a tide going out never to return.

That is what Christmas and New Year brought to me in 2019, turning 2020.

I can't help but continuously go over the past. I feel like I have a thousand pasts and no future.

Sweet suffering

I became robotic. It was my protection—being regimented in my ways to appear to get by. My military precision is an impermeable shell covering my inner numb turmoil. To my detriment, I became more comfortable with my own company and less with others. I am held up and kept buoyant by blind, emotionless and false efficiency. In my case, this has been magnified by having access to financial security and the support of personal assistants.

Long ago, sleep stopped being a physical necessity. It has now become an escape from reality. It's shallow and unfulfilling, but still, some respite from the pain is better than none.

I began to question myself and became fearful I'm losing my memory of Kim. I don't know if it's a memory, or a memory of a memory I am left with.

I continued to travel (by myself), at times having moments of heavy, deep grief. As time went on, I wondered why I kept travelling to the same places, the same hotels, the same restaurants and even the same art galleries.

I eventually came to the sad answer ... I was looking for Kim.

I've observed people in the same circumstances as mine. Hell, I know I'm nothing new or exceptional. Some seem to have the wherewithal to somehow move forward—even if it's the most minuscule progress.

Unfortunately, I don't think I'm one of them.

My love for Kim was such that I must stay where she last left me—caught in some time capsule.

Like a faithful yet unintelligent dog, I impatiently wait for a moment that will never be.

This week was the second year without her on our much-loved Valentine's Day. I've never felt so lonely. Losing Kim was like losing the rain. I kept most of Kim's cards and read them over and over again, sweetly torturing myself.

To my handsome brute who has never looked better or looked after me better in all our years together. Happy Valentine's Day.

To my husband, the man who has always appreciated a good bottom and thankfully still appreciates mine 26 years later.

"Come, my dear, grow old with me, the best is yet to be."—Robert Browning

Dear Ant, happy 27th anniversary. I give thanks for my partner sharing life's journey with me. Love, Kim.

Ant, happy 28th wedding anniversary. May we never stop enjoying each other. You are quite simply my life. Love, Kim.

Dear Ant,

"You take away my troubles, take away my pain and you give me love, love, love."—Van Morrison

I owe you my life—I always have, Kim. Happy anniversary. 29 years and many more to come.

Thirty years ago, we were young and beautiful. We stood together and made vows to each other to be true in sickness and in health.

You have been surely tested my love, and you have honoured those vows in a way neither of us could have imagined ... I fell behind but you waited for me.

To the love of my life, who over the last few months has demonstrated again and again and again his love for me. Now I owe the love of my life, my life. Happy Valentine's Day 2015. Love forever, Kim.

"Being so deeply loved by someone gives you strength, while loving someone deeply gives you courage."— Lao Tzu

Ant, you have given me life and you are my life.

THE GRIEF

Reuben

Reuben was so much more than our family dog.

Next to myself, nobody spent more time with Kim than Reuben. He was more than just company for Kim. He comforted her when she was frightened, which was pretty much any time I wasn't there with her.

When Kim passed away, Reuben was thirteen and beginning to suffer from arthritis. In the months after Kim's passing, he slowed down.

Finally, one morning, as I brought out his breakfast, he lay in his kennel. I looked into his eyes and knew he was dying. I gently lay by his side, stroked his head and whispered into his ear that no one could ask for a greater friend, and that we loved him. With that, I felt Reuben take his last breath and life leave his body. It is almost impossible to describe, bearing witness to life leaving a body. Somewhat sad, somewhat beautiful, completely surreal. I lay there with Reuben for a time, giving his eulogy in my mind.

It was as if in Kim's passing, he felt his job was now complete.

Reuben's business is now north.

Despite my manic efforts, I can't get rid of the stench of death in my car, which acted as a hearse to carry his dead body to the vet.

Losing Reuben cut deep into the boys, Lily and me. For me, Reuben was the last living proof of Kim's existence and memory. His passing now seems to have placed Kim even further away from me.

Before and after

It's now been nearly two years since Kim's passing and five-and-a-half years since this total chapter of pain and theft of my family's life began.

I become anxious as I find it hard to recall my life, our life, and my family's life, before this all began. My life before this all occurred seems a strange, distant and blurred memory. My future seems to hold nothing but this pain, and now depression, that I grapple with.

I have no past and no future, just this purgatory of pain that marks time. I'm sure it is no coincidence that almost on a dime at 2.00 pm, I have to run.

I run because I know that's when the 'black dog' knocks on my door—the exact time that it did for Kim each day.

I had a dream last night and woke with horrible anxiety and loss.

I dreamt Kim was alive.

We were together, but I had a deep sense we were drifting apart and becoming disconnected. Kim was falling out of love with me. I was panicking and attempting to call her to tell her I loved her. I couldn't get through. I tried to get her attention, but she seemed otherwise distracted.

She seemed to drift away, leaving me in a deep, dark despair with a sense of loss.

It's been nearly two years since Kim died. I'd rather be nowhere with Kim than somewhere without her.

I remember how I used to race home from work to be with Kim.

Dining each night was an event, a celebration. I'd be in the kitchen spiritually preparing the food and flavours that I alone knew Kim loved. Kim would perch up on the bench, chatting with me about almost everything. We'd open a bottle of wine and celebrate, wishing the night would never end, every night.

Now I drink so the night can end.

Change

Yesterday was 2 August 2020. It would have been Kim's and my thirty-fifth wedding anniversary.

As the anniversary loomed closer, so too did the angst.

I stood in our bedroom where I have some photos of Kim along with her ashes. Among those photos is a picture of us on our wedding day, barely adults, standing on the steps of St Joseph's College Chapel. Little did we know what lay ahead of us. Little did we know where each of us would be in thirty-five years' time.

I stood for a long time staring at that photo. I wanted to warn the young couple. Warn them, and somehow prepare them for what pain lay ahead.

My grief has now somehow evolved into a claustrophobic angst. The moment anyone becomes emotionally or physically close to me, I feel the need to run, to escape. I feel smothered. It has disappointed and confused not only the boys but also other lovely people, some of whom I deeply care about.

I'm contemplating some time away. I've become regimented, robotic and inflexible to contain my grief. I've also begun to harbour some bad habits. I'm constantly drawn to the only solution in my life to simply be with Kim.

The irony

Last weekend was Father's Day 2020. Yet again another milestone—you'd be surprised how many milestones there can be in relation to grief and the loss of someone. In fact, it's never-ending.

Again, the angst rose as the day approached. Never one who enjoyed the limelight of such celebrations, I secretly always enjoyed Father's Day. The boys being boys and oblivious, it was Kim in the background driving everything. What I loved was the message Kim was sending me:

'Ant, I love and appreciate the way you've been a father to our boys.'

That affirmation meant so much to me. Now that Kim is no longer with me, it's lost. The further irony of Father's Day was that weekend I was walking alone along Cronulla Beach, as I do most weekends. When I looked up, I saw a young man in the famous 'Cronulla Alley rip' screaming for help. I stripped down and rescued the man, only to find after bringing him ashore that my sacred wedding ring, which I wore on a chain around my neck—that very ring Kim placed on my finger at the altar—was gone.

The nightmare and dreams

Last night was bad. I had two very real dreams.

The first revolved around unsuccessfully continuing to phone Kim, not realising she was dead. Her refusal to answer my calls overwhelmed me, first with frustration and then with anxiety.

The second was frightening. I was in the cemetery where I found Kim's coffin. Despite people's cries for me not to open it, my need for Kim was so great that I did open it. I hadn't experienced such a nightmare for the longest time. The fear woke me up. The following morning, I still carried the fear of what it meant. The nightmare continues to haunt me.

The torture of anniversaries

The following photo has great significance. It was taken on 12 October 2014. Today is 12 October 2020. It was the very last photo taken of Kim pre-cancer.

MY BUSINESS IS NOW NORTH

It was a beautiful spring day, a Sunday which historically is our family dinner day. I wanted to do something special for them that day, so I hired a water taxi as a surprise to pick us up from Circular Quay and take us across to Manly for dinner.

Little did Kim and I know that in less than twenty-four hours—at approximately 11.00 am the following day—we were to receive the news that Kim had stage 4 terminal lung cancer.

I look at that photo often, somehow dreaming I can stop the clock so our family remains in that moment forever. The photo gives me painful pleasure.

My dreams continue with the storyline often the same. Kim either ignoring me or me having the feeling that I can't contact her and she's falling out of love with me. The nightmare of opening the coffin still haunts me.

Last week, I was again woken from my shallow slumber by my own weeping. It's a strange, sad and lonely feeling. I know I'm not coping. I still harbour these deep thoughts of wanting to be with Kim. It's prompted me to seek further help by returning to my grief psychologist.

After further reassessment, I've been formally diagnosed with severe PTSD (post-traumatic stress disorder). My clinician is a wonderful lady who also treated Kim, so she is intimately aware of the relationship between Kim and I.

Last week, we began our long road of EMDR (eye movement desensitisation processing) therapy. Its aim is to recalibrate my brain and mindset.

More than this

In this recent week, I experienced multiple nights of being woken in the middle of the night by my own crying.

Last night, I experienced a dream within a dream. I was away on holidays with Kim somewhere I can't recall. I became frantic as I had lost Kim's jewellery box. Kim attempted to calm my angst as I explained how important its contents were to me. Kim hugged me as I began to cry uncontrollably, explaining to her that I know this is a dream and that she is dead. We held each other for the longest time in a deeply sad moment as we both came to the realisation that even in a dream of a dream, she no longer exists.

I think I've come to the realisation that I will never be at peace until I'm back with Kim, wherever that may be.

The dreams continue. In my most recent dream, Kim is beginning to morph. My recollection of the dream is that I instinctively knew it was Kim, and she was looking slightly different. As is becoming a common theme in my dreams, she was attempting to dismiss me. As per usual, it gave me great angst.

'What do you think they mean, Ant?' my grief psychologist asked recently when discussing these with her.

'I think somewhere in my subconscious, it's trying to tell me to let go and accept Kim's death,' I replied.

I find that task almost impossible.

I'm tired of the grief and sadness.

I'm tired of being tired.

Playlist:
More than this, Roxy Music

Christmas 2020

Christmas 2020 marked the third Christmas without Kim.

Despite the joys that Christmas brings, there was an underlying sadness amongst the boys and me. As per Louis' and my tradition, we rostered ourselves onto the morning Christmas Day life-saving patrol on Cronulla Beach. In years gone by, I spent Christmas morning side by side with Louis on the beach, observing the swimmers and often laughing together as we shared stories—usually relating to one of Kim's Christmas meltdowns.

This year was different. Louis was especially sad this year. The two of us stood alone on the beach as he opened up to me about his incredible sense of loss and anxiety of 'where Mum is right now'.

Recently, I took myself up to Byron Bay to stay in a secluded villa for a semi-retreat. I walked many, many hours on the beautiful beach of Byron. I meditated a lot on what has happened and why I've become who I've become. The hours of thought have brought me to several conclusions.

I've often contemplated that if somebody had come up to me just prior to 12 October 2014 and outlined in detail what Kim and I were about to experience and embark on, I would have said, 'That's impossible.'

How could somebody with absolutely no symptoms except for a nagging pain in the neck, and who has never smoked in their life, be diagnosed with stage 4 terminal lung cancer?

How could someone withstand twenty-five major surgeries in four years?

How could I ever be in charge and become self-educated about Kim's life and her fight against cancer?

Could I ever imagine being given a marker pen by our surgeon, Dr Marc Coughlan, and asked to mark-up Kim as we were wheeling her into surgery, because he didn't have the time to view the scans, and this was an emergency operation?

Chemo.

Radiation.

Kim dying in my arms.

Rivers of tears and countless more stories.

Early in this chapter of our lives, Kim reached out, and I recognised she needed support. But the support she needed, I could not give her being the person I was. I needed to become someone different.

And so, the switch was flicked.

The switch that makes you messianic.

The switch that said to Kim:

'I will never give up, ever, ever. There will never be a time when I lay beside you and capitulate. I will never stop fighting, ever.'

This gave Kim great solace. That pleased me and it kept me in good stead whilst Kim was alive. But now that Kim has passed, I am like a soldier during peacetime. I don't feel like I belong.

The switch can't be turned off. And that's the point. It gave Kim so much solace because it is forever.

I meditated on this for a long time and concluded that this is why I am where I am. It is what it is. I would never have changed a thing.

I would never have changed a thing for Kim.

Last night, I dreamt that Kim and I were in the backseat of a car, being driven home from a night out. Kim was rabbiting on about something, but I wasn't listening. I was totally consumed by her beauty and how much I loved her. She belonged to me, and I belonged to her. I felt almost overwhelmed at the anticipation of us lying in bed together, holding one another. The car turned into the driveway, the front wheels jolting as it hit the kerb. My body froze, and I awoke alone in my own bed.

Playlist:
You're Missing, Bruce Springsteen
Stray Bullet, Bruce Springsteen
Chasin' Wild Horses, Bruce Springsteen
Moonlight Motel, Bruce Springsteen
My Funny Valentine, Frank Sinatra
I'll Stand by You, Bruce Springsteen
Iris, Goo Goo Dolls

Part Four:

The Strength

The Fight

I've talked about the battle a lot. Kim and I fought a battle.

Did I ever acknowledge the battle would be lost?

In a word; never. Perhaps this is why I struggled, and still do, with the grief of losing Kim. I was so deep in a mindset to fight and save Kim that there was no room for any inkling that we were going to capitulate. This continued right up until that moment on the floor of Mexico City Airport when her eyes rolled back and I screamed, 'Don't you fucking die on me! Don't you fucking die on me!'

Years before, I immersed myself in boxing, its history, its sad stories and its incredibly uplifting tales. But what really got me is how it reveals one's true character. Boxing can show an individual's real mettle. There is nowhere to hide physically, mentally or otherwise.

How does one react when pushing through the most incredible pain?

How is one's discipline during early morning roadwork in winter and while denying food and dieting to make weight?

Then there is the moment of truth in the ring with only two other people. One is your opponent, whose objective is to beat you to a pulp, and the other is the referee whose job it is to allow that to happen—well, until you are knocked out or counted out. Anyone who says they're not worried before they climb through those ropes is either a liar or a fool. It can be a very lonely place.

I got involved with combat sports all the way back in 1981, when I joined a local Tae Kwon Do school. Yes, this later became the 'Dog House'. After decades of training and commitment, I accomplished the level of fourth-degree Dan black belt and fought in numerous martial arts tournaments.

In my mid-thirties, I made the decision to commence my journey with boxing. Training at the Newtown PCYC (Police Citizens Youth Club) never bore a second thought. It was headed by the famous boxing trainer and mentor Johnny Lewis, and was the home of world champions like Kostya Tszyu, Jeff Harding and Jeff Fenech, plus other great Olympians and medallists such as Justin Rowsell. Not that I ever thought I could accomplish or had anywhere near their talent (or ever would), but such was my love for boxing, I wanted to be with the best.

Historically, I was good at training. Committed, persistent and with my years of experience practising martial arts, I had the ability to mentally and physically withstand great pain—yes, having ADHD does have its advantages. As time went on and I religiously went about my tortuous training regime, some of the serious fighters started taking notice, as did Johnny Lewis. It was there I was christened with the nickname, 'The Energiser'. I wear this name as a badge of honour because it was given to me by the boxing fraternity of the famous Newtown PCYC. I had many hard spars there and, while considered 'late in life' as a boxer, was given no free rides. There was a saying at Newtown when you were sparring—'Never say sorry.'

'It's boxing, not ballet!' Johnny Lewis would scream whilst standing on the apron of the ring during those legendary sparring sessions.

Later, I would be honoured by Johnny when he requested I sit on the Board of the Newtown PCYC with him. Over the years, I fought unregistered in bouts as a 'pro-am' (professional-amateur, unsanctioned). I couldn't be registered as an amateur due to my age or as a professional due to being considered a novice. Fighting on these cards in professional conditions (no headgear and three-minute rounds), I maintained amateur status by donating any money earned to Westmead Children's Hospital.

The biggest of these bouts was a ten-rounder where I took on the Ukraine Super Middleweight Champion, who had recently immigrated to Australian shores. It was a war (for me, anyway), and the longest ten rounds of my life. The odds were stacked against me. At one stage during the fight, the referee came to my corner as they were madly trying to repair a cut over my closing left eye and explained that if the cut opened wider, he would be stopping the fight.

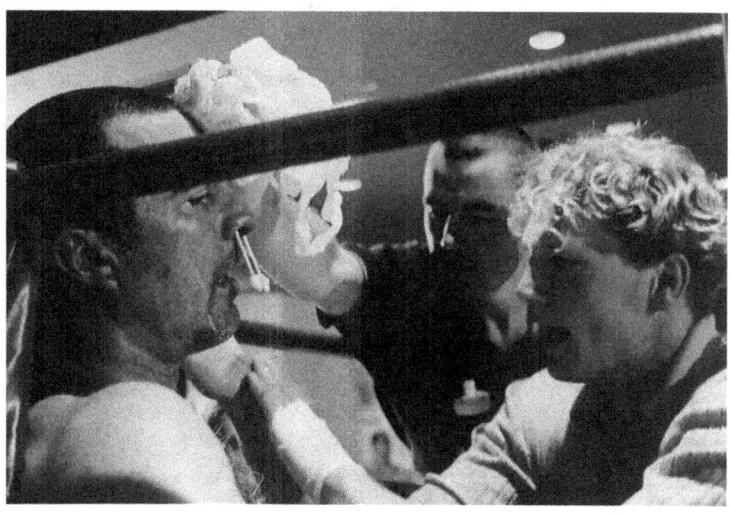

I turned to my cut man and screamed, 'Fix that eye. I am ready to fucking die tonight!'

Quite rightly, he looked at me like I was a lunatic. At the end of the fight, with a damaged left retina, closed left eye and dislocated right jaw, I nearly passed out in the shower. Kim, who had been waiting for me in the dressing room, frantically ran to get the fight doctor. The Doc sat me down, asking me the usual post-fight concussion questions. Of course, I replied that I was ok. I knew how many fingers he was holding up but when he asked me who the Prime Minister of Australia was (it was the famous Liberal leader, John Howard), my reply was, 'I should know the answer, shouldn't I?'

Not knowing the answer to that question, and with a strained retina, closed left eye and a right jaw that kept popping out, brought a temporary hiatus to my boxing career and I took a break for a while.

If you hadn't already worked it out, my hand wasn't raised by the referee at the end of that bout. In fact, I didn't win a single round of that ten-round fight. However, I did win the respect of my opponent who remains a friend to this day. It is not uncommon for two fighters to become close friends afterwards—particularly when it's a brutal fight, which this one was. At the height of the battle, at its most vicious, something quite intimate transcends boxing, something you rarely share with another human being. You have both been to a place that no one else but the two of you can understand. After that fight, I worked the corner for a number of my Ukraine friend's fights. As for Kim, she was annoyed, anxious and proud of me all at the same time. The truth was that no one expected me to even last those ten rounds with the Ukrainian champion, but I knew with Kim by my side, I could do anything. Perhaps this is why I truly believed together we could beat the diagnosis of terminal cancer.

Did this whole chapter of boxing in my life affect my mindset in relation to Kim's and my fight against cancer? I will simply state, 'How could it not?'

The Dog House

It's ironic. In normal circumstances, if someone trains often and conscientiously, they reap positive results—and believe me, Kim trained like a demon. But as the disease progressed, and with the side effects of chemotherapy, radiation and approximately twenty-five major surgeries, Kim's health continued to decline. Albeit not as rapidly as if she didn't train, but nonetheless it declined.

Hidden from the public, the Dog House was our escape from the world.

We listened to Bruce Springsteen blaring as I encouraged her to push through her pain and receive the euphoric endorphin high that comes with exhausting exercise. Sometimes Louis attended, lending his expertise. Kim loved having 'her Lou' by her side.

In the beginning, Kim walked through the gym, then with the aid of a walking stick, then with a walker, until eventually I wheeled her in a wheelchair to work out with light hand weights.

At times, she cried at the thought of entering through the doors of the Dog House.

'Ant, I just can't do this anymore.'

But, without exception, at the completion of every session, she explained how much better she felt.

More than two decades earlier, I took over the martial arts combat gym which became known by the Sobb Family as the Dog House, broadening its scope to include boxing and MMA (mixed martial arts).

Think of an old underground boxing gym like something out of Rocky and that's pretty much the Dog House. Kim often commented that it looked more like a museum and reeked of sweat and liniment. I rather thought it had character and the aroma was the perfume of hard work. Either way, little were we to know how important this sanctuary was going to become.

Back in 2000, it became a constant criticism of Kim's as a financial burden because it barely ever broke even.

'Kim, it's a service to the community. It's not meant to make money,' was my defence, but this certainly didn't cut the mustard with the ever-pragmatic Kim.

However, as the years went by, both Jackson and Louis trained and fought out of there, immersing themselves in the importance of fitness and discipline.

Fast-forward to 2014.

With Kim's diagnosis, I needed to focus with no external distractions taking me away from her wellbeing. I ceased classes and access to the public, turning my once-commercial combat gym into a private one for Kim.

The Dog House didn't save Kim's life, but by God, it gave us some respite.

The Support

On graduating from St. Joseph's College, I certainly wasn't considered an academic. In fact, quite the contrary, I was a victim of the then archaic concepts of learning and the education system. Once a month whilst at boarding school, we were allowed out for the day, returning at 8.00 pm that Sunday evening. Religiously, we would dine out as a family prior to my returning to the rigours and virtually inedible food of Joey's. Possibly magnified by the poor quality of boarding school food, I loved those nights dining out with the family, usually in Sydney's famous Chinatown, gathered at a round table (yes, complete with that lazy Susan).

I loved the ceremony of dining. It gave more than just physical sustenance and heightened palate satisfaction. It gave me a feeling of connection synonymous with family. I believe it was here I began my love affair with being of service to people and all things hospitality.

Fast-forward to 2000 and, after working in numerous hotels, restaurants, and clubs, I applied for the position of CEO at Fairfield RSL. The club was considered a large one with the footprint of a whole block, and had two stories with several dining outlets, a large auditorium, function facilities, bars and 330 gaming machines. In its heyday back in the 1980s, it was a booming venue and an entertainment hub for the area. By 2000, it was a tired, maturing organisation, trading poorly with an even worse culture rooted with unsavoury characters, gangs and regular physical altercations. All this created not only an unhealthy organisation, but an unhealthy financial balance sheet. I remember arriving with Kim to 'case the joint out'. We were immediately met with disinterested and unfriendly staff, and the smell of stale beer and smoke. I can still hear Kim's voice echoing, 'Ant, what are we doing here? You already have a great job.'

Today, Fairfield RSL is considered an industry leader as a leisure facility that offers a variety of high-quality dining experiences. It has a reputation for engaging and efficient service in a designer environment peppered with beautiful pieces of art. The facility is something I am proud of, and its transformation was only achieved due to the incredible support of staff, managers and the Board alike. Kim saw the transformation and became proud of the facility. On news of her diagnosis in October 2014, both the Board and senior management closed ranks to ensure that not only was I supported in the workplace, but that I had the flexibility to be wherever I needed to be when it came to Kim's wellbeing and treatment. Without their support, things would have been very different. Whilst I will forever be in their debt—at the risk of sounding arrogant—regardless of anyone's support, I would have made things happen for Kim.

The Medical Profession

I retain a huge amount of respect for the medical profession. Without them, Kim and I would not have had the time we did have. When writing the emails over those four years, out of respect for the professionals who we interacted with, I didn't always share the rationale behind our medical decisions, especially when we took certain matters into our own hands.

You can see we made radical decisions about diet, exercise, treatment and recuperation. What you do, if you are ever unfortunate enough to be faced with cancer, will depend on your circumstances, your background, the current state and understanding of medical options and a myriad of other factors.

On reflection in the years since, I can share a little more about why we made the decisions we made.

The oncologists
We changed oncologists often—five times to be exact. This is uncommon for people in our situation, but we were anything but the norm. Kim was extraordinary, and I was a fighter. After the initial shock of the diagnosis, I transformed and went into fight mode. The first oncologist suggested we simply sedate Kim, write her will and, for some reason, added that Kim would not see Oscar (then in Year Nine) graduate from high school. Fuck him.

The next was a professor with little to no bedside manner who obviously found me quite annoying due to asking him multiple questions in relation to Kim's treatment. After Kim's fourth chemo treatment of the highly toxic cisplatin, he announced at our regular checkup that he could give no more cycles to Kim. He wasn't aware I had done my own research and knew for a fact that you could receive six cycles should the patient appear fit enough. Nobody knew how fit Kim was more than I did. This was why we trained her body so hard, so she could withstand this treatment and the disease. An argument broke out in his office where Kim had to placate me. Needless to say, that was our last appointment with him. Fuck him, too.

The next was a lovely lady with an excellent bedside manner, but she simply lacked the drive I was looking for.

Others followed, ones that I could stand over and who would give in to my demands. The thing is, I discovered that not all doctors are the same. Whilst they may have the same qualifications, someone came first in the class, and someone graduated last. Some doctors immerse themselves in dogma, whilst others open their mind to different possibilities and the latest treatments. Some are incredibly intuitive to their patient's needs, whilst others are not so. I was brought up in a time where you never questioned a doctor or a priest. Hasn't that now changed? In Kim's journey and our fight with cancer, we needed like-minded people. That is the advice I give. Get alternative opinions, immerse yourself in resources that enable you to absorb knowledge, for knowledge and wherewithal are not exclusive to doctors or academics. If you have the want, you will find the way. We did not want to capitulate and so, in turn, wanted warriors by our side. If you didn't intend to fight 'the fight', then you had no place in our tribe.

The doctors and surgeons

When putting any team together, you need specialists. Knowing Dr Marc Coughlan was prepared to fight for us, he became an excellent resource forfinding other like-minded specialist doctors. Marc became my litmus test and resource for cohorts. Without a like-minded team, the treatment and progress can become fragmented. Be a part of choosing your team. Be proactive in researching them. You have a choice.

Surprisingly, there is an abundance of information available should you wish to research doctors. There were red flags during our research odyssey into doctors and their performance—or lack of. Bedside manner and an intuitive nature to understand and listen were often reflected in basic social intelligence.

- Was the doctor engaging?
- Did they ask questions?
- Were they really listening to our answers?
- Did they appear to prepare for our consultation, or did they 'wing it'?

As I mentioned before, whilst all people in the medical profession have a particular qualification, someone graduated last, and someone graduated first in their class. We also need to remember that doctors are human. Just because they are doctors doesn't mean that they do not make mistakes, have oversights, get tired and even become complacent or apathetic. This is why you get second opinions. This is why you need to self-educate. This is why you need to take note that when a radiologist in the past has given an incorrect report from a PET or MRI scan, you decide not to utilise them again. Learn to have some understanding of how to read these reports. Learn to understand their language, 'turn of phrase', jargon or, at the very least, key terminologies. I was (and always will be) far from an academic, but it is amazing what you can become when the life of someone you love so much is in the balance.

If you are prepared to judge a doctor's (or anyone else's) performance, you, too, must arm yourself with knowledge. This knowledge became an important part of my preparation. I immersed myself in the world of cancer and its treatments. On top of that, I also took on the role of home nurse and trainer, so I intimately understood Kim's body, well-being, and mindset. All these factors, in and of themselves, can drive and empower you.

I was a desperate man. This was a desperate situation, and I simply couldn't fathom the thought of losing My Kim. So, I did everything within my power to ensure Kim received first preference. Put bluntly, I ingratiated myself to whatever medical team I was dealing with. First and foremost, my approach was to treat everyone with dignity, courtesy and respect and if that didn't work, then they had better be prepared for a fight. Virtually all senior doctors held in high regard are in incredibly high demand, so they are time-poor. As laser-focused as I was, I was always mindful not to waste their time, so I, too, prepared at length prior to appointments. The good doctors respected my reciprocating preparation. There was very little blubbering or jabbering, and I think they appreciated that.

My other secret weapon was acknowledging the doctor's 'gate keeper' and support staff. Show them dignity, courtesy and respect. Acknowledge their value, always bring a chocolate for each of them and from time to time, send flowers. Somehow, mysteriously, you seem to get those important appointments just when you need them!

Dr Marc Coughlan

Marc Coughlan grew up in South Africa and, with several medical professionals in the family, was drawn to medicine from a young age, especially the technical aspects of the surgical field.

He obtained his medical degree from the University of Cape Town and then spent a year working in a bush hospital in Natal where he was exposed to a lot of heavy-trauma surgery. That cemented his interest in surgery, and he went on to spend the next thirteen years specialising in neurosurgery, eventually receiving his Neurological Fellowship in South Africa in 2003. He met world-renowned cardiac surgeon, Christiaan Barnard, several times, and was fortunate enough to spend eleven years at the renowned Groote Schuur Hospital, where Dr Barnard did the world's first heart transplant.

Living in South Africa, Marc saw lots of pathology and trauma, and from early on he got broad exposure and a lot of hands-on experience as a doctor. Around his sixth year in neurosurgery, he went to a conference in Cape Town where he got to meet Dr Charlie Teo. At the time, he expressed to Charlie that he'd love to get over to Australia and do some work there.

'Just get in touch with me and we might be able to arrange a fellowship,' responded Dr Teo and Marc did just that.

Because of Dr Teo, Marc underwent a significant learning experience. When it comes to Dr Charlie Teo, few things are impossible. Dr Teo has never been afraid to take on conditions that other surgeons would consider inoperable. He opened Marc's eyes to what's possible, especially when it comes to surgery.

These days, Marc still does a few brain surgeries, but most of his surgeries are spinal reconstructions, of which a subgroup is cancer or tumour surgery. Most of what he works on relates to degenerative spinal conditions. Spinal tumours are not that common, but when they occur, they're like Kim's where the cancer has eroded part of the patient's spine.

Dr Coughlan met Kim and I in late 2014, soon after Kim had been diagnosed with lung cancer and the secondary spinal tumours had been identified. She had seen a surgeon at another hospital who said to us, 'Look, it's too dangerous to do anything and you've got a metastatic disease, so your prognosis is not good. It's not worth throwing everything at it.'

This was hard to hear, especially because Kim was still mentally so robust and physically so strong. However, the reality is that by the time you've got metastatic disease where it's eroded away a lot of your spinal column, the prognosis is not good on paper.

Some patients come to Dr Coughlan looking for advice, while other patients come looking for answers. Kim and I, however, came in ready to fight. On the face of it, her situation was hopeless. However, coupled with her physical strength, she had her attitude and a supportive partner who would not take no for an answer. Marc realised that if we could physically and mentally keep things together, we could change what the future holds.

He understood the power of not being curtailed by textbooks, prognoses and people telling us 'this is your amount of time left'. With him, we underwent radical surgeries, including putting in 3D-printed prosthetic parts.

At every stage, Marc said to me, 'Haven't you had enough surgery?'

'No, we want to fight this,' I'd reply.

He'd get me to sign all the consent forms and review the information and the risks, but I really trusted Marc. I was keen to take the risk, and it did pay off. It paid off for many years. Kim and I got to travel together, have a good quality of life, keep fit and healthy and train in the gym for many years.

Cancer treatment is starting to move more towards biological solutions around using antibodies and genetic markers rather than surgical solutions. We're seeing advances in treatments like immunotherapies, and maybe we are getting to a stage where we don't have so many surgeries. However, despite all the advances, patients are still coming to see Dr Coughlan with their spinal columns riddled with tumours. Even as we make advances in treatment, it doesn't make a big difference to the patients who have already got spinal fractures from cancer.

Even towards the end, I was still coming to Marc with options. Right until the end, we just wanted to fight. As a surgeon, he questioned how many times you can operate on someone. We looked at the alternatives and there weren't any.

I'd say to him, 'What would you do if it was your wife?'

Marc said he would do the same.

There are many mental and physical things we can do each day to buy time and have a good quality of life. Most of all, Marc thinks patients need a reason to fight. He knew Kim and I had our boys and that we had goals and milestones to reach. Marc also knew we were a devoted couple with an amazing partnership and an amazing bond. He knew I didn't mind if my wife was in a wheelchair, or if I was carrying her to bed every night. Marc knew I was so in love with Kim that every day was special.

When Kim passed away, I helped Marc with a charity called PNG Angels by fundraising through the RSL Trust I work with. It has allowed Marc to travel to PNG to help people with cancer. Few people have access to cancer treatment there, so he sees the drastic end-stages of the disease. Just recently, Dr Marc saw a child with facial cancer who was waiting for an implant. Within a matter of days, he and the engineers looked at the child's scans and on the last trip over, Dr Marc took a 3D- printed jaw to implant in the patient. It's just amazing.

And yet, for all his surgical background, Dr Marc, too, would like to see cancer treatments move more towards preventative and targeted biological solutions. This would mean less of the surgeons doing the physical mopping up, and more systemic treatments such as injecting cancer- killing viruses into patients as these become more effective. The Holy Grail may lie with stem cells and cellular-focused treatments that preferentially kill off the cancer. Sadly, for a lot of patients, they're cut off from these newer, more radical treatments because they're being managed by their local oncologists who haven't thought outside the box. So, the future is also about changing doctors' thought processes. Doctors practise what they think is appropriate, safe and peer reviewed. For Marc, it's exciting how we are merging science and engineering with surgery. The sad thing is that there is not more collaboration across medical disciplines.

There are opportunities for patients like Kim, who are determined and ready to fight regardless of the possible outcomes, and who have the courage to undertake those procedures, even with a lot of unknowns and risk. Nurture and develop your relationship with a surgeon you trust implicitly to work together with full honesty about the potential outcomes.

In Kim's journey and our fight with cancer, we needed like-minded people on our side. Knowledge and wherewithal are not exclusive to doctors or academics. If you have the want, you will find the way. We did not want to capitulate and so, in turn, wanted warriors, like Dr Marc, by our side.

Part Five:

Travelling North

El Camino (The Way)

On Sunday 4 June 2023 at 11.15 pm, I sent a text to my sons.

'Tomorrow, I take my first step of the long journey, full of trepidation and an anxious heart. Will I find calm and peace? I don't know. I expect nothing but yearn this trip will be everything. The only constant I know is that (despite my anxiousness) I must do this. I must face all the pain and memories the journey is going to bring. The alternative is simply the abyss. Deliver me from nowhere and Godspeed.'

In 2019, in the depths of deep grief, barely functioning, I recognised I had to do something—anything—to break the grip of the dark shadow Kim's death had cast on me.

I have often found inspiration through the arts, and as an avid lover of cinema I viewed a movie called *The Way*. Written and directed by Emilio Estevez, and starring his father, Martin Sheen, the movie tells the true story of a father who learns his son has died early along the route of the famous Catholic pilgrimage known as 'El Camino'. The father sets off on the pilgrimage himself to complete the trek on his son's behalf.

The Camino de Santiago, known in English as the 'Way of St James', is a network of pilgrims' ways or pilgrimages leading to the shrine of the Apostle St James the Great. Tradition holds that the remains of the apostle are buried in the Cathedral of Santiago de Compostela in Galicia in northwestern Spain. Many still follow its roots as a path or retreat for their spiritual growth. The distance from Roncesvalles to Santiago de Compostela through Leon is about 800 kilometres. There are numerous sections to choose from if you are unable to do the complete trek. I decided to do the final chapter, which commences in the town of Sarria in Spain, trekking more than 115 kilometres over six days and finishing at the Cathedral in Santiago.

My initial intention was to continue with the bad habits I had developed and do the trek alone, in silence, carrying Kim's ashes. But as happens with great friends, Greg Russell 'The Stayer' (as my grief counsellor christened him because he continued to ring me every day to check on my welfare) knew better.

'Would you mind if I came along?' Greg politely requested during one of our meetings.

And so began our plans to trek the Camino together.

The COVID pandemic came and went, and in June 2023 we flew out of Sydney to make our way to Santiago in Spain. Travelling to the starting point in Sarria was arduous, taking over thirty-one hours. Sydney to Dubai, Dubai to Barcelona, a connecting flight from Barcelona to Santiago, then transport from Santiago to Sarria where we would commence the 115-kilometre trek back to Santiago.

Greg, being the pragmatist that he is, had planned well. In the months leading up to the trek, he embarked on an almost military fitness and diet regime, losing twenty kilos while preparing his body for the trek. He also ensured we both purchased the appropriate hiking attire, leaving no stone unturned.

So, on Sunday 5 June 2023, at approximately 8.00 am, travelling with light backpacks, we ceremoniously took our first steps of the 115-kilometre, six-day odyssey, known as El Camino.

I carefully placed a vial of Kim's ashes in my pack.

When preparing this vial, I recalled an incident tattooed on my memory that occurred back in 2018, a few weeks after I returned home from Mexico carrying Kim's ashes.

* * * * *

Thinking I was alone in the house, I summoned up my courage and decided to open the box that contained Kim's ashes for the first time. It was a stained wooden box with a crucifix, about the size of a shoebox. I gently laid a sheet on our kitchen table, brought the box down from our bedroom, and placed it on the sheet across the kitchen table.

I was acutely aware that the contents were Kim's remnants. I had never opened a box of cremated ashes—I'm guessing not many people have—so I did it with great trepidation, care, and caution. The stained wooden box was just that: a façade disguising the ugly truth it contained.

Opening the box, the remains of my beautiful Kim were in nothing more than a clear plastic bag. I'm not sure what I expected, and I am not sure what else they could have been put in, but there was something almost cold and disrespectful about the remnants of my Kim in that plastic bag.

As I gently opened the bag to put her ashes into a number of vials I had prepared, an immense anxiety swept over me. Among the ashes were all the prosthetic pieces of metal, the bolts and pins that had held her fragile body together, along with large pieces of bone. My God, they couldn't even give her the dignity of preparing her ashes properly.

Gently, I started to separate the metal screws and bolts like they were almost a part of her living body.

The back door suddenly opened behind me and gawping at the surreal scene was Louis. We both stopped and stared at one another for what seemed like an eternity, like we were in a trance. Louis knew exactly what I was doing, and he was in shock.

'Get out of here, just get out of here! Go now,' I said, breaking the silence.

He quickly turned and walked away, and we never spoke about that moment again.

* * * * *

Our first day heading off on the trek from Sarria was notable for Greg's and my complete lack of wherewithal. Our first steps felt like two astronauts stepping out into unknown space, on a journey and mission about which we knew very little. Initially, we shared some small talk to quell our trepidation, but that evaporated quickly as we consumed the beautiful Spanish countryside.

With the first twenty kilometres in front of us, and zero trekking experience, the great journey began. While we had gone to great lengths to deck ourselves out with all the right equipment and accessories, we had done zero planning on our strategic approach to accomplish this demanding trek. With that, and for a reason that God only knows, we consumed the first day's trek in record-breaking time with no breaks, except for brief moments to consume water and gently spread some of Kim's ashes at a beautiful lookout.

Greg and I finished the twenty kilometre trek barely able to walk and wondering if we had chosen an impossible task. That evening over dinner, we held a deep discussion, recognising we needed to slow down and, rather than think about the final destination in Santiago, look no further than just the day at hand. This approach would have been useful earlier that day!

With the new strategy at hand, we started the second day's twenty-kilometre trek.

EL CAMINO (THE WAY)

Again, I spread some of Kim's ashes early on the trek and we set out, finding our rhythm. We spoke little and Greg led the way. I wanted it that way. With Greg leading, I marched directly behind him, not having to think about the task at hand and being able to transcend and contemplate my thoughts.

And that is what I did.

The fatigue and pain from the first day's suicide run bore heavily on us both. It was thirty-degree heat and an undulating surface caused our already aching feet to burn. With my mind free to wonder, I went to one of Kim's bucket list travel destinations.

* * * * *

We were at the Halong Bay beach in Vietnam. The beach has a famous lookout at the top of approximately 500 metres of steep stairs. I could hear the trepidation in Kim's voice as she agreed to join me in what was, to any able-bodied person, a challenging physical feat. So, hand in hand, we set off. Kim, with one lung, riddled with cancer and a body poisoned by countless amounts of chemotherapy and radiation, followed me.

I remember that incident like it was yesterday.

I could almost feel her delicate hand grasping mine. After approximately twenty minutes of climbing stairs, and with not one murmur of complaint, we made it to the top.

Kim was exhausted.

'Isn't this magnificent?' I turned to her and said, consumed by the incredible Halong Bay view from this height.

Kim didn't look at the view.

She looked deep into my eyes and said six words I will never forget. Six words that I meditate on to this very day.

'Ant, are you proud of me?' she said, her voice fragile, her body exhausted.

Here was Kim, in Vietnam, at the top of the Halong Bay lookout, with terminal cancer and physically exhausted.

And the most important thing to her was that I was proud of her?

* * * * *

For approximately eighteen kilometres, I meditated on that.

The responsibilities a partner has for the other ...

The responsibilities of what one does with that power, physically, emotionally ... and otherwise ...

Of how, along with that power, comes the courage to surrender yourself to your partner and allow yourself to become completely vulnerable ...

That nothing is more important than your partner's needs ...

And with both partners, there comes the balance ...

Your needs are secondary to your partner's, and, in turn, your partner's needs are secondary to yours ...

Of course, being humans, we are flawed. I am certainly aware I never fulfilled those responsibilities all the time, but that doesn't mean that I didn't strive for that and, at the very least, recognise it ...

I meditated on that for a long time—one's responsibilities in a relationship ...

And then it happened ...

In midday's thirty-degree heat, on a hot, black, tarred road during the final two kilometres up a steep incline, the valve burst, and I was now spiralling out of control.

In the beginning, Greg politely commented on the abrupt increase in pace. My silence and lack of visual contact answered him. I wasn't there. I was somewhere else. I was gone, and on my own pilgrimage. Even if he wanted to, Greg knew he could not walk this walk with me. All Greg knew was that he had to be there when I came back.

In the midday heat, on a hot, black, gravel road, up a two-kilometre steep incline, I took off.

I wanted pain. And I wanted it now.

I needed to feel pain.

I needed to somehow connect with Kim.

Kim had suffered so much pain and I couldn't stop it.

And now she is dead, and I felt like I failed her.

I couldn't inflict enough pain on myself.

This was my self-inflicted penance for failing her.

I was almost running up that hill.

Greg later recalled fellow pilgrims simply shaking their heads as I took off. Finally, at the top of the hill, and in complete exhaustion, I sat by the side of the road and the tears came as a flood of emotions physically poured out of me, like the floodgates of a giant dam bursting.

Eventually, I felt a hand reach across my shoulder, and it was Greg.

He didn't have to say anything.

Greg always appreciated silence, and he instinctively knew there was nothing to say. Eventually, the tears subsided. I had nothing left. Emptied of this flood of emotions, I slowly started to breathe again. The flames of grief and guilt had been extinguished, though the charcoal remnants of their fuel remained.

There we were, two lone astronauts lost in space with only each other and no ground control, somewhere on the El Camino in Spain.

After I don't know how long, we both stood up together and finished the rest of that day's trek. Possibly walking a little lighter.

The moment finished as dramatically and quickly as it had started.

That night, Greg and I talked at length, not about my 'moment' but rather our approach to the way we trekked. You see, as the days rolled on, Greg and I gathered wherewithal. We decided to not only slow our pace down but committed to stopping approximately every five kilometres at an appropriate spot. At that stop, we usually had a coffee or rehydrated. We would reflect on the last five kilometres and contemplate the upcoming five.

We consumed and digested the El Camino experience. It was at this time on day three that Greg and I truly embraced the El Camino.

Days four and five brought rain, sometimes heavy, sometimes light, but rain. The trail, at times, became a muddy bog as we donned our wet weather gear. We both strangely enjoyed the challenge of rain. It bore witness that this truly was a challenging trek, as opposed to a walk in the Spanish countryside. It gave us a reason to believe.

Day five also brought a further moment.

* * * * *

Six days prior, on the day Greg and I flew out to begin the trek, I visited my sister Camilla in hospital. Approximately four months earlier, she was diagnosed with cancer and was now in a hospice receiving pain-relief management.

I had brought her a coffee and sandwich from her favourite delicatessen. We sat in the hospice's sun-drenched common room, consuming our lunch and talking about everything and nothing. She was in good spirits as we talked and laughed, making plans for how I could assist her on my return.

As I departed and we said our farewells, I watched the elevator door close and witnessed Camilla painstakingly move along with it, as if to ensure she could maximise her view of me before it completely closed.

I didn't know it at the time, but that was the last moment I would see her alive.

* * * * *

After completing our twenty-kilometre trek on day five, I checked my texts, where I received the news that Camilla had passed away a few hours earlier.

Up until then on the trek, completely spent and exhausted, I slept like I had never slept before. That night, after receiving the news about Camilla, I lay awake most of the night contemplating life, its purpose, our purpose, and where both Kim and Camilla were right now.

I felt numb.

Greg and I started day six, our final day, with anxious excitement. This was it. We were going to finish the 115-kilometre pilgrimage known as the El Camino. It was almost surreal.

It certainly became real approximately half way into the final day.

With over one-hundred kilometres covered, our bodies began to feel the fatigue. We had both prepared physically for this, but we weren't young men. At some point, our bodies were going to say enough is enough.

I emptied the last remnants of Kim's ashes into a beautiful, flowing river about an hour outside of Santiago. I took a photo of the river and sent it to the boys. They each texted back immediately with their own messages. It gave me great comfort, as I was in a deep moment of sadness, still missing my Kim.

This is the river where I spread the last of my vials of Kim's ashes. I'm hoping the river will carry her through the Spanish countryside. I miss you, Kim.

Throughout the trek, Greg, ever the pragmatist, counted off the kilometres. As we approached the end, and fatigue set into our weary bodies, I requested he start counting down by the hundred metres!

The final kilometres were arduous, until finally, at approximately 11.50 am on Sunday 11 June, we entered the famous Santiago de Compostela, the end point of the famous El Camino.

It was done.

Greg and I stayed two nights in Santiago, immersing ourselves in the culture, breaking bread together, both of us becoming emotional at times as we pontificated on what we had just done and what it meant to us.

I told him I could not have done it without him, and no man could ask for a greater friend.

Days after we returned home, both of us recalled how we felt a little odd not being out trekking together. It occurred to me just how potent and concentrated the events that took place over those six days were.

Trekking the El Camino with Greg was no panacea to all my grief, but it delivered me from nowhere. And sometimes that's enough.

Travelling North

'We go to liberate, not to conquer.

We will not fly our flags in their country.

We are entering Iraq to free a people and the only flag which will be flown in that ancient land is their own.

Show respect for them.

There are some who are alive at this moment who will not be alive shortly.

Those who do not wish to go on that journey, we will not send.

As for the others, I expect you to rock their world.

Wipe them out if that is what they choose.

But if you are ferocious in battle remember to be magnanimous in victory.

Iraq is steeped in history.

It is the site of the Garden of Eden, of the Great Flood and the birthplace of Abraham.

Tread lightly there.

You will see things that no man could pay to see

—and you will have to go a long way to find a more decent, generous and upright people than the Iraqis.

You will be embarrassed by their hospitality even though they have nothing.

Don't treat them as refugees for they are in their own country.

Their children will be poor, in years to come they will know that the light of liberation in their lives was brought by you.

If there are casualties of war then remember that when they woke up and got dressed in the morning they did not plan to die this day.

Allow them dignity in death.

Bury them properly and mark their graves.

It is my foremost intention to bring every single one of you out alive.

But there may be people among us who will not see the end of this campaign.

We will put them in their sleeping bags and send them back.

There will be no time for sorrow.

The enemy should be in no doubt that we are his nemesis and that we are bringing about his rightful destruction.

There are many regional commanders who have stains on their souls and they are stoking the fires of hell for Saddam.

He and his forces will be destroyed by this coalition for what they have done.

As they die they will know their deeds have brought them to this place. Show them no pity.

It is a big step to take another human life.

It is not to be done lightly.

I know of men who have taken life needlessly in other conflicts.

I can assure you they live with the mark of Cain upon them.

If someone surrenders to you then remember they have that right in international law and ensure that one day they go home to their family.

The ones who wish to fight, well, we aim to please.

If you harm the regiment or its history by over-enthusiasm in killing or in cowardice, know it is your family who will suffer.

You will be shunned unless your conduct is of the highest—for your deeds will follow you down through history.

We will bring shame on neither our uniform nor our nation.

(On Saddam's chemical and biological weapons.)

It is not a question of if, it's a question of when.

We know he has already devolved the decision to lower commanders, and that means he has already taken the decision himself.

If we survive the first strike we will survive the attack.

As for ourselves, let's bring everyone home and leave Iraq a better place for us having been there.

Our business now is north.'

Lieutenant Colonel Tim Collins' Eve-of-Battle Speech, 2003

Part Six:

And So It Goes

And So It Goes

There is a strange, unfamiliar echo in the house. This large home, Kim's and my first place, held the 'Sobb circus', and is where we brought up all three of our boys from the hospital after their births. Tears, laughter, fear, pain, and a kaleidoscope of all the flotsam and jetsam that comes with a family growing up together now has an eerie, echoing silence. It feels like an old, abandoned theatre that was once filled with larger-than-life cast characters and excited audiences.

The silence is deafening in my home right now.

The boys have all moved out and I am an empty nester.

Strangely, I embrace our home becoming this as it dilutes my emotional connection to it. I am preparing to move out to start a new chapter in a newly purchased duplex, a stone's throw from my beloved North Cronulla beach.

It's 2024, and nearly six years since Kim went to that place I could not follow.

It's a large house with three floors, but Jackson, Louis and Oscar have moved out and are pursuing their lives as young men. Of course, I don't begrudge that. It's the circle of life, but it certainly has not made it any easier—for me, anyway.

Jackson married his lovely partner, Nikki, who Kim adored. He is a successful CEO of an innovation company that is about to revolutionise recycling. He and Nikki live not far from me, and both lead very active lives. He always seems so busy, but that doesn't stop his outpouring of love and gratitude when we do reconnect.

Louis moved out about a year ago with his long-term partner, Sarah. She used to be Kim's hairdresser. They, too, live not far from me. Louis still calls me every day and we remain incredibly close. He owns a successful and popular cocktail bar and continues to train hard at the Dog House whenever he can, periodically attempting to curry my favour to join him in a campaign for another fight. He is looking to expand his bar business and, from time to time, he entertains me with stories of overzealous, possibly inebriated, male patrons being put in their place and of how he reminds local young men full of Dutch courage of who Louis is and what he is capable of.

Oscar left home about a year ago, moving into a share house in the inner city with his dearly beloved Joey's boarding schoolmates. I think the excitement and adventure lasted all of about three weeks until he rang up one day saying, 'Dad, can I come home for the weekend? I need a break from that animal house.' Thankfully, the boys' housekeeping skills got better, and they all live harmoniously in a semi-organised, 'clean-ish' environment. He now works as the youngest accredited National Rugby League player-manager and spends his weekends scouting young future NRL stars. He recently came back from a trip to Canada with his partner, who is Canadian. I was touched when he approached me, asking if he could take a vial of Kim's ashes and lay them where she was born in Toronto, Canada. He really has matured since that frightened little boy whose only way of coping with his mother's terminal illness was to ignore it.

Lily is still my number one little girl and has a younger brother called Budrick, who, too, is an English Mastiff. The two of them are inseparable. I often look at them and am reminded of Kim and I.

As for me? Since Kim's passing, when not at work, I have immersed myself in surf life-saving. Whenever I am not on the beach or driving an inflatable rescue boat, I am patrolling on a rescue jet ski—there's no fool like an old fool. During the recent floods, I accompanied the State Emergency Services on two tours into regional New South Wales, tackling the treacherous rural floods.

I have a lovely, lovely partner. I worked with her nearly forty years ago. She is incredibly patient and understanding.

Through my grief over this chapter of my life and the loss of Kim, I have come to understand that it never really goes away. My grief is certainly still there but, as time goes by, I've just learnt to manage it and accept it. I recently read a quote that said, 'Just because someone carries it well, doesn't mean it isn't heavy.'

And so it goes.

My business is now north.

The Complete Playlist

January 2015
Alan Watts, *The Mind*, courtesy of alanwatts.org

May 2016
Across the Border, Bruce Springsteen

October 2016
Should I Fall Behind, Bruce Springsteen

May 2017
Two Hearts, Bruce Springsteen
Alan Watts, *Live Fully Now*, courtesy of alanwatts.org

June 2017
With Every Wish, Bruce Springsteen

July 2017
Hunter of Invisible Game, Bruce Springsteen

August 2017
Tunnel of Love, Bruce Springsteen

October 2017
The Power of Love, Frankie Goes To Hollywood

December 2017
This Must Be the Place, Talking Heads

THE COMPLETE PLAYLIST

February 2018
Badlands, Bruce Springsteen
I Wish I Were Blind, Bruce Springsteen

May 2018
I'll Work for Your Love, Bruce Springsteen

Travelling South
Sky High, Jigsaw

The Grief
More Than This, Roxy Music
You're Missing, Bruce Springsteen
Stray Bullet, Bruce Springsteen
Chasin' Wild Horses, Bruce Springsteen
Moonlight Motel, Bruce Springsteen
My Funny Valentine, Frank Sinatra
I'll Stand by You, Bruce Springsteen
Iris, Goo Goo Dolls

And So It Goes
And So It Goes, Billy Joel

Further Reading and Viewing

Collateral Beauty, 2008, directed by David Frankel and written by Allan Loeb, performances by Will Smith, Edward Norton and Helen Mirren. Warner Bros. Pictures.

Frankl, Viktor. 1946. *Man's Search for Meaning*, Beacon Press (English).

Into the Wild, 2007, directed and written by Sean Penn, performances by Emile Hirsch, Marcia Gay Harden, and William Hurt. Paramount Pictures. Based on the 1996 book by Jon Krakauer.

Kubler-Ross, Elizabeth. 1969, (Reissued 2014). *On Death and Dying*, Simon & Schuster/Touchstone.

Mad Max 2, 1981, directed by George Miller and written by George Miller, Terry Hayes and Brian Hannant, performances by Mel Gibson and Bruce Spence. Kennedy Miller Productions.

Springsteen, Bruce. 2016. *Born to Run* Simon & Schuster.

The Shape of Water, 2017, directed by Guillermo Del Toro and written by Guillermo Del Toro and Vanessa Taylor, performances by Sally Hawkins and Michael Shannon. Fox Searchlight Pictures, Double Dare You, TSG Entertainment.

The Way, 2011, directed by Emilio Estevez and written by Emilio Estevez, performances by Martin Sheen, Emilio Estevez and James Nesbitt. Icon Entertainment International.

Watts, Alan. *The Mind*, courtesy of alanwatts.org

Watts, Alan. *Live Fully Now*, courtesy of alanwatts.org

Acknowledgements

To Greg 'The Count' Russell — You were the quintessential 'stayer'.

To my friends at North Cronulla Surf Life Saving Club — You knew I needed to be left alone, whilst not allowing me to feel lonely.

To the team at Fairfield RSL (my workplace) — The ghosts who walked along my side.

To Julie and Dany, my trusted scribes — Your stoic nature gave me courage.

To Cathy, our travel agent — Who in the later stages of life made Kim's dream of travel possible when others thought it impossible.

To Rananda Rich, my personal editor and advisor on the path to publication — You gave me the encouragement to fight 'one more round'.

To Bonita Mersiades and her team at Fair Play Publishing — For recognising the value of this story, lending it your expertise and giving it a place in this world.

About the Author

A dedicated family man and successful businessman, Anthony was married to Kim for over thirty years.

Encouraged during his boarding school years at St Joseph's College in Sydney, Anthony built a career around his passion for food, wine and bringing people together. Travelling the world with Kim by his side allowed him to pursue his appetite for bringing new tastes and experiences back to Western Sydney.

While Anthony understands the power of sharing sustenance to forge relationships, he firmly reset his boundaries in the last years with his wife, keeping all others at arm's length. Though Anthony and Kim needed no one but each other, he nevertheless found catharsis and comfort from relaying an increasing flow of words through a careful, controlled channel to a close, concerned network.

He has remained focused on supporting his three sons and holding his family close.

Now, after shutting out the world for over a decade, Anthony is ready to share his story. Today, through this book, he supports those who face a similar journey.

MORE REALLY GOOD BOOKS FROM FAIR PLAY PUBLISHING

Just Because

Shirley's Story

The Bipolar Runner

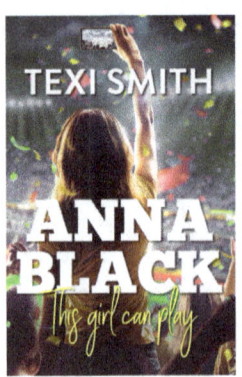

Anna Black
This girl can play

High Heels and
Low Blows

Jarrod Black
Chasing Pack

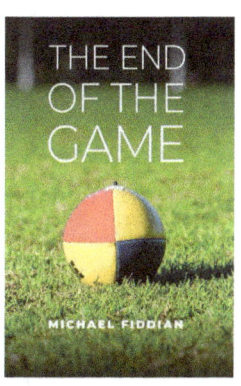
The End of the Game

Turning the Tide

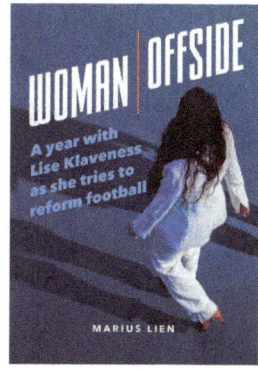
Woman Offside

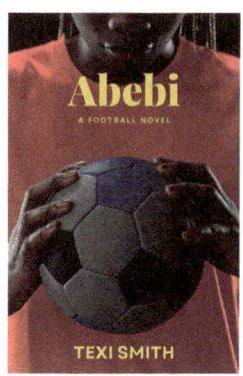
Abebi

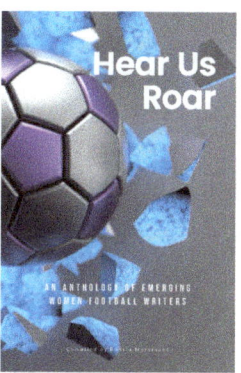
Hear Us Roar

Chappuis

www.fairplaypublishing.com.au

www.ingramcontent.com/pod-product-compliance
Lightning Source LLC
Chambersburg PA
CBHW072047110526
44590CB00018B/3066

My Business Is Now North

When Anthony Sobb's wife, Kim, was diagnosed with stage 4 lung cancer, they chose to confront the illness with unwavering determination, embracing life with all its beauty and uncertainty.

My Business is Now North takes readers on a journey through the emotional and physical challenges of fighting a devastating diagnosis, pushing the boundaries of what it means to live and love, and finding a way forward after an unthinkable loss.

"A purpose in life is to love well.
Who and what you love is debatable.

Anthony Sobb (Ant) loved his wife in a way that challenged me. His love was deep, tender, aggressive and purposeful. He wanted her to live well as long as she could.

This book has helped me to love my wife differently—
with fewer conditions and more sacrifice.
Men should read this book."

Dr John P Best, FACSEP FFSEM
Sports and Exercise Medicine Physician

PEPPER PRESS

WWW.FAIRPLAYPUBLISHING.COM.AU
PUBLISHED IN SYDNEY

www.ingramcontent.com/pod-product-compliance
Lightning Source LLC
Chambersburg PA
CBHW072050110526
44590CB00018B/3116